AMERICAN
DYNASTIES
TODAY

AMERICAN
DYNASTIES
TODAY

by the Editors of
The Wall Street Journal

DOW JONES-IRWIN, INC.   *Homewood, Illinois 60430*

© Dow Jones-Irwin, Inc. 1980

Printed and bound in the United States of America
10 9 8 7 6 5 4 3 2 1

Library of Congress Card number: 80-68102
International Standard Book number: 0-87094-228-X

CONTENTS

INTRODUCTION

B ECAUSE THIS BOOK is about some of the great families of American business, it might well be expected to be a compilation of triumphs: fortunes made from meager beginnings, social mountains climbed, power wielded in many areas of national life, and wealth and distinction enough for generations past and future.

It is that in part, of course. All of the families included were selected for a 1979 series of articles in *The Wall Street Journal* titled "The Founding Families" for the pioneering nature and continuing importance of the enterprises that bear their names. Those names are as well-known today as they have been at any time since they first reached the national consciousness—no mean feat in light of the changes that have taken place in the intervening years.

Most present-day members of the eight clans profiled herein live in comfort, if not luxury, and come and go as they please. If they do not, it is by choice rather than necessity. The old saw about wealthy American families going from shirt-sleeves to shirt-sleeves in three generations gets little support here. If one of *the* McCormicks, for instance, is seen in public in shirt-sleeves almost 150 years after his illustrious forebear started the company that was to make his name famous worldwide, it is almost certainly because it is very warm outdoors.

Basically, though, the stories that follow are ones of decline. While the wealth of the corporation-builders' heirs still is plentiful, most of them have lost or are losing control of the enterprises in which their position and influence are grounded. The process by which this has occurred is noteworthy because it is the result of some of the major forces that have shaped corporate life in America.

In one case—that of the descendants of Richard Warren Sears, the dominant founder of Sears, Roebuck & Co., the world's largest retailer—the split between family and corporation has long since occurred. Indeed, 65 years or so after Sears's death, his grandchildren have become so removed from any connection with their famous forebear's identity and company that they were surprised to hear from a newspaper reporter and interested to know how he tracked them down. The sole male-line descendant of Sears is a hobbyist, handyman, and hardware-store clerk who shops at Sears Roebuck, just as the rest of us do, and whose charge account there sometimes gets fouled up.

Bill Guggenheim, one of the few direct descendants of Meyer Guggenheim, who in the early 1900s dominated the world's metals-mining industry and established one of the greatest American fortunes, lives modestly in Lakeland, Fla., not far from Disney World in Orlando. His working life has included stints as a securities analyst and as the owner of a store specializing in selling paper dresses. He also has written a sex manual that sold 25,000 copies. More recently, his occupation has been that of "mystic counselor." In that capacity he has collected and catalogued material on spiritual topics and conversed with people who, like himself, believe they have received messages from "beyond the grave." Control of the companies Meyer Guggenheim founded has long since passed from family hands. Bill and his family live off the income from a trust fund that contained just a tiny chunk of the once-huge Guggenheim pile.

Most present-day descendants of John Jacob Astor, that intrepid fur-trader and landowner of the early days of the Republic whose name is so much a part of the American landscape, live in England. They are still well-off financially, but their once-vast United States landholdings have been sold. They lack the immense riches of old John Jacob and his sons, and the political distinction of the first Astors who settled in England around the turn of the century has faded.

Brooks McCormick, the great-grandnephew of Cyrus McCormick, whom history books credit with inventing the reaper and thereby revolutionizing world agriculture, has retired as chairman of International Harvester Co., Cyrus's corporate descendant. The family's ownership share in the company has shrunk to insignificance, and Brooks McCormick, speaking of his line functioning as managers of the giant concern, calls himself "the last of the Mohicans."

That fate already has befallen the mighty du Ponts of Delaware. The last member of that family to head the chemicals company founded in 1800 stepped down in 1971. Only three members of the enormous clan were even still employed there in recent years, none above the middle-management level. The du Ponts still own 35 percent of the company's stock, which means that many of them are very wealthy. Moreover, a few have made their mark in other fields, ranging from government to sports. Yet there seems to be little likelihood that a du Pont will ever again run the corporation that made the name famous around the world.

The Mellons still live around Pittsburgh, still are enormously rich, and still hold sizable ownership stakes in such companies as Gulf Oil Corp., Aluminum Co. of America, Koppers Co., and Mellon Bank, the nation's 17th largest. But the family has become leaderless, with its members going in their own directions and apparently paying little attention to the affairs of "their" corporations.

Even the Fords—perhaps the best-known of America's industrial dynasties—in 1979 saw the first break in family leadership of the company started in 1903 by Henry the First. Their 40 percent share of the voting stock of Ford Motor Company seemingly ensured that they could regain the chief executive's reins if they chose, but no clear successor had emerged, and a nephew of Henry Ford II and his surviving brother and sister was suing to gain control of a large block of stock his father had left. It all set Henry to wondering aloud about what might happen to the family's solidarity in voting their company stock if a serious intra-family rivalry ever developed.

Indeed, of the eight clans profiled, the one that seems to be holding up best is the Cabots of Boston, and it is noteworthy that their distinction is based more on their record of civic and political leadership in their home city than on any single great fortune. Some Cabots believe that family members have done as well as they have at least in part because few of them have enough money to devote full time to spending it. (The Cabots, however, have long been prominent in New England business, and one family branch controls Cabot Corp., a large maker of industrial products.)

Whether the somnolence of the founding families of American industry is real or feigned has been a subject of considerable debate for many years. Prominent on one side of the argument are Adolph A. Berle and Gardner C. Means, whose 1933 book, *The Modern Corporation and Private Property,* contended that as major United States companies have grown and become more complex, their operations—and, in fact, their control—have passed from the hands of the heirs of their entrepreneurial founders to those of hired professional managers, who run them as they wish. Berle and Means state that even members of founding families who own stock in and serve as directors of their companies typically know only what their "hired-hand" officers tell them about corporate affairs, and thus can exercise no real control over decision-making.

On the other side is Ferdinand Lundberg, author of the book *The Rich and the Super-Rich,* published in 1968. He contends that a relatively few very-rich families (including most of the ones in this book) not only exercise control of their enterprises when it counts, but also "run" the American political process through their power to give or withhold campaign contributions and their indirect power over newspapers, magazines, radio and television through advertising. He writes that this control often is disguised and always is cleverly rationalized, but its consistent effect has been to maintain the status quo on issues of vital interest to the perennial holders of wealth and power.

The family profiles in this book are journalistic, basically anecdotal in nature, and weren't written with the aim of proving or disproving either of these notions about the efficacy of the American wealthy. But while it would be simple-minded to conclude that the rich don't have more political power (and everything else money can buy) than the rest of us, the families' stories don't bear out any theories of conspiratorial political control. Moreover, if the families chronicled here (and others of equal prominence, such as the Rockefellers, Armours, Vanderbilts, Morgans, Westinghouses, and Harrimans) are any guide, maintaining control of vast companies becomes more difficult with each passing generation and appears ultimately to be a losing cause.

Some reasons why this should be so stem from the way modern corporations develop and grow. Just about every big company started out as a small one, usually owned not by nonrelated shareholders but by an individual or a small group of partners. If the idea for the enterprise is a good one, it grows and so does its need for capital. The bigger the company gets, the more money it needs. Two options commonly present themselves: borrowing, or selling to the public stock representing shares of ownership. As much as the owner or owners enjoy keeping things in their own hands, the lure of "going public" through the sale of stock often proves irresistible. Borrowed money must be repaid on schedule and with interest. Money raised through the sale of stock is "repaid" through dividends based on the company's profits, if there are any. And it has become common for even very profitable companies to plow all of their earnings back into the business and leave their shareholders to find their rewards in the appreciating value of their shares on the public stock markets.

Some companies have been able to attain great size without resorting to public ownership, but their number is small and shrinks annually. Once begun, dilution of the control of publicly-held companies by the heirs of their original owners inevitably continues by way of death and taxes. As the example of the Mellon family clearly shows, very rich families can utilize gifts, private holding companies, and the creation of charitable foundations to keep the vast bulk of their wealth from the public treasuries, but their ownership proportions in their corporations are usually diminished. This trend has accelerated in recent years: a fairly new law that limits to 20 percent the proportion of stock in a company that a charitable foundation can hold has all but eliminated foundations as alternative repositories for a family's corporate interests, for example.

Public ownership is inhospitable to family control for other, less tangible reasons. Although any close observer of American business knows that high-level nepotism isn't absent in publicly-held companies, the practice certainly is less prevalent there than elsewhere.

When the corporate door is open to descendants of the founder, such an "opportunity" often is a mixed blessing at best. The code of individualism—which holds that it is noblest to succeed on one's own—runs deep in America, and the sons and grandsons of the rich enter their families' businesses at their own risk. Those who do it often find themselves in a "no-win situation," according to John Gates, author of a history of the du Pont family. "If they don't make it, they are considered hopeless. If they do, their co-workers say it's because of their name," Mr. Gates explains.

Scions of the rich have many career options, including that of not working at all. When they do choose to work, it is often in an occupation that affords them the chance to succeed or fail on their own. Incredible as it may seem, at least a few inheritors of great wealth regard their riches as a burden. Steven Rockefeller, Nelson's son, told Peter Collier and David Horowitz, authors of a 1976 history of his family, that he saw his family's fortune as "an anachronism, a dinosaur that is trying to keep me from getting out and getting involved in American life just like everyone else."

Such thinking affects parents as well as children. "The old line, 'Son, some day all this will be yours,' is more European than American," asserts Robert Sobol, an author and professor of business history at Hofstra University in Hempstead, New York. "The wealthy American father is more likely to tell his son that someday he will be able to do whatever he wants to do."

To be sure, a closely-knit family can be a superior business instrument and often is wielded as such. As any proprietor of a "mom and pop" store knows, family members will work longer and harder in their own businesses than any outsiders who might be hired, and for less money. Business secrets tend to stay secret in family-run companies, and the bonds of loyalty between family members who work together can be far stronger than those that link nonrelated partners or employes and employers. It's no wonder that the great majority of American businesses are family-owned and stay that way.

But the very strengths of family ownership of a small business can turn into liabilities once a company becomes large. That has been the firm conclusion of a number of articles on family-run concerns carried in recent years by the *Harvard Business Review,* a leading periodical devoted to management subjects.

In the July-August 1964 issue of *Harvard Business Review,* Robert G. Donnelley writes that problems in the large family firm frequently stem from conflicts between the goals of the business and those of the family that operates it. "Immunity from institutional restraint (of the sort that obtain in publicly held companies) allows important company needs to be thwarted by family considerations," he writes. "Such a situation may lead to one or more of the widely catalogued problems of family firms, including capital shortages, misguided financial secrecy, ingrown company policies, a lack of profit discipline, ineffective utilization of nonrelated management talent, nepotism, and, most seriously, family conflicts." He continues:

> Unlike a company value system, which ideally determines a person's authority, responsibility, status and financial benefits on the basis of his demonstrated competence in accomplishing the goals of the firm, family norms usually stress the obligation of providing for the needs of the family. In the resulting confusion

of values, company requirements may lose out to family obligations.

Harry Levinson, head of the Levinson Institute in Cambridge, Mass., approached the subject from a psychologist's perspective in a March-April 1971 *Harvard Business Review* article. Family businesses, he says, tend to be fraught with so many internecine rivalries that they are "possibly the most difficult to operate."

Levinson says that the difficulties of the family business typically start with the founder, who goes into business for himself because unresolved conflicts with his father make him "uncomfortable when being supervised" and eager to escape the authority of "more powerful figures." For him, the business is simultaneously his "baby" and his "mistress"—"an extension of himself, a medium for his personal gratification and achievement above all." No matter what he may tell his son or sons about his desire that they someday succeed him, he hangs on, often as to life itself.

Not surprisingly, sons stepping into that sort of situation have problems, too, stemming from their own guilt over supplanting their fathers and from the need to correct institutional flaws that inevitably develop in a company long dominated by a single individual, Levinson writes. Furthermore, "while he is acting to repair the organizational weaknesses left by his father, he is subject to the criticism of those persons who, envious of his position, are waiting for him to stumble. They 'know' that he is not as good as his father. If he does less well than his father . . . he is subject to the charge of having thrown away an opportunity that others could have capitalized on."

Other conflicts can intrude upon a family firm, Levinson goes on: brother-brother rivalries, those between the wives, daughters, and sisters of the men who are vying to run things, and more complex ones that develop as more family members come onto the scene. He writes:

> A business in which numerous members of the family of varying ages and relationships are involved often becomes painfully

disrupted around issues of empire and succession. Its units tend to become family-member territories and therefore poorly integrated organizationally, if at all.

Salvation, he concludes, can't be expected without large and frequent transfusions of new blood: "I know of no family business capable of sustaining regeneration over the long term solely through the medium of its own family members."

It is a discouraging picture for the would-be dynast, and perhaps the wonder of it is that a few families such as the Fords and McCormicks have been able to keep things in the family and running well for so long. This book didn't set out to provide answers to the question of how this was achieved, either, but it does provide some clues. The Fords, it seems, have done it by vesting supreme corporate authority in one individual: first Henry, the founder, and then (after a brief and uncertain period when Henry's son, Edsel, was in charge) Henry II. So complete was Henry II's sway over Ford Motor Co. affairs that when he announced his retirement as chief executive officer, his brother, William, said he would believe it when he saw it. "They may have to carry his chair out of here with him in it," William said. But Henry did step down, although remaining as chairman.

For the McCormicks, the "secret" seems to have been the ability to absorb members of subsidiary family branches into the corporate fold. Brooks McCormick, the latest (and perhaps last) of a long line of McCormick managers of International Harvester, is descended not from Cyrus McCormick of reaper fame but from Cyrus' younger brother, William Sanderson McCormick, whose role in the founding of the company was small.

An even better example of a family prolonging its control over its company by extending opportunities to distant relatives was the du Ponts: Many of the men who ran that huge and highly successful company for 170 years until 1971 were cousins of main-branch du Ponts, or the husbands of those cousins. They brought to the firm ambitions for the wealth and position that main-branch du Ponts had by right of birth.

There is, of course, more to the histories of the great American business families than business. Through their philanthropies, many of them have been benefactors of legions of worthy projects on the national or international scene: witness the far-reaching effects of grants made by the Ford Foundation, the United States's largest; the gifts of the various Mellon-family funds that have built and expanded the National Gallery of Art in Washington; and the stipends to individual artists by the foundations created by the Guggenheims.

(It is also worth noting that some foundations have gone off in directions that have displeased prominent members of the families that funded them. In 1976, Henry Ford II resigned as a trustee of the Ford Foundation with a blast at the organization for "spreading its resources too thin" and for not doing enough to aid "competitive-enterprise" institutions that helped him and his father make the money that made the whole thing possible.)

There have been scandals involving the rich that have variously, and sometimes simultaneously, titillated and appalled us through the years: Henry Ford II's Jet Set cavortings; the marriage of 32-year-old Fowler McCormick to the 51-year-old mother of one of his Princeton classmates; the parties at the Astor estate at Cliveden at which call-girl Christine Keeler gamboled with the British elite and touched off the notorious "Profumo affair"; the conviction of a prominent Mellon heir for making an illegal political contribution to Richard M. Nixon.

There's also whatever instruction can be gleaned from reading about how the rich got rich, even though the history of American business tells us again and again that making a great deal of money is largely a matter of being in the right place at the right time with the right idea, and of possessing the unusual ability to ignore all the smart people who say that the idea will never get off the ground.

In the final analysis, though, watching the rich and their offspring is popular because so many see it as more than a mere spectator sport. Which of us has not thought that with a lucky break or two, we and our children could be right up there, making all that money and doing all those wonderful things?

"In a way, it's a very democratic interest," says Professor Sobol of Hofstra University. "Most of us don't resent the rich, because we can aspire to be like them. We look at ourselves and our families and wonder how we'd act if we had the advantages money can bring. The fact that most of us believe that we'd handle things better than the people who have it only adds to the fun."

I

The Cabots

Here's to good old Boston,
  Land of the bean and the cod,
Where the Lowells speak only to Cabots,
  And the Cabots speak only to God.

F OR THE CABOTS of Boston, that ditty is "The Poem."
Originally recited at a Harvard University function in 1905 by a
now-forgotten Midwesterner, and revised a few years later by a
Holy Cross College man, it has come to symbolize the family and
their city.

"Everybody knows it," Henry B. Cabot, III, a Boston investment
banker, says with a sigh. He recalls that he once crossed the
Allenby bridge from Jordan to the nascent state of Israel, handed
the border guard his visa and was greeted with a rendition of the
poem.

"Outside of Boston, people constantly ask, 'Are you one of *the*
Cabots?' " says Charles C. Cabot, a Boston lawyer who has run
unsuccessfully for the Republican nomination for attorney general
of Massachusetts. "I just tell them that I'm a Cabot and I'm from
Boston," he shrugs.

What the poem indicates, of course, is that there is something
special about the Cabot name and the Cabot family. The name by
itself sets them apart from the Smiths, Johnsons and O'Reillys.

By and large, being part of a particular family doesn't mean much in America. There isn't any legal aristocracy with particular titles and privileges. An outsider can't easily tell which families are socially important. But social commentators say a sort of American aristocracy exists simply because Americans seem to want one.

"Americans have always rather missed having a royal family, so we cast about for the equivalent," theorizes Stephen Birmingham, the author of a number of books on American society. When American wealth was developing in the 1800s, there wasn't an indigenous system for "surrounding money with the trappings of gentility," he says. So members of wealthy families turned to the British system of nobility as a model for legitimizing the prominence they acquired with wealth.

In America's oldest cities along the Eastern seaboard, families like the Cabots trace their position in society back to revolutionary times, when the leading Royalist families had been driven out and society's upper echelons were vacant. Even though they had helped overthrow the king, they quickly filled the gaps created by the loss of a legally-appointed aristocracy.

Insofar as there still is an aristocracy in America, the Cabots are certainly part of it. In Boston, where names and family ties matter more than most places, the Cabot family stands out. "They're a very important family," says Rose Walsh, society editor for the *Boston Herald American.*

Family members have played prominent roles in Boston ever since the first Cabot arrived in America in 1700. Cabots have been senators, judges, administrators, and ambassadors. They have written books, designed buildings, and pioneered in medicine and inventions. Cabots helped open the China trade, start America's first cotton mill, and provide funds for America's early railroads, copper mines, and even the telephone. Family members have pushed for abolition of slavery and keeping the U.S. out of the League of Nations.

Even today, the Cabots in Boston seem to typify the popular image of a dynasty, with wealth, position, and ties by marriage and history apparently providing influence across a wide sphere. The mere list of their accomplishments, their titles and their directorships suggests a web of influence extending through Boston and Cambridge, the northern hub of America's eastern seaboard.

Consider that Louis Cabot, chairman of Cabot Corp., served as chairman of the Federal Reserve Bank of Boston for six years from 1973 through 1978 and is also an alumnus overseer of Harvard University. His Father, Thomas D. Cabot, a trustee of several Boston-area universities, has endowed two professorships at Harvard and one at Massachusetts Institute of Technology. Often regarded as the "First Citizen of Boston," Thomas Cabot helped preserve Boston's pre-eminence as a medical center by spearheading the drive to build a huge medical complex.

Paul Cabot, a second cousin of Thomas Cabot, is in his 80s and is still chairman of State Street Research & Management Corp., which manages millions of dollars for mutual-fund investors. Until 1965, he was Harvard's treasurer, steadily increasing the size of the university's huge endowment. Donald Fleming, professor of intellectual history at Harvard, says, "It's a defensible point that he has been the most important man in the recent history of Harvard." Today, his nephew Walter Cabot runs the endowment.

Then there is Anne Cabot Wyman, Paul Cabot's niece, who is editorial-page editor of the *Boston Globe,* the city's most important newspaper and a liberal voice nationally.

A listing of the influential Cabots might seem to imply substantial economic pressure being used to support family interests. But it apparently doesn't happen that way.

There isn't any evidence, for example, that Cabot-controlled money has aided Cabot Corp., a big but stodgy chemical firm. All the family ties to Harvard and MIT aren't sufficient to get unqualified scions admitted. Henry Cabot Lodge jokes, "My sons tell me I couldn't get in today." Cabots certainly don't influence the intellectual attitudes at the two schools. In fact, Louis Cabot wrote an article for the *Harvard Business Review* arguing that corporations should donate money to colleges even if teachings there criticize capitalism.

Being a Cabot wasn't enough to get Charles Cabot, an admittedly inept campaigner, nominated for attorney general of Massachusetts. Noting that the Cabots don't seek personal gain through public trust, one Republican politician, himself a member of an old-line Boston family, says, "One nice thing about raising money from the Cabots is that it comes with no nephews attached."

While the Cabots can boast a variety of accomplishments and prominent family members, few Bostonians would recognize a Cabot on the street. Moreover, the self-effacing Cabots prefer it that way.

Even though the Cabot family doesn't "run" Boston and doesn't fulfill the popular image of a powerful dynasty that can control public events to its own ends, it continues to exist as a family entity, as it has for hundreds of years. That in itself is a difficult accomplishment in America, where the old saw has it that a family goes "from rags to riches to rags in three generations." The fact that the Cabots have kept producing prominent individuals for all that time is a remarkable feat that even family members can't explain.

Families in America don't remain notable simply on the basis of a wealthy ancestor. Even huge fortunes can be dissipated rapidly by profligate heirs and huge inheritance taxes. A lack of male heirs quickly eliminates a family name. Family members often scatter across the nation or the world, quickly losing the influence that a concentrated family group can have.

But the Cabots have been around so long that the generic family is more important than any single member. Unlike most prominent American families, the Cabots don't trace their position to any individual ancestor who single-handedly built a vast fortune. Nor is their status tied to a single enterprise like Ford Motor Co. or Du Pont Co.

Instead, the Cabots' high status results largely from the fact that the family has been around so long by U.S. standards. John Cabot arrived in Massachusetts Bay Colony in 1700, and by the end of the century the Cabots had become wealthy through privateering and trading in rum, slaves, and opium.

Since they established their position in the upper crust, the Cabots have shown a remarkable skill in remaining there. They and other 18th-century Bostonians "endeavoured to establish an aristocracy comparable to England's," says Robert Dalzell, professor of history at Williams College in Williamstown, Mass. "They began a tradition of civic responsibility" as well as privilege, he says. "The remarkable thing is that they created a pattern that is still being maintained."

Money is the primary basis for social position in America. But it isn't enough. Status often depends upon how old the family's money is, rather than how much there is. Top society in Dallas traces its origins back to cattle and cotton money and sneers at the *nouveau riche* oil millionaires. In Detroit, lumber and mining for⁺ ..es are considered more respectable than automobile fortunes. In Boston, the trick is to trace money back to a daring sea captain. Even though Cabot fortunes from managing money and from such inelegant chemical products as carbon black dwarf any sums passed down from the earlier shipping trade, it is the tie to the sea that firmly establishes their high place in Boston's society.

Mere heritage, however, isn't enough to explain the Cabots' success through the years. Many Cabots still feel that, because of their tradition, they have certain duties in society. Some unconsciously reflect novelist John P. Marquand's *The Late George Apley,* the definitive portrait of a self-righteous Boston Brahmin. Godfrey Lowell Cabot, the millionaire industrialist who died in 1962 at the age of 101, once wrote, "The best heritage that we can leave to our children is the habit of industry and the earnest, poignant desire to render service to others."

Some Cabots still feel their name confers a responsibility. "The sense of responsibility that all of us have is one of the traits that has kept this family together and kept each of us doing something well," says Walter Cabot, the Harvard endowment manager. "There's an inner kind of standards-building in the family. Life is not soft. It's not just to go sliding around in. I felt it. My kids feel it. Certainly, my forebears felt it," he says.

Thomas Cabot, the elderly "First Citizen of Boston," recalls that the sense of duty was firmly driven home for him as a child by his often-tyrannical father, Godfrey Cabot. "We have a strong feeling in most of the family that we have a certain duty to do something for the benefit of the world," he says. "When I was growing up, everything was duty. I studied art and music because it was a duty."

Today that sense of duty appears in the service many Cabots do on various charitable boards and civic organizations. Walter Cabot says that the family ideals don't call for devoting 24 hours a day to a job. "There should be a balance between home, business and community," he says, and the community service is a very important aspect of family duty.

Most of the Cabots over age 30 are involved in one charitable function or another. "They're just full of good works. They're the absolute upper crust," says one woman, herself a Brahmin. One Cabot heads the board of the Perkins School for the Blind, one of the nation's oldest and most distinguished schools of its kind. Others are on the boards of various private schools in the Boston area. Few charitable fund drives in Boston lack a Cabot name on the list of sponsors.

The name appears in some unexpected places, reflecting diverse interests of family members. Godfrey Lowell Cabot, the crotchety entrepreneur who amassed the largest fortune in family annals, sponsored numerous interests. He established a foundation to study solar power at MIT and one to study wood energy at Harvard. The Cabot Prizes at Columbia University were established by Godfrey's son, John Moors Cabot, a diplomat who served in several Latin American countries. The prizes are given to Latin American journalists who promote understanding among the Americas.

The Cabots' social position, of course, makes it much easier for them to do good works. A Cabot is commonly invited to join a board of trustees because his family name and reputation make him a logical candidate. Certain charitable functions in Boston, particularly in connection with the Boston Symphony Orchestra, the ballet, or the Museum of Fine Arts are inextricably tied into society. A Cabot woman would be asked to help out in arranging dinners or receptions that a newcomer to Boston wouldn't even be invited to attend.

While many of the Cabots have a certain sense of *noblesse oblige,* they generally don't take themselves too seriously. "We're basically a very bourgeois family," says Ann Cabot Wyman, the *Globe* editor, who says the family is notoriously blunt and down-to-earth. They have never been particularly noted for intellectual achievements, in contrast to the other great Brahmin family, the Lowells, whose members have included three noted poets, one a Pulitzer Prize winner, a famous astronomer, and one of Harvard's greatest presidents.

Thomas Cabot is emphatic in stating that family members don't go around with their noses in the air and a holier-than-thou attitude. "We may be screwballs, but I'll deny we're snobs," he says, commenting on the theme of "The Poem."

Few Cabots seem conscious of social position in evaluating their place in Boston. "There's no society with a capital 'S' here," says Henry B. Cabot, the investment banker. "You don't see anyone clamoring to get in. It isn't like New York."

Nonetheless, to some outsiders, the Cabots' position is enviable. Boston's high society isn't normally attainable through social, intellectual, or business achievement. A proper Bostonian must virtually be born into the social register. Social historian Cleveland Amory asserts that the rolls of Boston Society closed in 1878 with the death of the last of the China traders. Everyone high in Boston society since has been a descendant of those who were then at the top of the social structure.

Just as great wealth won't get someone admitted to Brahmin society, it isn't a prerequisite for staying in society. "You don't need a tremendous amount of money," says Henry Cabot, the banker. "People accept you."

Indeed, not all of the Cabots are well-to-do. Besides the children of Godfrey Cabot, who received large inheritances of stock in Cabot Corp., few Cabots have started out their careers with big fortunes. Inheritances are generally under $100,000, a substantial sum but not nearly enough to make possible a jet-set life style for long. "There aren't many of us who have been able to live off our inheritances," says Walter Cabot, Harvard's money manager. "We've had to earn our own way."

Some Cabots believe that family members have done as well as they have partly because they have never had enough money to devote full time to spending it. Cabot money is enough to give scions a good start in life with education at top-notch private schools, travel to Europe, and college at Harvard. After that, Cabots are expected to use that background to make their own way.

The Cabot name may be enough to get them entry-level jobs in Boston's tight-knit community of money managers or at Cabot Corp., but it isn't enough to get them very far after that. The Cabot name also will get a family member into Boston's exclusive clubs.

"West of the Hudson the most important man in the country club is probably the man with the most money," says one local Brahmin. "Here, that isn't true. The leading member of the club would probably be a Cabot because the name means so much."

No doubt the Cabots do owe something of their continuing prominence to the mores of their home city, where a "name" is apt to mean more than it would elsewhere. A Cabot in Chicago or Los Angeles mightn't be notable, but in Boston any talent or achievement is burnished by possession of the name.

The recognized importance of the name in effect makes the Cabots and a few other American families aristocrats. And being a member of the clan certainly adds luster to personal achievements. Not all Cabots have accomplished great things, but enough have demonstrated great abilities to make observers note other Cabots who appear on the scene.

Contrary to common assumption, the Cabots are not descended from John and Sebastian Cabot, the father-son navigator team that made the first English-sponsored voyage to North America in 1497. Those Cabots were Italians who adopted an English surname when they lived in that country.

Early in the 20th century, some Cabots who were concerned about their genealogical underpinnings hired professional researchers to try to trace the Cabot name back to noble forebears.

One branch of the family even briefly adopted the coat of arms of the noble Chabot family of France. But the New England Genealogical Society, the official arbiter on the issue of heraldry, maintains the Cabots of Boston aren't entitled to that coat of arms, or any other.

In fact, the family can't reliably trace its history much further back than John Cabot, the first member of the family to come to this country. John Cabot was a 20-year-old shipwright from the Isle of Jersey who emigrated to the town of Salem in 1700, about seven years after the witch trials. A 700-page privately-printed family history completed in 1926 by Boston historian Vernon Briggs says that John Cabot prospered in Salem but that his most remunerative action was marrying Anna Orne, the daughter of a wealthy local merchant. At his death, Cabot owned two schooners, a warehouse, and a wharf.

His eldest son and namesake became the first of about 100 descendants to attend Harvard, graduating in 1727. He became a medical doctor, establishing another family tradition.

Others among the founder's nine offspring married well—three to scions of the well-to-do Higginson family. With that sort of replication, Cabot and Massachusetts genealogies quickly became intertwined and hopelessly confusing. A century later, one Cabot woman commented in frustration that it seemed "it isn't uncommon for a Cabot daughter to be a great aunt before she is born."

It was the founder's youngest son, Joseph, who preserved the family name and added to the fortune, fathering a large brood of children who began to achieve the real prominence that put them in the forefront of colonial society. Joseph's oldest boys, the third generation of Cabots on this side of the Atlantic, started the merchant firm of J&A (for John and Andrew) Cabot in Beverly, Mass., a seaport near Salem, northeast of Boston.

The firm prospered, and evidence of their ultimate importance can still be seen in Beverly, now a posh seaside suburb where several Cabots dwell. The main street is Cabot Street. The current town hall was the house of one brother, and the Beverly Historical Society was the home of another.

As time went on, the Cabot brothers prospered by trading cargoes of fish to Spain, and they brought brothers and sisters into their enterprises. But it took the Revolution to put them into big money and high social status.

The Cabots don't seem to have vacillated. Stephen Cabot, who would soon die of unrelated causes, marched for Concord as soon as word of the battle there reached Beverly in April 1775. He got there too late for the battle and returned home after just three days in uniform. That was the only Cabot experience in the revolutionary army.

But the Cabots quickly saw the chance for profit in the war. John and Andrew and their younger brother George (who had dropped out of Harvard and gone to sea as a cabin boy in 1767 when his father died) outfitted their ships as privateers and preyed on English shipping. The privateers were essentially a private navy authorized by their government to attack and capture enemy shipping. They, not the government, made the profit from selling off captured vessels and cargoes.

Privateering was a very risky business, because even merchantmen often carried extensive armaments, and the British navy was always on the look-out to capture the lightly-armed privateer ships. The British, understandably, tended to regard privateers as little better than pirates, and they were treated harshly if captured.

Nonetheless, the Cabots prospered mightily. By the end of the Revolution they had invested in a total of 39 privateer ships, more than any other rebel family. Although some ships were lost, profits from others easily made up the losses. Just a few weeks before the peace treaty was signed, the Cabots' ships captured several British West Indiamen worth over 100,000 pounds sterling.

Even before the Revolution ended in 1783, the Cabots' growing wealth attracted considerable attention. Samual Curwen, an envious loyalist who had exiled himself from Beverly to England shortly after the war began, wrote, "It is a melancholy truth that while some are wallowing in undeserved wealth that plunder and rapine have thrown into their hands, the wisest, most peaceable and most deserving are now suffering want. . . . The Cabots of

Beverly, who had but five years ago a very moderate share of property, are now said to be by far the most wealthy in New England."

Historians doubt their wealth exceeded that of John Hancock, for example, but there isn't any question that the Revolution had been good for both the Cabots' fortune and their social standing. After the war had ended, with many of the leaders of prewar society gone to England, *nouveaux riche* families like the Cabots found it possible to use their wealth to establish themselves as a veritable aristocracy.

"The upper level of society in Boston was decimated by the Revolution. It was easy for bright young boys from the boondocks to come in," says historian Robert Dalzell. In fact, in the 20 years after the Revolution, many of the Cabots did move to Boston from the still-sleepy village of Beverly.

Among those who moved was George Cabot, the erstwhile cabin boy, who became the first truly prominent Cabot. George, born in 1751, had a remarkable business career by the time he retired at age 40. A skilled and daring sea captain before he was 21, he had been a big contributor to the success of J&A Cabot as merchants. By the time of the Revolution, he was already a principal in the firm.

George Cabot had a sharp eye for the coincidence of private gain and public need. After the Revolution ended and the Cabots had to return to ordinary trading, George Cabot became active in Federalist politics and developed a friendship with Alexander Hamilton.

He helped encourage the new nation's trade policies. Among actions he favored was establishment of import duties of 50 cents a ton on goods imported in foreign ships, compared with 6 cents a ton on goods entering in American bottoms. He wrote letters in favor of another duty system that allowed American ships to pay duty at just one port per voyage along the American coast, while foreign ships had to pay duty at each port entered.

George Cabot and his brothers didn't limit themselves to seaborne enterprises, either. They were among those signing for the charter for the first textile mill in America, which was built at

Beverly in 1787. A few years later, George Washington visited the three-story mill, which ran on horsepower, and had breakfast with George Cabot.

Unfortunately, the mill design wasn't particularly efficient, and it lost money. George Cabot proposed to Hamilton that the U.S. should run a national lottery to finance the mill, arguing that it would benefit the nation as a whole. That source of finance wasn't forthcoming, and the Cabots finally closed down the mill, concluding it was cheaper to import hand-woven cotton from Madras, India, than it was to weave it on inadequate machines in Beverly.

By 1791, George Cabot had tired of business and gone into politics. He was elected a U.S. Senator. During his term, he moved from Beverly to a 90-acre estate in Brookline, just west of Boston.

After four years in the Senate, George Cabot, disgruntled by the in-fighting and factionalism there, resigned and returned to Massachusetts. He was appointed president of the Boston branch of Hamilton's controversial Bank of the United States.

In 1796, George Cabot was named the first Secretary of the Navy by George Washington, but he turned down the post a day later. According to his great-great-grandson, Henry Cabot Lodge, the former vice-presidential candidate who has George Cabot's commission hanging in his stairwell, "He never took the oath because he didn't feel up to it physically." Other historians say George Cabot just wasn't interested in another public post after his unpleasant experiences as a Senator.

After the turn of the century, he moved into Boston. The Senator was semi-retired for years, growing bitter as Jefferson's Democrats ran the country. Especially upsetting to him and to most Bostonians was the War of 1812 against the British, which nearly destroyed merchant trade. In 1814 George Cabot was among those who attended the Federalist convention in Hartford. He was elected president of that gathering, which asserted the right of states to disassociate themselves from the U.S., an assertion that was regarded as bordering on treason by the Democrats in power. The budding Federalist revolution was defused by the American victory in the war, and the Federalist party was forever discredited.

George Cabot renewed his interest in commerce and concentrated on expanding his fortune. Among other interests, he took over the presidency of the Boston Marine Insurance Co. from his brother Samuel, who retired.

Several of George Cabot's descendants would become as notable as he was. George had married a Salem merchant's daughter, Elizabeth Higginson, his double first cousin—his father was her mother's brother; his mother was her father's sister.

Their descendants include Sen. Henry Cabot Lodge, the isolationist Republican leader who successfully fought to keep the U.S. out of Woodrow Wilson's League of Nations. Sen. Lodge wrote a warm biography of George Cabot in which he recalled growing up in 19th-century Boston in the house of his grandfather, Henry Cabot, who was the son of George Cabot and was notable for the skill with which he augmented George's fortune.

The third Senator in the line was another Henry Cabot Lodge, now in his 70s, who himself had a distinguished public career. He served a term as Senator, eventually losing his seat to John F. Kennedy. He also served as U.S. ambassador to the United Nations and later to South Vietnam, and ran for vice-president on the ticket with Richard M. Nixon in 1960. In his retirement, Mr. Lodge is giving lectures and serving as head of the World Affairs Council, a prominent private group.

While George Cabot was making a national name for himself, several of his brothers and dozens of nieces and nephews were filtering into Boston, marrying into other first families, and establishing their own fortunes. The most successful was Samuel Cabot, the youngest of Joseph's sons and the first of nine consecutive generations of Cabots to carry the name Samuel. He went to Boston in 1784 and established a business at Store 17 on Long Wharf. He prospered, eventually becoming president of an insurance company and fathering a large and successful brood.

Samuel Cabot served on a U.S. commission sent to England to discuss war damage claims against the British, becoming one of the first Cabots involved in diplomacy. But he is best remembered for a bitter dispute with portrait painter John Singleton Copley. Samuel Cabot was Copley's agent and represented the Boston native's affairs, because Copley spent most of his artistic life in England. In 1795, shortly before Charles Bulfinch's State House was erected on Beacon Hill, Cabot, representing the painter, sold Copley's lands on Beacon Hill to a group of real-estate speculators. The lands became much more valuable shortly afterward, and the bitter Copley accused Cabot of conniving with the speculators. Cabot denied the charges and was supported by other Boston merchants.

Samuel Cabot married Sarah Barrett, a descendant of Mary Chilton, who came to America with her parents on the Mayflower. The marriage gave his descendants three Mayflower ancestors, a considerable claim to respectability.

His son, Samuel, made another in the long history of lucrative Cabot unions, wedding Elizabeth Perkins, daughter of Thomas Handasyd Perkins, the wealthiest shipowner of his day. Perkins was perhaps the prototype of the wealthy 18th-century Boston merchant. As a so-called supercargo in charge of ships' freight, he had been among the first Bostonians involved in the China trade and had made his fortune by the time he was 30, trading furs from the Pacific northwest to Canton and Shanghai.

In 1795 Perkins smuggled George Washington's godson, George Washington Lafayette, out of France and sheltered him in Boston for a period before removing him to Mount Vernon. A man of considerable self-confidence, he is said to have turned down the proffered post of Secretary of the Navy, noting that his fleet was larger and thus more important than that of the budding nation.

Perkins also dressed with considerable style, but he was notorious for wearing his watch on a leather thong. One day he was approached on the street by a jeweler who urged him to get a gold chain because it was more suited to "a man of your position." Perkins replied, "A man of my position can wear his watch on a leather thong."

Samuel Cabot was a successful merchant in his own right, with voyages to France and a partnership in Philadelphia by the time he married Elizabeth Perkins. After the marriage he was made a partner in Perkins' firm, cementing his fortune.

Reflecting on that match and others, Thomas D. Cabot says today, "How did my ancestors come into real money? They married it."

Samuel Cabot, by all accounts, was successful in managing the affairs of the Perkins firm. Like other Boston merchants, they carried a variety of cargoes, among the most lucrative of which were slaves to the West Indies and opium to China. Some of his brothers and children were brought into the firm as sea captains and supercargoes. In 1834 Samuel Cabot assessed his net worth at $340,879.18, a substantial sum. A few years later, his father-in-law's firm was dissolved and Samuel Cabot retired to concentrate on managing his money.

D URING THE EARLY 1800s, another Cabot relative was taking actions that would arguably have a greater effect on the history of Massachusetts and the U.S. than those of any other upper-crust Bostonian before or since. Francis Cabot Lowell, son of Susanna Cabot and Judge John Lowell and great-grandson of John Cabot, the founding Cabot, was beginning the American textile industry, a first step in the American industrial revolution.

Having been graduated from Harvard in 1793, Lowell served as supercargo on a few merchant voyages and then set up shop on Long Wharf in Boston, buying and selling cotton and other goods and speculating in real estate during the first decade of the century. His business, like that of other Boston merchants, fluctuated from boom to bust with changing political currents. With Britain and France at war, both countries were threatening American shipping. President Jefferson, whose political base lay outside New England, sought to avoid being embroiled in war by closing U.S. ports. The embargo was lifted for a while, and business boomed, but then the embargo was reimposed before the War of 1812.

Lowell came close to having a nervous breakdown and sought to escape the pressures of business by traveling to Europe. As a cotton merchant, he became interested in Britain's huge textile mills of Lancashire and toured them extensively. The British, knowing their technological advantage, had outlawed the export of textile machines or blueprints, but they willingly let Lowell wander through the mills, where he asked questions and observed closely. The British had lost their lead in thread-spinning technology when Samuel Slater had taken the knowledge in his head to Rhode Island to set up spinning mills. But U.S. home weavers didn't present a big market for thread, and the key machines were the weaving looms.

When Lowell got back to Boston in 1813, he encountered considerable skepticism about his plan to make cloth. Bostonians questioned the size of the labor pool, the need for such huge amounts of cloth, and the desirability of creating a non-agrarian working class. But Lowell and his brother-in-law, Patrick Tracy Jackson (who was married to Lydia Cabot, another of the founder's great-grandchildren), persevered in raising funds. However, none of the Cabots, presumably remembering the experience with the Beverly mill, would invest.

Lowell's mill at Waltham, Mass., on the Charles River nine miles west of Boston, was opened in 1815 and within a few years was spinning out 30 miles of cloth a day. Although the first two years were difficult, customers eventually began buying the American cloth, and the merchants who had invested in the mill began to get a better return on their investment from the mills than they did from the riskier and more nerve-racking shipping enterprises. The first mill was established with an investment of $100,000, and shareholders got dividends starting in 1817, averaging almost 20% yearly and rising as high as 27½% in 1822, a handsome return indeed in a pre-inflation era.

Even while he was developing the first mill, Lowell was working on a scheme for making his new industry a social experiment as well. Lowell conceived the idea of getting labor from the farms of New England by providing proper, supervised boarding houses for Yankee farm girls to live in while they toiled in the mills. These women, who worked in the mills for only a few years while they built themselves dowries, were in sharp contrast to the proletariat of the English mill towns who worked in terrible conditions because the alternative was starvation. Lowell's system had to be more appealing than farm life to attract workers. ;

Francis Cabot Lowell died in 1817 at age 42 without seeing either the industrial success of the industry or the social success of his mill-town ideal. But as the industry boomed and new mills became necessary, his partner and other Boston merchants did establish a new town along his idealized lines. When it was created on farmland on the banks of the Merrimack River in 1821, the new town was named Lowell.

During this era, the business and financial outlook of Bostonians began to change. Men who had created fortunes in terribly risky sea trading had created pools of capital they wanted to preserve. These pools of capital weren't available elsewhere in the U.S., because merchants hadn't been as successful. Their existence helps explain the development of industry in New England. But this wealth held the seeds of Boston's demise as a center for swashbuckling risk-taking.

While the founders of most Boston dynasties were farsighted men who willingly staked huge sums on a single voyage to Canton, by the 1820s they were often trying to ease their sons out of such risks.

Various theories are propounded to explain the perceived decline of productivity among Boston's first families in the mid-1800s. Russell B. Adams, Jr., whose book, *The Boston Money Tree,* anecdotally traces the history of Boston financial dealings from colonial times to the present, argues that just as Boston was the first city to engender large fortunes, it was the first city to grow preoccupied with conserving them. He notes that Boston developed the testamentary trust, a device that took control of inherited funds from the heir and placed them in the control of a fiduciary who was pledged to handle the money responsibly and avoid the risk of an irresponsible child plunging his birthright on newfangled ideas. People like Samuel Cabot, rather than working steadily till the day they died, began to retire from active business affairs and merely manage their estates. Adams attributes this to timidity.

Historian Robert Dalzell also notes the withdrawal of Boston families from active business management, but he argues that the men were choosing to pursue more important matters than business, rather than fearfully shrinking from challenge.

He argues that investment in textile mills was "less a way to make money than a place to put it once you had it—put it and keep it." By developing the textile industry, which could be run by others and depended on to provide a relatively steady flow of dividends, Dalzell says, the Boston aristocracy was able to pursue higher ends than commerce.

Take John Lowell, Francis Cabot Lowell's nephew. Rather than going actively into his uncle's mills, he lived off his capital, traveling the world until his unexpected death in India. His greatest achievement was his philanthropy, for he established the Lowell Institute with a $250,000 gift. The institute was set up to present educational lectures for the people of Boston, and it augmented the city's reputation as the Athens of America. The institute, still headed by a Lowell, now is a major source of funds for Boston's public-television station.

While the Cabots didn't limit themselves to philanthropy, the next generation tended to ease out of commerce and engage in a variety of pursuits. The eldest of Samuel and Elizabeth Perkins Cabot's children, Handasyd, who followed his father into the China trade, died of malaria at age 21 in Canton. But Samuel's other children entered a variety of fields. For example, Edward Cabot was an architect who designed the Boston Athenaeum, a private library, now a historic landmark standing on Beacon Hill. Edward's design wasn't expected to win the competition, but it developed that the other architects had failed to design a building that wouldn't encroach on the Old Granary Burial Ground, where Paul Revere and other patriots are buried, as specified in the competition rules. As a result, Edward won the competition almost by default. He also designed a number of other Boston buildings.

James Eliot Cabot became a close friend of Ralph Waldo Emerson. After the essayist's death, he served as his literary executor and wrote a two-volume authorized biography of the Sage of Concord.

Stephen Cabot, "who wasn't considered very bright" according to one family member, achieved his greatest distinction during the Civil War. Like many other wealthy Americans, he avoided service in the Union Army. But when the anti-draft riots occurred in New York with poor Irish immigrants protesting the fact that rich people could get out of the draft by hiring a substitute, the violence threatened to spread to Boston. Stephen Cabot, as an officer in the Massachusetts National Guard, was responsible for defending the arsenal against the rioters. Although he had been ordered not to shoot at the protestors, he apparently panicked, gave the order to fire, and dispersed the demonstrators. The riot ended without the hundreds of deaths that occurred in New York.

Among the most interesting of that generation of Cabots was Samuel, the third to bear the name. Samuel Cabot graduated from Harvard and became a medical doctor by studying at the Sorbonne. He combined social and political concerns with dedication to both a career and an avocation—a style typified by the Brahmins of the 19th century. His life set an attractive ideal for what was outwardly best about the society—its intellectual curiosity, social consciousness, and civic spirit.

Studying in Europe wasn't unusual for Brahmins of that era. Most went to Europe repeatedly through their lives in almost a replication of the "Grand Tour" that had been considered necessary for the upbringing of a proper British gentleman a century earlier. But Samuel Cabot didn't return contentedly to Boston after his stay in Europe.

His exploratory spirit unquenched, he managed to get himself appointed physician for the Stephens-Catherwood expedition to Mexico's Yucatan peninsula, which discovered the Mayan ruins in 1841. Samuel Cabot, a devoted ornithologist all his life, discovered one ancient temple while chasing after a parrot he had wounded and wanted to stuff as a specimen.

His granddaughter, Eleanor Cabot Bradley, now an octagenarian herself, recalls being told that one of the skills he had developed at the Sorbonne was a surgical technique for correcting cross-eyes. At one point on the Yucatan expedition, he cured that affliction in

Godfrey Lowell Cabot, who amassed the largest fortune in family annals. He made his money from gas and carbonblack. A prodigious walker, he tramped the backwoods buying acreage and drilling wells. This photo was taken in 1961 on his 100th birthday.

Thomas Cabot, considered "First Citizen of Boston." After recovering from a severe illness he spent less than half his time on his father's business, concentrating only on major issues.

Louis Cabot, son of Thomas and Chairman of Cabot Corporation. Under his leadership, the firm has grown steadily. *Credit: Schalkwyk.*

Paul Cabot, who founded the first
mutual fund to the United States.
Credit: Harvard University News Office

Walter Cabot, Harvard University
Endowment Fund Manager. "There
aren't many of us who have been able
to live off our inheritances."
Credit: Harvard University News Office

a native guide. "Next day, his tent was surrounded by natives," she says. "He feared some sort of native insurrection." But it turned out they were all cross-eyed and desired to be cured as well.

Samuel Cabot's skill in correcting cross-eyes was also appreciated by his sister, Elizabeth Cabot, who was "a very pretty woman except for her cross-eyes," according to family lore. Samuel Cabot corrected her condition and she subsequently married Henry Lee, another Brahmin.

Samuel Cabot had inherited a comfortable fortune from his father. He married his double second cousin, Hannah Lowell Jackson. She had previously broken off her engagement to the poet James Russell Lowell, who dedicated several poems to her. The family was often short of money. Samuel Cabot frequently treated poor people free. And though he wasn't a scientific pioneer, his medical instincts were apparently sound. He theorized that the crowded conditions of Boston's tenements were the cause of tuberculosis, and he once prescribed that a poor woman should live in a tent on the roof because he knew she couldn't afford to go to the healthier country air.

As a surgeon at Massachusetts General Hospital, he was reportedly respected by his fellow doctors, although he never received the professional admiration that two nephews, sons of Emerson's friend James Cabot, would achieve in the early 1900s.

Among Samuel Cabot's passions was abolitionism, a popular position in Boston at the time. He was a good friend of abolitionist John Brown, and his granddaughter, Eleanor Cabot Bradley, says one of her aunts "remembered his coming to the house. He was a very courteous and dignified gentleman." That image of Brown contrasts with the historical picture of him as a fire-breathing insurrectionist.

Samuel Cabot backed Brown by financing families to move to Kansas in the bloody effort to make Kansas a free state. He also worked against slavery closer to home, and his house on Boston's Park Square was a stop on the "underground railway" for escaped slaves.

Cabot practiced ornithology assiduously; on his death he bequeathed a collection of some 3,000 birds, most of them stuffed by him, to a Boston museum.

Despite his variety of interests and frequent money shortages, Dr. Cabot ultimately broadened the family wealth through shrewd or lucky investments. According to family lore, he consistently made investments on the basis of patriotism or friendship that turned out well financially.

Once when James Fisk had cornered the gold supply and U.S. Treasury bonds plummeted to a value of only 30 cents on the dollar, Cabot went to his wife and said he wanted permission to put all the family's money into the bonds to help preserve the country. When the bonds returned to par, patriotism proved a good investment.

Better yet was his investing in a Michigan copper project being developed by Alexander Agassiz, son of a Harvard professor who had married into a Brahmin family. When young Agassiz couldn't get bank financing to develop a promising copper lode, he canvassed Boston families, and Samuel Cabot, like others, backed him from a sense of family loyalty. The Calumet and Hecla mine repaid the Bostonians many times both in principal and yield for their investment. Over the fifty years it operated, shares bought at a price of $12.50 produced dividends of more than five times that amount; in addition, the stock appreciated to as much as $1,000 a share at its peak.

By the time he died in 1885, at the age of 70, Samuel Cabot left an estate of a half million dollars.

Among his children was, of course, another Samuel Cabot. That Samuel had a scientific bent; he went to MIT and later studied chemistry in Switzerland. Pushed by his Uncle Edward Cabot, the architect, he developed a stain for the wooden shingles that were becoming popular in the design of the era at fancy cottages in Newport and Boston-area resorts. The stain business, based in a factory across the river from Boston and using coal tars as a chemical base, was moderately successful from the start, according to his grandson, also Samuel, who until recently was president of Samuel Cabot Inc.

His grandfather "was a great one for wanting to find a use for any product," says the current senior Samuel Cabot. On family vacations at Chatham on Cape Cod, he became intrigued by the eel grass growing in salt water. Thinking that dried eel grass might be a good insulator, he developed a series of experiments for testing its efficiency. His son Samuel was kept busy as a small boy reading the thermometers used for the tests. The eel grass did prove good insulation, and Cabot's quilts, made by sewing the grass between large sheets of paper, were a preferred insulating material for years, being used to protect the weather station atop Mt. Washington and to provide sound-dampening in Rockefeller Center.

Samuel's success, however, pales in comparison with that of his youngest brother, Godfrey Lowell Cabot, whose name, his biographer Leon Harris notes, combined all three deities referred to in "The Poem."

GODFREY, BORN IN 1861 as the Civil War began, was a bumptious runt in his family who recalled his terror at the tough "Micks" whom he had to confront while tobogganing as a boy. He went to MIT for a year, then to Harvard. After graduation, he went to Europe for a period. On his father's death he set himself up as a chemist in Boston, later associating himself with his brother Samuel's firm. Samuel was by then interested in producing carbon black, used in making inks and dyes. It was produced by burning carbons, first coal distillate and later natural gas that had become cheap and abundant in Pennsylvania following the discovery of oil there.

Godfrey went to the hills of Pennsylvania, "because he wasn't satisfied with getting 4 percent on his money," like many Proper Bostonians, according to his son Thomas. There he developed the carbon-black business, eventually buying out his brother for $5,-000. He acquired gas rights to thousands of acres for $1 an acre. While selling carbon black was marginally profitable in the 1890s, the gas business was the source of his early fortune. Godfrey, a prodigious walker, tramped the backwoods of Pennsylvania and later the even more primitive hills and hollows of West Virginia, buying acreage and drilling wells. In a period when roads were nonexistent in the state, he supervised laying pipe from his wells to the cities.

The gas was profitable. John D. Rockefeller's Standard Oil Trust was worried that Godfrey would go into the municipal gas business in competition with the trust, so it bought all his gas at the going rate. (Godfrey himself was doubtful about the efficacy of trusts. When his firm later was invited to join a carbon-black trust, he refused, explaining to his sons: "Never be party to a gentleman's agreement, for you'll soon find you are the only gentleman party to it.")

The carbon-black business began booming after the turn of the century because the material was an essential ingredient for toughening the rubber used in automobile tires. After that period, Godfrey began spending more of his time in Boston, as the money rolled in, and less time in West Virginia and Pennsylvania.

He ran his business primitively and never learned double-entry bookkeeping. Well into the 1900s, when the business volume was millions of dollars a year, he calculated his annual profit merely by subtracting the bank balance at the beginning of the year from the balance at the end. The system, of course, merely recognized cash flow and ignored such niceties as the difference between capital investment and operating expense, as well as the intricacies of depreciation. Reconstructing corporate finances after the income-tax amendment to the Constitution was passed in 1916 proved an arduous task for a team of accountants and lawyers, who finally had to negotiate a settlement with the government.

Godfrey Cabot ran his business with an imperious elan. Although his sons Thomas and James took over operating control during the 1920s when Godfrey was in his 50s, he never relinquished stock control. Even in the 1950s, he frequently embarrassed Thomas at board meetings by giving specific instructions on where to drill gas wells in the West Virginia hills.

Despite his primitive practices, Godfrey Cabot, whose awe-struck nephews called him "Uncle God," was entranced by many scientific and technological developments. His greatest fascination was with flight, and he followed the Wright Brothers' success with interest, writing them to inquire about the possibility of transporting carbon black by air, and writing his cousin, Sen. Henry Cabot Lodge, to urge the U.S. government to become interested in military applications of air power.

When World War I started in 1915, Godfrey, then 54 years old, tried to join the Navy to go to flying school. When he was rejected, he bought his own sea plane, learned to fly it, and voluntarily patrolled the Massachusetts coast searching for German submarines. He never found a German submarine, but frightened residents of coastal Winthrop, Mass., once fired at him.

Eventually his persistence won him a commission as a lieutenant in the Naval Reserve. He commanded a unit in Boston for a while, paying for ammunition for the rifles himself when the Navy objected to the expense. Later, he was transferred to a Naval air station at Norfolk, Va. All the while he ran his business, chiefly supplying gas to Standard Oil for the busy factories of Pittsburgh, but also producing carbon black for use in gas masks at the front.

He insisted that his two oldest sons learn to fly, although Thomas recalls in his autobiography that the tailless biplanes on which they learned were so unlike standard models that the training was of little use. Nonetheless, each ended up getting a commission in the Army Air Force. Godfrey Cabot's flying career ended after the war, but his involvement with flying didn't stop. He became active in the National Aeronautic Association, a booster group, and worked two years in Washington, D.C., as association president, hobnobbing with Charles Lindbergh, Eddie Rickenbacker, and Howard Hughes, while his wife explored Washington society.

Godfrey Cabot's sense of duty extended beyond passive charity (from his early 20s on he was wont to give West Virginia cities gifts like horse troughs or planted trees) and patriotism (he granted the country his patents for devices for midair refueling). He wanted actively to improve society.

His greatest involvement in this regard was through Boston's notorious Watch and Ward Society, which supervised the morals of the city and made the phrase "Banned in Boston" a national joke during the first half of the 20th century. Cabot joined the society in 1900. By 1915 his growing wealth and generosity got him the office of treasurer of the Society, a post he held until 1940, when he was 79 years old.

During the early years of the century, the Watch and Ward engaged in active investigations of houses of prostitution and gambling halls, gathering evidence for police and aiding them in raids. But it became best known for its censorship activities. While its legal power to ban books was limited, it carried considerable weight because of the economic and social clout of its members, who could boycott a play or a bookstore. Cleveland Amory, whose book *The Proper Bostonians,* published in 1947, remains a classic piece of social history, records that the society's annual report contained a list of several Brahmins who were its directors and the following boast: "Our honored list of Officers and Directors is, we believe, a guarantee that our work has the confidence of some of New England's foremost citizens and is directed by men of social experience and ability."

These citizens had their biggest year in 1927, when they banned 68 books, including works by Sinclair Lewis, Ernest Hemingway, and Sherwood Anderson. Cabot himself generally read second-rate novels of lower artistic (but perhaps higher moral) quality.

It was Godfrey Cabot's high moral standards that brought him his biggest fight. In a classic confrontation, the aged Brahmin fought and finally bested a crooked Irish district attorney. The dispute grew out of Godfrey's reputation. It seems a young Boston woman was seduced in the course of treatment by an unscrupulous doctor. Upset, she went to Richard Cabot, a leading physician of the day, who decided her complaint was moral and sent her to his cousin Godfrey.

Godfrey Cabot reported the young woman's story to District Attorney Joseph Pelletier, who laughed at it and, instead of prosecuting the doctor, allowed him to leave town. Infuriated, Godfrey Cabot investigated Pelletier and discovered that he was regularly bribed, through local lawyer Daniel Coakley, to avoid prosecuting individuals. Upon further investigation by the Watch and Ward

Society, Cabot discovered that the two men had actually set up a blackmail ring: Women would lure wealthy men to hotel rooms, where the men were arrested by police. The embarrassed men would then pay off Pelletier and Coakley for not prosecuting them for fornication and would pay hush money to the women.

Cabot's fight to prosecute the two became a consuming passion between 1913 and 1920. He hired dozens of detectives to shadow Pelletier. He pushed a bill in the state senate to remove Pelletier. He himself narrowly avoided being trapped in a blackmail attempt by a woman who offered him secret information about the ring.

Pelletier and Coakley fought back cleverly and strongly. Pelletier referred to Cabot as the "archfanatic" after learning that Cabot's will had been amended to pay for continued investigation if he should die. Coakley, a former sportswriter, attacked Cabot in the newspapers, contrasting his own humble Irish origins with "those on whom Fortune had pinned the blue ribbon." Pelletier was eventually able to prosecute Cabot for theft because one of Cabot's detectives, working undercover in Pelletier's office, was caught stealing papers. Cabot got off.

Eventually, though, the burden of evidence discovered by Cabot was enough to have Pelletier and another district attorney disbarred. Coakley was later sent to jail. The fight cost Cabot personally $78,000—an indication of the moral indignation of which he was capable.

Events like the fight against Pelletier added to the awe that Cabot engendered naturally by his imperious manner. Like most Cabots, he was unconcerned with civil niceties. "My father's generation was notorious for bad manners," admits his daughter, Mrs. Bradley. "They'd say, 'Why should I greet someone on the street? We already know each other.' "

He was stern and penurious with his family. He forbade alcohol, tobacco, and even coffee for them and required open windows, even in winter, cold baths, and long walks. The family remained in unfashionable Cambridge for years after Cabot was earning hundreds of thousands of dollars a year. His penury was augmented by his wife, Minnie, who lived in constant fear of poverty. Mrs.

Bradley recalls that while she was growing up, life seldom seemed luxurious, and she adds that the "only reason I ever got any money was that my older brother died (in 1930, when she was 37), and the company had to start paying dividends to support his widow."

From the 1920s on, Godfrey's sons, Thomas and James (until James's death in 1930), and son-in-law Ralph Bradley, took over the operations of the company and led it through its great expansion. Godfrey's actions began to look more eccentric, but in the great tradition of Brahmin tolerance, they were regarded as evidence of character.

His love of a fight led him to insist that the company build a gas pipeline from a small field in Pennsylvania to Rochester, N.Y., to supply Eastman Kodak Co. The plan was bound to be unsuccessful since the field was too small for the needs, and it was fought vigorously by his sons, by every railroad and coal company that foresaw losing business, and by the Rochester electric utility. Godfrey told his sons he would call a stockholders meeting if they didn't follow his orders—a viable threat, since he owned or controlled almost all the stock. He hired agents to buy options on rights of way across New York to Rochester. He triumphed in court by outmaneuvering the utility's lawyer. And he apparently took it in stride when he ran out of gas and had to buy his way out of the Kodak contract.

In another quixotic struggle, he ran for mayor of then-heavily Irish Cambridge in 1923 as a reform candidate. Predictably, he lost.

He continued going to his spartan office until he was well into his 90s. Henry B. Cabot III, the investment banker, recalls that in the early 1950s, he could look out of his office window onto Boston's busiest intersection, "and precisely at five to nine the traffic cop would stop traffic and Godfrey Cabot would walk across, looking neither right nor left."

As he aged, he continued to enjoy a good fight and fomented many with his obstreperous letters to local newspapers. Generally he castigated liberal politicians such as Roosevelt, but during the 1950s he argued against dismissing Harvard and MIT professors accused of Communism.

He refused to do any estate planning until he was well into his nineties, stoutly maintaining that it was unnecessary because the Republicans would abolish inheritance taxes as soon as they came to power. By the time he was convinced this hope was vain, late in the Eisenhower administration, he was unable to protect much of his estate. Although he left an estate of just over $100 million when he died in 1962 at age 101 (at the time the largest estate ever left by a New Englander), taxes took a huge chunk of it.

He was an anachronism—the last of the old Brahmin Breed that accepted without question the old Boston society, believing that with all its eccentricities, bigotries and snobbism, it represented the best produced on the planet.

During Godfrey's lifetime, Boston changed from a society run by the blue-blooded Yankees with little regard for the first- and second-generation Irish immigrants (the poor, underprivileged majority, as one account put it) to a city where political clout or business skill could offset a lack of breeding. Godfrey Cabot's children could never be quite as sanguine about their place in the world as he was. And although he made his fortune far from Beacon Hill, he never shed the self-righteousness he acquired growing up within sight of it.

Parochial as Brahmin provincialism seems today, Boston before 1950 gave the firm impression that the Brahmins did rule most aspects of city life. City hall and judgeships were generally controlled through the election or patronage systems, of course, but the few thousand Boston Brahmins were the leaders in almost every field.

In Godfrey's immediate family was an older brother, Arthur, who became a doctor and remained a bachelor all his life. A noted *bon vivant* whose hedonism contrasted with Godfrey's Puritanism, Arthur served for many years as one of five Fellows of Harvard Corporation, the university's governing body.

A sister, Lilla Cabot Perry, was an artist of some skill who actually studied with Monet in France. Like many other long-lived Cabots, she didn't let the passing years slow her down. When she was approaching 90, she painted for five hours daily and confided to friends that she was confident she was steadily improving.

A cousin, Henry Bromfield Cabot, was prominent in developing the Boston Symphony Orchestra into one of the nation's great cultural institutions. He served as a trustee and later chairman of the board.

A younger relative, Stephen Cabot, headed the Judge Baker Foundation, one of Boston's largest philanthropies around the turn of the century. Stephen, like other Cabots before and since, was regarded as difficult to approach. He himself told the story of being accosted one day on the Boston Common by a beggar asking for some money. Cabot forthrightly denied him, saying, "My man, you've been drinking." The beggar replied, "It would take a couple of drinks before I could ask a man like you."

Then there was Judge Frederick Pickering Cabot, a juvenile-court judge who pioneered in developing rehabilitation programs for delinquent children as an alternative to punishment. Judge Cabot, though himself a resident of suburban Brookline, was well known in the fashionable center of Boston because twice a week he would sell eggs from his henhouse to blue-blooded residents there.

Judge Cabot was also active with the board of the Boston Symphony. Helen Howe, who wrote a memoir about turn-of-the-century Brahmins called *The Gentle Americans,* recalls that at one children's concert given by the symphony, the distinguished Judge Cabot stepped forth to introduce the program and was greeted by the shout, "It's the egg man."

The brothers Richard and Hugh Cabot were among the nation's most distinguished doctors. During World War I, one headed the Harvard Medical School medical unit and the other the Massachusetts General Hospital medical unit. Richard Cabot is noted for his work in medical social service. He developed a system for providing follow-up social service to the indigent patients who had been treated at the hospital. Hugh, a urologist, later taught at the University of Michigan medical school in Ann Arbor.

THROUGH THE FIRST half of the 20th century, Cabots continued to be prominent figures. As recently as 1946, no less than 10 Boston Cabots were prominent enough to be listed in *Who's Who in America*. Although the number has since declined to four, the Cabots and other Massachusetts blue bloods have kept playing a remarkable role in national life. Lodges and Saltonstalls and Peabodys and Sargents have continued to show up in the U.S. Senate and the Massachusetts State House. Brahmins with the blessing of a Harvard education and a cosmopolitan background have held prominent posts in the Washington bureaucracy, and particularly the State Department. Others have been notable in Boston.

The generation of Godfrey Cabot's children produced a number of prominent family members, and several of them today carry on the tradition of family service and innovation, even though their perception of the world is less parochial than that of their parents.

Take the four sons of Henry B. Cabot, who headed the board of trustees of the Boston Symphony Orchestra for many years. All four went to Harvard, but their later careers varied greatly. The eldest, Henry B. Jr., who married the wealthy Olivia Ames, maintained the family tradition by heading the Boston Symphony Orchestra for 23 years. While he suffered from an early attack of tuberculosis, which kept him from practicing law, he was a revered figure around Boston, serving as trustee of various family trusts, doing "a lot of hand-holding" in the best tradition of Boston trustees, says his son Henry B. III. The current Henry B., an investment banker, recalls that his father and another prominent lawyer were trustees for one account under which they had to go down to the bank vault together once a month to clip coupons on bonds.

Despite Henry Jr.'s aristocratic upbringing, his greatest pleasure was in his New Hampshire farm, where he worked vigorously on weekends. "He could shovel more manure with one lung than most men could with two," his nephew, Walter Cabot, says admiringly. Henry Jr. died in his 80s in 1974.

His brother, Powell M. Cabot, had literary ambitions and worked for a time for the Boston *Transcript*. This unusual daily for 111 years presented proper news to Proper Bostonians; finally closing in 1941 with its circulation down to some 15,000. When Powell tired of reporting, he started a publication called *The Sportsman Magazine* in partnership with Christian Herter, who later served as Secretary of State in the Eisenhower administration. The magazine died in the Depression, and Powell became Chief Marshal of Harvard, a job in which he ran commencements and entertained visiting dignitaries.

The youngest brother, Charles C. Cabot, was perhaps the most public-spirited. Also a lawyer, he was an associate justice of the Massachusetts Superior Court from 1943 to 1947. He was an alumnus overseer of Harvard for six years, president of the Harvard Alumni Association, and for 18 years president of the trustees of Wellesley College.

At age 66 he accepted the arduous task of chairing the Massachusetts Bay Transit Authority, a scrappy amalgamation of conflicting political authorities that supervised the rail and bus systems of eastern Massachusetts. He held the post for three years.

But the most remarkable of the brothers and the sole survivor is Paul C. Cabot, a blunt-spoken character, now in his 80s. He founded what he argues was the nation's first mutual fund. The spry financier still goes daily to his office at State Street Research and Management Co. in a modern office tower overlooking the harbor where his ancestors' ships sailed. He served as treasurer of Harvard University for 23 years, building its endowment "with a rising market and considerable luck" from about $200 million to over $1 billion.

Paul Cabot got his B.A. from Harvard in 1921 and his Masters from the Business School, where he was second in the class, in 1923. Then he went to work for First National Bank of Boston in its London office. While there, he learned about the Scottish investment trusts that pooled the funds of many investors and put them into such vehicles as American railroad bonds.

When he came back to the U.S., he left the bank to develop a similar plan in the U.S. with the added twist of investing in common stocks. In partnership with Richard Saltonstall and his first cousin, Richard Paine, he started the firm in 192 . "The business appeal was that you could get your money out any time you wanted," he says, which made it considerably safer than direct investment in such less-liquid securities as unlisted stocks. "I talked to every big shot in investments, including J.P. Morgan. Without exception, they thought I was insane to establish a company that could be liquidated by its shareholders," Paul Cabot recalls.

The partnership began selling mutual-fund shares in 1923, Cabot says. However, it didn't incorporate until late in 1924, three days after another mutual fund, Massachusetts Investment Trust, had filed incorporation papers. Both firms have since claimed to be the first mutual fund.

Paul Cabot's service to the mutual-fund business didn't stop with founding it. His nephew Walter tells of the time when "Uncle Paul went to see President Roosevelt to save the mutual-fund industry." It seems an administration official had proposed taxing mutual-fund dividends both when they were paid to the fund and then when they were distributed to shareholders. They had been taxed only as shareholders' income, as the payment to the fund was just passed through.

Cabot traveled to Washington to explain to the administration why the law would be unfair. He arranged an appointment with President Roosevelt, but after being kept waiting for hours, he was finally told the President couldn't see him. Cabot said, "Damn it, I'm going to see him," and marched into his office, Walter Cabot says. He said, "Mr. President, someone is pushing you to make a very bad law, and you ought to know about it." Roosevelt listened to the argument and killed the proposal, preserving the mutual-fund industry.

Cabot's success with State Street Research & Management Co. helped make common stocks acceptable investments in conservative Boston, where many fiduciaries emphasized bonds as the wise way to handle money.

Boston had become a money center through the financial daring of the China traders and textile barons. Later in the 19th century, those fortunes were augmented through risky but successful investments in things like western railroads, the telephone, and the Calument and Hecla copper mine.

But more and more money was tied up in fiduciary trusts, with trustees operating under the so-called prudent-man rule propounded by a state court in 1823. The rule required trustees to invest their charges' money the way a prudent man would, and thus avoid chancy ventures. Boston investment advisers generally put a conservative interpretation on the ruling and took refuge in bonds. Banks wouldn't even accept common stocks as collateral for loans.

Cabot remembers that while New Yorkers "gambled like hell" in the stock market, Bostonians were much more conservative. "Common stocks were considered a wild gamble" in Boston, Cabot says, but he was able to help change this thinking. Starting in 1924, when Charles Francis Adams was treasurer of Harvard, Paul Cabot began advising the university on initial investments in common stocks. Under his direction, the university slowly began showing more interest in these securities.

In 1948 he was asked to become treasurer of Harvard. He refused to abandon State Street Research. So the university allowed him to keep his chairmanship there on the theory that the tools the firm possessed would be helpful in running the Harvard endowment. Much of the endowment had been Boston land, but Cabot, feeling that common stocks had much greater potential than the declining inner city, successfully moved the portfolio into stocks.

Despite the fact that he was considered somewhat fiscally reckless for his emphasis on common stocks, Paul Cabot never accepted the idea that charitable institutions should spend principal from the endowment as well as interest to take advantage of the rapid growth some stocks were recording in the late 1960s. The idea, endorsed by the Ford Foundation, caught on with a number of institutions, including Harvard's archrival, Yale University.

Although he retired as Harvard treasurer in 1965, Cabot fought vigorously a proposal that Harvard follow such a course. In 1972, he wrote an open letter to Harvard president Derek Bok to dissuade Harvard "from adopting this dangerous, unfair, unwise and possibly disastrous policy." In the best tradition of Boston's money managers, he wrote that "If one spends capital . . . it really amounts to robbing the future to take care of the present." Harvard refrained from dipping into capital gains for operating expenditures, avoiding dependence on growth stocks, a policy that looked prescient two years later, when the growth stocks crashed.

Even today, the conservative money manager, who eschews electronic calculators in favor of his trusty slide rule, fumes about the evils of spending principal. On meeting a Yale man, he mentions that he received an honorary degree from the university and then explodes: "I wish to God Yale would learn something about running their stupid finances."

Godfrey Cabot's branch of the family has also managed to make quite an impression in Boston. His oldest son, James, died in 1930 of a misdiagnosed strep abscess. But his other sons had remarkable careers. John Moors Cabot, the youngest son, went to Groton, a prestigious preparatory school, and on to Harvard, Oxford, and Georgetown University's School of International Affairs before embarking on a diplomatic career. He served in consulates and embassies all over the world, concluding with stints as ambassador in Brazil, Colombia, Sweden, and Poland.

But it is Thomas Dudley Cabot, Godfrey's second son, who perhaps best typifies the Brahmin and Cabot ideals of useful service coupled with business success and personal satisfaction.

Now a courtly octogenarian, Thomas Cabot is usually considered Boston's leading citizen. He recently published an autobiography entitled *Beggar on Horseback* (a reference to a line in Robert Burton's *Anatomy of Melancholy:* "Set a beggar on horseback and he will ride a gallop," which in turn is a reference to Cabot's reputation as an organizer of charitable drives who won't brook small pledges). The organization of the autobiography itself gives an indication of the breadth of his life. Unlike most such books by business leaders or world travelers, it isn't a chronology of the events of a lifetime woven around a single career drive. Instead, the chapters deal with different aspects of his life. One describes his career as a businessman, another deals with his experiences as an Alpinist, and others detail his canoeing, sailing, traveling, and State Department service.

Even as a young Harvard graduate, when he was setting up a home in the wilds of West Virginia with his new bride, he found pleasure in his work of riding the hills, checking his father's gas pipelines, and occasionally confronting moonshiners who found tapping the pipes gave them a cheap source of fuel. On week-long horseback trips (there weren't any auto roads in most of the state in the 1920s), he and his wife, Virginia Wellington, a member of another prominent Boston family, stayed in lonely farmhouses on straw ticks and ate corn pone and sour-belly.

The Cabots stayed in West Virginia less than two years, returning to Boston to straighten out his father's income-tax problems and then continuing to operate the company when Godfrey Cabot went off to Washington with the National Aeronautic Association. The Cabot firm, by then incorporated as Godfrey L. Cabot Inc., prospered as the automobile industry grew after World War I, requiring tons of carbon black for tires. Thomas, who had noticed the huge gas fields of Texas while in flying school in the war, developed a number of carbon-black plants in the Southwest.

When the Depression struck, the company was hard hit as volume dried up. Worse, James Cabot was struck by the strep infection that killed him in 1930, and Thomas got a similar infection that forced him to leave the business for several years. Operations of Godfrey L. Cabot Inc. were left largely to the founder, in his 70s, then to his son-in-law Ralph Bradley, and Edward Billings, Thomas's Harvard roommate who had joined the firm.

After his severe illness, Thomas Cabot never concentrated as fully on the family business, spending less than half his time at work and engaging in a variety of other interests. He says today that the diversification, by keeping him out of operations and making him concentrate only on major issues "made me a better businessman." He was involved in Cabot's development of a system for pelletizing carbon black for bulk handling, saving the expense of bagging it. He even designed the special hopper cars needed to carry the material. Although Thomas supervised most of the family firm's growth during the 1930s and 1940s, as it expanded into a multimillion-dollar business with 10,000 employes, it wasn't until the 1950s, when Godfrey Cabot was in his 90s, that he finally relinquished the title of president to Thomas.

After his illness, Thomas Cabot began serving on the boards of other companies, including United Fruit Co., the huge Boston-based banana-growing and importing firm. After World War II, directors became concerned because the dictatorial Samuel Zemurray, who had built the firm to pre-eminence, was 73 years old and giving no sign of picking a successor. With Zemurray's reluctant assent, they named Thomas Cabot president of United Fruit. Cabot now says, "It was the biggest mistake I ever made. He and I started to pull the company apart. The vice-presidents, who all owed their jobs to him, just played it cozy." Frustrated, Cabot resigned after only one year as president. He remembers selling his stock at $85 a share. "Later it dropped to $2," he adds with satisfaction.

Outside of business, Thomas Cabot's career was equally remarkable. He was an avid canoeist from boyhood, struggling with heavy but fragile canvas-covered canoes around the salt marshes of Cambridge and Boston. After his marriage he and his wife began running the rapids on New England rivers, becoming proficient at the difficult technique of poling the canoe through rapids, with Mrs. Cabot paddling in the bow and Thomas standing in the stern of the unstable vessel with a long pole to control the craft's course. His knowledge of New England rivers led him and a friend to publish a book, *Quick Water and Smooth,* describing all the canoeing waters of New England south of Maine. It was the first such guide for the region.

After World War II, Grumman Corp., which had developed new techniques for shaping aluminum, asked him to design an aluminum canoe. The design he proposed, with buoyant flotation pockets in the bow and stern and with lower ends than traditional designs to reduce wind resistance, is still used by Grumman and is the design of at least half of the canoes made today. At the age of 80, he was invited to canoe the wild St. John's River of northern Maine, which is threatened by a proposed hydroelectric project. The trip was reported by naturalist and writer John McPhee in the *New Yorker* magazine.

During his 20s, he and his wife became mountaineers, making first ascents in the Canadian Rockies and narrowly losing races to be the first to conquer several peaks in the South American Andes. His autobiography recounts narrowly missing death several times in the Swiss and French Alps. His wife once slipped hundreds of feet down a glacier there, and he and his son were once nearly trapped between crevasses on the Mer de Glace at Chamonix. He nearly froze to death one winter night in Canada while trying to build a fire during an expedition to view a large herd of caribou.

A skier since his youth, he led family expeditions to the new ski areas in New England and the Canadian Laurentians. His nephew Ralph Bradley says admiringly, "Tom Cabot can ski faster on less snow and canoe quicker in less water than any man I know." He is still remembered by the skiing pioneers of Sun Valley, Idaho, and various areas of Colorado. He remembers with embarrassment that he once advised a friend against building a resort in Colorado after skiing in the wilderness there. The friend disagreed, and the area is now Aspen.

Thomas Cabot collects islands the way some other wealthy men collect Renoirs. He has bought dozens along the coast of Maine, where he still frequently sails his 50-foot schooner, Avelinda. He leaves most of them alone, arguing that under his ownership their delicate ecology is untrammelled, whereas if he gave them to the state as parks, they might be spoiled by hundreds of tourists. He and his wife, who are indefatigable travelers, have toured islands from Greenland to Tierra del Fuego.

Always curious, Cabot is proud that he wrote several papers that were the first in their field. In his autobiography, he cited a report he wrote about a lake in central Africa where extractable methane gas is trapped under hundreds of feet of clear water. He notes that his article was the first in English on the phenomenon. During the

1920s, he and his wife explored reports of a 10,000-foot mountain on Santo Domingo that was described in atlases. The Cabots proved that there weren't any peaks there higher than 4,500 feet. Also during that period, Cabot wrote what he says was the first article on liquefying natural gas by keeping it very cold, for storage in tank facilities. Forty years later, his interest in the field led to a Cabot Corp. investment in a liquefied natural gas project, an investment that resulted in a $35 million write-off, he admits ruefully.

Cabot has also done considerable government service and philanthropic work. During the Korean War he served under Secretary of State Dean Acheson as Director of International Security Affairs, negotiating on the contributions of various NATO allies to the war effort in Korea. After the post was eliminated by Congress, Cabot continued to serve in various capacities, including leading a mission to the new government of Egypt. He recalls he came back full of plans for contributing to the Aswan Dam, but Secretary of State John Foster Dulles refused to see him. It turned out the Cabot family was considered suspicious by the McCarthyites because the obstreperous Godfrey Cabot had written a letter to the Boston newspapers arguing that America's enemies were the Stalinists, that Communism by itself wasn't inherently evil, and that Jesus Christ was probably a Communist.

Closer to Boston, he headed the commission that developed Logan International Airport on salt marshes across the harbor from downtown Boston. But his greatest services were as a philanthropist. He has given millions of dollars to Harvard and has endowed two professorships there and one at MIT. He spearheaded the drive to combine a cluster of Boston hospitals at one center, raising $15 million in the process. His fund-raising reputation became so great that once, when traveling in the Fiji Islands, he introduced himself to an American woman who said, "Why I know you. You're the biggest beggar in Boston."

Thomas Cabot's son, Louis Wellington Cabot, to whom he turned over leadership of Cabot Corp. in 1962 when he was 63, comes close to filling his father's shoes as a prominent Bostonian.

Louis Cabot is a short, stocky man with a shock of white hair. In the years he has run Cabot Corp., it has expanded substantially outside the original carbon black and oil and gas fields—not always successfully, as evidenced by the controversial and costly liquefied natural gas project. But Cabot Corp. has grown steadily, diversifying by acquiring a large metal-alloys company.

Widely respected in the business community, Louis Cabot has been very active as an alumnus of both Harvard and the Harvard Business School. Like his father before him, he served as an alumnus overseer. He wrote a long article for the *Harvard Business Review* criticizing a growing trend among conservative businessmen to avoid making financial contributions to schools because of the perceived leftist teaching at the schools. "What comes through is a message perilously close to 'Teach that of which we approve or expect no support from us,' " he wrote. "Such efforts play right into the hands of critics who jump on every opportunity to charge that the free enterprise system is so flawed it wants to substitute indoctrination for the free exchange of ideas."

Louis Cabot also served as an MIT trustee, and he has been a member of the Commerce Department's Business Ethics Council. His long tenure as chairman of the Boston Federal Reserve Bank, a post not unlike that of his ancestor George Cabot, who headed Hamilton's Bank of the United States, has made him well-known in the Boston business community.

Younger Cabots like Walter Cabot, the Harvard endowment-fund manager, and Anne Cabot Wyman, the *Globe's* editorial-page editor, already assure that the prominent role of Cabots in Boston will continue.

T HE CABOT FAMILY now is spread out in many parts of the country. One grandson of Thomas Cabot, Jeremy Black, is a movie actor who was seen in *The Boys from Brazil*. Thomas's son Robert, who wrote a novel called *The Joshua Tree,* now lives in British Columbia. One of Henry B. Cabot's grown sons left for Vermont to live in a religious community.

Many of the Cabots preserve their strong sense of family. While few have grandfather on the brain, to use Cleveland Amory's felicitous phrase, there is considerable consciousness of the family tradition.

Many Cabots hew to the activities of their forebears. Mrs. Eleanor Cabot Bradley, in her 80s, proudly lists her many uncles, nephews, and grandchildren who are practicing doctors or planning to go to medical school.

Samuel Cabot Inc., which celebrated its 100th anniversary in 1977, still exists as a family enterprise. Located in a restored brick building near Boston's trendy Quincy Market, the current president, Samuel Cabot, is only a few blocks from the spot on Long Wharf where his namesake set up an office eight generations earlier.

Samuel Cabot Inc. is a dwarf compared to Cabot Corp. It produces about $7 million worth of stains and varnishes a year, and "we make money every year," Samuel Cabot says. He took over the business at age 38, when his 68-year-old father retired. But the senior Samuel Cabot still comes to the job regularly. So does Samuel Jr.'s sister Ellen, who is manager of data processing.

Cabot Corp. itself lists in its roster Louis W. Cabot as chairman; John G. L. Cabot, senior vice-president and director; and John M. Bradley, director. (John G. L. Cabot and John M. Bradley, who runs a plastics firm, are grandsons of Godfrey Cabot, as is Louis.)

The Cabots' recreations tend to be hearty and active, like skiing and sailing, gardening and chopping wood. "Rather than going to the country club, I like to work with my hands," one says. Paul Cabot's branch of the family regularly vacations at Cabotville, a rustic retreat on an island near Pulpit Harbor, Maine. The unpretentious collection of 10 houses there, sometimes packed with as many as 40 Cabots, contrasts with the posh formality of nearby Bar Harbor.

Cabots, like Bostonians generally, disparage jet-set glitter. Boston "isn't gaudy. There are no fancy clothes, fancy jewelry or fancy society," says Walter Cabot, the Harvard endowment manager. "I guess this city just came from the Puritan ethic."

Even by Boston standards, the Cabots are notoriously practical. Anne Cabot Wyman, the *Globe* editor, recalls that on the death of

Walter M. Cabot, three Brahmin families who were related to the deceased got together to divide up his personal effects. "The Paines took art. The Forbeses took books. And the Cabots all took furniture," she says.

This is in line with the Cabot penchant for coming straight to the point. According to one old Boston saying, "The Cabots are a curious clan with customs but no manners." Even today, Anne Wyman admits, "I've heard it said with pride. We do have manners in terms of decency and compassion. But there's no curled finger on a tea-cup or that sort of thing."

"If manners is defined as the niceties according to Emily Post, we might not be the greatest," admits Walter Cabot. "We're not known for small talk and pleasantries. I'll go in a direct route. I won't beat around the bush. I have no intention of being rude. But it's a busy world."

That is certainly in keeping with a long tradition. While Godfrey Cabot was noted for his blunt rudeness and his insistence that conversation be limited to topics of interest to him, he was by no means unique in his family. Dr. Richard Cabot, when introduced to the husband of a distant cousin, was invited to dinner by the man. The distinguished doctor replied, "Really, I have so many people I should like to dine with but never get around to, I should not pretend that I ever would do it."

Thomas Cabot concedes that when he first became active in the State Department, his new colleagues were shocked by the directness with which he criticized proposals by distinguished European diplomats.

One family anecdote illustrates the precept that Cabots don't set much store by propriety. One time Paul Cabot and his brother Henry B. were in Paris for a wedding. For a little exercise, they went to a tennis club, but were told they couldn't go on the courts without white attire, which they had neglected to bring. Undaunted, they stripped to their underwear and proceeded to rally away. Undoubtedly, their ancestor Thomas H. Perkins, who said "A man in my position can wear a leather thong," would have approved.

In the Victorian generation of Cabots, there was a notable lack of open emotion. Godfrey Cabot's children have criticized him for his lack of affection and his inability to compliment them or show affection. Judge Charles Cabot once said, "My wife's always telling me I can run a community drive but I don't know how to give a Christmas present."

Cabots maintain they aren't cold within their families today. But they still often present a gruff exterior.

Inside the family, the Cabot name sometimes is treated as a joke. A sign at the family retreat in Maine reads "Cabotville—No Lowells here." Godfrey Cabot, late in life, was introduced to a southern man who said with mock surprise, "I thought the Cabots spoke only to God." Cabot responded, "Why sir, I thought you were God."

But to many in the family, the name seems a burden. "Certain people do things with that name," complains Ellen Cabot, the data-processing manager at Samuel Cabot Inc. "They assume all kinds of odd things about you." Her brother, who says he felt comfortable entering the family firm only after first proving himself as a banker, says "the relationships are kind of beaten into you."

Charles Cabot, a corporate lawyer in Boston, admits that just possessing the name once made him uncomfortable, but as he got older and accomplished more, "it bothered me less than it used to."

In some senses, it seems, being a Cabot forces the bearers of the name on to greater accomplishment. Walter Cabot, who as manager of Harvard's endowment has certainly achieved a measure of success, says, "When I was a kid, the name always made me feel a little uncomfortable. Now, to a degree, we've all earned our own way. Until you begin to do that for yourself, you feel uncomfortable."

II

The Sears

I T W A S A common credit-card snafu, the kind that happens to everyone sooner or later. The victim was a suburban Chicago homeowner who had placed an order with Sears, Roebuck & Co. for a kit with which to build a two-car garage—one of those home products for which the giant retailer is well known. The price of the kit was $3,800, but when the bill arrived it was for slightly more than $10,000.

The man did what anyone else would do under similar circumstances: he called the store and asked, nicely, if things would be set straight. He was assured, nicely, that they would be. That little scene was repeated several times over the next six months, but the bills for $10,000 kept right on coming.

So, reluctantly and in desperation, the fellow played his trump card. He informed the store that he was the grandson of the company's founder. "The first few people I talked to didn't believe me, which was what I was afraid would happen, but I finally got through to someone who did," says Carroll Sears. "He got things fixed up."

The folks at Sears, Roebuck & Co. might have been forgiven for thinking the man on the telephone was bluffing. Sears, after all, is a fairly common name, and no member of the family had been associated with the company since Richard Warren Sears, the promotional genius who started it in 1893, died in 1914, fully 65 years before.

They might have been even less willing to believe Carroll Sears's story if he had told it in person. Sears is a bulky, bearded man of 36 years who favors casual garments such as lumberjackets, cotton "washpants," and ankle-topping work boots. He looks like what he is: a hobbyist, handyman, and sometimes hardware-store clerk. The fact that he works out of choice, not necessity (he has a good-sized income from an inheritance), and owns a four-acre estate north of Chicago fronted by an iron gate that is controlled from inside his house doesn't affect his image of himself.

"I'm a plain guy who likes to work with his hands," he says. "I have never made a big deal out of being Richard Sears's grandson. The thing about the garage was my first contact with the company other than as an ordinary customer."

Sears Roebuck feels much the same way about the descendants of its founders. Its public-relations department keeps a list of the children and grandchildren of Richard Warren Sears and Alvah Curtis Roebuck, the erstwhile partners, but it is sketchy and doesn't specify their whereabouts. The company has made little effort to keep in touch with them over the years. "Why should we?" asks a spokesman for the company. "That's all part of the past."

That attitude, which might seem cruel to some, is the prevalent one in the impatient world of American business. Families like the Fords, McCormicks, and du Ponts, whose members were active through many generations in the pioneering concerns created by their forebears, are very definitely exceptional.

The reasons for this are several and well known. Students of management are fond of pointing out that the men of vision who start new enterprises often lack the skills and temperament to run them after they get going, and they depart soon after their seminal function is completed. Public ownership—the eventual form of almost all United States corporations that grow to large size—tends not to be tolerant of nepotism and mediocrity, although public companies certainly are not devoid of either. As is illustrated in other chapters of this book, family control over business enterprises is inevitably dissipated by stock sales made to pay (or avoid paying) inheritance taxes.

There is also the deeply-rooted American code of the individual, which holds that it is noblest—indeed, imperative—to succeed on one's own. "The old line, 'Son, some day all this will be yours,' is more European than American," says Robert Sobol, professor of business history at Hofstra University in Hempstead, New York. "The wealthy American father tells his son that someday he will be able to do whatever he wants."

The offspring of some famous American business families, such as the Rockefellers and Harrimans, followed that course to distinction in a variety of fields over the years. More often, though, it leads to obscurity, sometimes consciously chosen.

That this should happen to the descendants of Richard Sears is noteworthy, because the company he founded, with a small assist from Alvah Roebuck, is one of the best-known enterprises around. A retailing and mail-order colossus, its sales of more than $18 billion a year make it far and away the largest such chain in the United States, with a revenue equivalent to almost 1 percent of the entire gross national product, the annual sum of all goods and services produced in the country.

Sears's 800-odd retail outlets and more than 2,500 catalog centers make it a ubiquitous part of America's Main Streets and shopping centers. Its mail-order catalogs, distributed at a rate of 50 million annually, have a circulation surpassed only by the Bible. Some 32 million Americans, or more than one of every three adults, hold Sears credit cards, and most use them fairly frequently to buy items included in the company's vast line of merchandise.

The company has 460,000 employees and 278,000 stockholders. Its 110-story headquarters building in downtown Chicago, a pyramid of rectangles as solid and unstylish as the company itself, ranks as the world's tallest building; its 4.5 million square feet of floor space make it the largest office structure anywhere.

"No single institution, including perhaps the Government itself, so nearly reflects so many aspects of the daily life of the American people," wrote Gordon Weil in *Sears, Roebuck, U.S.A.,* the latest (1977) of several books about the company.

S EARS ROEBUCK WAS important historically as well. Although Richard Sears did not invent the mail-order business on which the company was based, he did develop it into one of the major homogenizing forces of the turn-of-the-century United States. The 1894 Sears catalog—its first to offer what amounted to a complete line of goods—was included among the most significant documents of the American past by historian Daniel J. Boorstin in his book, *An American Primer.*

"The Sears catalog changed the pattern of distribution of goods in this country—it was a system of mass distribution to match our emerging system of mass production," says John E. Jeuck, professor of business at the University of Chicago and co-author of *Catalogues and Counters,* the definitive history of the company. "It set a standard of value for products of all sorts. It was a major transmission belt of middle-class culture and tastes."

The company that was to do all this had a very inauspicious beginning by any standard. Formed in Minneapolis in 1886 by 23-year-old Richard Sears, it was first called the R.W. Sears Watch Co., and it sold cheap timepieces through a mail-order catalog composed by its creative proprietor.

The year before, the young Sears had been a railroad stationmaster in the small town of North Redwood, Minn. He had taken the job several years earlier, partly because it enabled him to practice telegraphy, his hobby, and partly because the second floor of the Minneapolis and St. Louis Railroad depot, where he worked, provided living quarters for himself, his mother, Eliza, and his two sisters, Kate and Eva. His father, Warren, a Civil War veteran who had failed as a farmer, blacksmith, and gold miner, had given up on making a living. He left it to his only son to support the family.

Young Richard Sears, however, was not long for humble tasks. He always had a strong bent for commerce, which he got a chance to exercise when a shipment of watches that a local jeweler refused to claim wound up in his station house. He contacted the Chicago manufacturer, and he was told he could buy them for $12 each and sell them for whatever he could get. He said that sounded fine and offered the watches to other stationmasters on his line for $14 each. Since the timepieces were fetching about $25 at retail locally, they were happy to accept, thereby affording the young man a quick profit. Richard Sears so enjoyed the experience that he soon embarked for Minneapolis, the nearest large city, and went into the watch-selling business full time, using the mails as his merchandising medium.

ALVAH CURTIS ROEBUCK came along in 1887, when the R.W. Sears Watch Co., having moved to Chicago because of that city's advantages as a transportation center, advertised in the *Chicago Daily News* for a repairman to handle the heavy volume of defective timepieces that customers were returning. Roebuck, also 23 years old (he was one month and two days younger than Sears), was earning $3.50 a week repairing watches in Hammond, Ind., near where he was born. When he answered the ad, he and Sears hit it off immediately, and the two soon became partners. After several corporate transmutations—one of which found Roebuck buying out Sears for about a week—Sears, Roebuck & Co. was formed in 1893, offering a broad range of goods through the mails.

It is hard to imagine two more different individuals than Sears and Roebuck. Sears was a full-bodied, active, almost peripatetic person, given to sudden enthusiasms and rapid-fire speech when he was expounding upon a subject that interested him, as happened frequently. He was a promoter—an idea man who always kept pencil and paper handy so he could jot down his ideas before they were pushed out of his head by other ideas.

To say that Richard Sears's sense of business ethics was deficient, at least by modern-day standards, would be to give him the benefit of considerable doubt. His credo was sell, sell, sell; he did not much care how he did it.

The best account of the early days of Sears, Roebuck & Co. is the book, *Send No Money*, by Louis E. Asher, an early employee of the concern. Asher, who became the company's general manager and was a close friend of Sears, relates that Sears consistently advertised for sale goods that he did not have, assuming he could obtain them later, after the orders had come in. This did not go down well with many customers, Asher wrote:

> The volume of letters complaining of delay frightened Richard Sears's associates. They were ready to discontinue the advertising until the factories could catch up and the orders on hand had been filled. But Sears continued the barrage of printers' ink. He believed it was of greater importance to spread the news of his bargains quickly, to entrench the business by making as many customers as possible in the shortest time, even though his procedure brought some waste through cancellations and some dissatisfaction through delays.

> A classic in the apocrypha of the early history of Sears, Roebuck & Co. is the letter from the customer who wrote: 'We are waiting for the special $5.95 baby buggy we ordered for our little son. Better change the order to a single-barrel shotgun and a plug of chewing tobacco. The kid is growing up.'

Alvah Curtis Roebuck was quite the opposite sort. He was a sparely-built, quiet person whose religious feelings, always strong, came increasingly to the fore after he adopted the Christian Science faith upon his marriage in 1900. He was clever with his hands—indeed, he was a mechanical genius—but he had little taste for the rough-and-tumble of the marketplace.

In 1939, when he was 75 years old, Roebuck wrote a brief autobiographical chapter for a history of the company he was preparing (it never was published). Of his earliest years with Sears, the following is one of the few things he chose to set down for posterity:

> During the two years I worked for the R.W. Sears Watch Co. from April 1887, to March 1889, I had the best lathe and set of attachments and other tools I could buy. . . . Every evening at closing time, instead of leaving my lathe, attachments and other tools, etc., exposed on the bench, as most workmen do, my careful nature prompted me to wipe off all perspiration marks, etc., with a piece of chamois skin, enclose it in a cotton flannel bag, remove it from the bench and place it in a vault for safekeeping, as a result of which, after nearly three years of service,

instead of having the appearance of an old lathe, it was almost as
bright as new.

A man of such temperament could not be expected to counte-
nance the sharp business practices of Richard Sears, or the chroni-
cally precarious financial condition of the fledgling corporation in
which he found himself a partner. By 1895, his stomach had "gone
back" on him and his nerves had become so "jumpy" they frightened him, he later told an interviewer for the *New Yorker* magazine. He sold his one-third interest in the company to Sears for a
sum variously recorded as $20,000 or $25,000.

Roebuck stayed on in a managerial role for several years after
the sale, then left to design and manufacture equipment for the
infant motion-picture industry. He made some money there, invested it in real estate around St. Petersburg, Fla., and lost it all in
the crash that accompanied the Depression of the 1930s.

Needing a job, he applied at Sears, Roebuck & Co. in 1933, 19
years after the death of Richard Sears. He was hired as a low-paid
clerk in the patents-research department. He spent the years immediately before his final retirement from the company in 1940
touring Sears's retail stores so customers could get a look at the
surviving founder of a chain that had grown to enormous size.
(Sears Roebuck had begun opening retail stores in 1925.)

It was an assignment that pleased him, he told associates. It was
not taxing, it gave him a chance to meet people under comfortable
circumstances, and it allowed him to tell the gentle jokes that
delighted him. A favorite went like this: "A minister visited a new
family in his parish and greeted the wife at the door by saying, 'I
am your minister of the Gospel.' The wife then turned and told her
husband, 'The man is here about the gas bill.' "

In his later years, Roebuck occasionally confessed to having
some regrets about selling out so cheaply to Sears. But he thought
that, all in all, he had not fared too poorly in his life.

"Sears made $25 million—he's dead," Roebuck told the man
from the *New Yorker* in 1938. "Skinner (the company's first gener-
al-merchandise manager) made $1.25 million—he's dead. (Julius)
Rosenwald (Sears's later partner and long-time head of the compa-

ny) made $100 million—he's dead. Me, I am 75 years old, and I never felt better."

Roebuck died in Tujunga, Calif., in 1948, at age 84. Perhaps no one whose name adorns a major American corporation did so little to earn such a continuing notoriety. (Goodyear Tire & Rubber Co., the world's largest tire manufacturer, is named for Charles Goodyear, the developer of rubber, but the designation is purely honorary. Neither Mr. Goodyear nor any member of his family was ever involved in the company.) Over the years, Sears, Roebuck & Co. officials have several times discussed dropping Roebuck's name, but whenever word of such a decision leaked out, enough customers protested so that the plans were halted. Nonetheless, the Roebuck name is being quietly phased out of company operations— the corporation's logo, for instance, consists simply of the name "Sears" encased in a black rectangle—and it may not survive much longer. No descendant of Roebuck has ever worked for the company.

Meanwhile, back in 1895, Richard Sears already was doing fine without Alvah Roebuck. After buying him out, he took on as partners Aaron Nusbaum, who was in the business of manufacturing the pneumatic tube systems that whisked cash, receipts, and other paperwork around department stores, and Julius Rosenwald, Nusbaum's brother-in-law.

Rosenwald, a manufacturer of men's suits, had had dealings with Sears, Roebuck & Co. One day, Richard Sears came into Rosenwald's factory asking to see some suits. A salesman offered to show him a selection, but Sears brushed him aside, quickly examined a few that were on hand, and ordered 50 of them. He had already sold them, he explained, so fast delivery was essential; if he received orders for more, he would be back.

Rosenwald was impressed with a man who could do business like that, so when his brother-in-law offered him the chance to join Sears, he took it. On Aug. 23, 1895, the company drew up new articles of incorporation that left Sears with 800 shares and Nusbaum and Rosenwald with 350 each. The total of $75,000 the two paid for the stock came in handy for the capital-short company.

Later, Sears sold each of them some of his own shares, and they became equal partners.

Aaron Nusbaum and Julius Rosenwald gave Sears, Roebuck & Co. the managerial competence it had lacked, and the concern grew apace. But so did friction between the brothers-in-law, who found that being related by marriage did not mean they could work together. The showdown in 1901 found Sears and Rosenwald on one side and Nusbaum the odd-man-out. Sears and Rosenwald purchased Nusbaum's shares for $1,250,000, a sum that in itself was testimony to the company's rapid growth. Rosenwald assumed the "inside" managerial role alone and filled it well, bringing order to the company's finances and formerly chaotic order-filling and warehousing processes. Between 1900 and 1910, annual sales climbed from $10 million to $60 million, surpassing those of Montgomery Ward & Co., which had been in business 20 years when Sears Roebuck was formed in 1893. Over the succeeding years, Sears and Ward's were to fight it out on many a merchandising battleground, but Ward's, although a large and prosperous company in its own right, almost always came out second-best.

Historians agree that while Rosenwald's executive skills played a vital role in Sears Roebuck's early success, most of the credit should go to Sears. He had, they say, a unique talent for writing advertising copy that tapped the material aspirations of rural Americans, the primary audience for his justly-famous catalogs.

COMPARING PRESENT SEARS ROEBUCK catalogs with those composed by the company's founder in its early days is like comparing a corporate annual report with a Ringling Brothers, Barnum and Bailey Circus brochure. Sears's catalogs were wild, exuberant things, wordy and full of bombast and inflated claims. Their object was to sell, and sell they did, with page upon page of illustrations of products and florid descriptions of their wonders down to the smallest details.

Sears, Roebuck & Co., its catalogs proclaimed, was "The Cheapest Supply House on Earth" and "The Great Price Maker." Goods offered for sale were routinely described as "marvelous," "most

Richard Sears got his start in commerce in 1886 when he accepted a shipment of watches refused by the original purchaser. He resold the watches to other agents, starting a business that grew into Sears, Roebuck and Co.

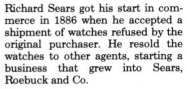

Alvah Roebuck was hired to repair the many broken watches returned to Richard Sears' small company. He soon became a partner, but sold out in 1925 for about $20,000 because the tremulous nature of his partner's management was effecting his nerves.

Richard Sears poses with the catalog credited with changing the system of distribution of goods in America.

Julius Rosenwald was a clothing manufacturer who was impressed with Richard Sears' brash purchasing practices. He joined the firm as a partner and brought order to the firm's finances and formerly chaotic order-filling process. He was Chairman from 1924 to 1932.

The first Sears retail stores opened in 1925 and were well received.

Single Generator Gasoline Stoves.

No. 15781. The **Acme** Single Generator Gasoline Stove, No. 122, has two burners on top and one powerful double burner on step; a single generator serves all burners; every generator provided with a union joint coupling at bottom of stand pipe, and all generators have separate channels; size of main top, 20x27 inches; step top, 36x14 inches; high shelf, 7x22 inches; height to main top, 30 inches; height to top shelf, 44 inches; shipping weight, 105 lbs. **This is our Leader** in this class of stoves, and is as strong, handsome and durable a stove as any one could wish. Price, with tin oven, **$14.25**; with Russia oven.............................**$15.00**
Full directions for operating with each stove.

1897 Acme Process.

Finest on earth. Greatly improved for 1897. These improvements to be had only in the Acme.

Leading Points:

All Stoves are strongly and substantially built. All stoves are beautifully finished and elegantly designed. All competitors attest to the superiority of our stoves as regards finish and design. All hot air and vaporizing tubes are connected with removable cast iron elbows, easily taken apart, so that the vaporizers can be taken out and cleaned. All vaporizers are made of perforated brass and of the latest scientific construction. All burner drums are of the best sheet brass, and have

NOTE REDUCED PRICES.

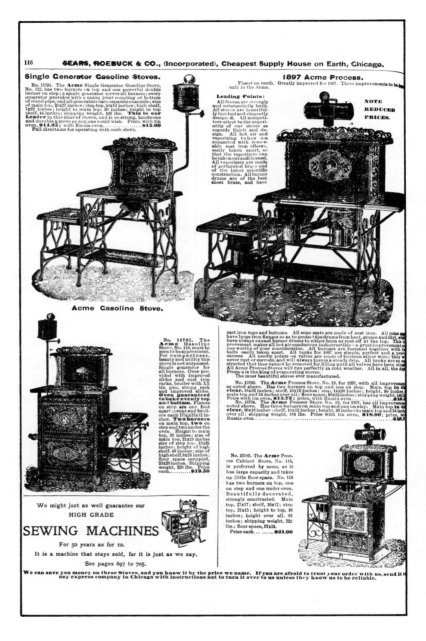

Acme Gasoline Stove.

No. 15782. The **Acme** Gasoline Stove, No. 118, must be seen to be appreciated. For compactness, beauty and utility this stove is not surpassed. Single generator for all burners. Oven provided with improved slides and cast iron racks, broiler with XX tin pan, strong rack and improved slides. **Oven guaranteed to bake evenly top and bottom.** Flames on step are one foot apart; ovens and broilers each 17½x15x12 inches. **Two burners** on main top, two on step and two under the oven. Height to main top, 35 inches; size of main top, 21x28 inches; size of step top, 15x21 inches; height of high shelf, 49 inches; size of high shelf, 8x23 inches; floor space occupied, 23x28 inches. Shipping weight, 220 lbs. Price each...........**$19.50**

cast iron tops and bottoms. All cone seats are made of cast iron. All cone seats have large iron flanges so as to protect the drums from heat, grease and dirt, which have always caused burner drums to either burn or rust off at the top. This improvement makes all hot air conductors indestructible—a great improvement, one worthy of your consideration. All burners are fastened together with bolts easily taken apart. All tanks for 1897 are simple, perfect and a positive success. All needle points on valves are made of German silver wire; they will never rust or corrode, and will always insure a steady drip. All tanks are so constructed that they cannot be removed for filling until all valves have been closed. All Acme Process Stoves will run perfectly in cold weather. All in all, the Acme Process is the king of evaporating stoves.
The most beautiful stoves ever manufactured.

No. 15783. The **Acme** Process Stove, No. 18, for 1897, with all improvements as noted above. Has two burners on top and one on step. Main top **in G clear**, 16x22 inches; shelf, 16x12 inches; step, 14x20 inches; height, 30 inches; main top and 54 inches over all; floor space, 38x22 inches; shipping weight, 145 lbs. Price with tin oven, **$15.75**; price, with Russia oven..............................**$16.**

No. 15784. The **Acme** Process Stove No. 19, for 1897, has all improvements noted above. Has three burners on main top and one on step. Main top **in H clear**, 36x16 inches; shelf, 16x12 inches; height, 30 inches to main top and 54 inches over all; shipping weight, 164 lbs. Price with tin oven, **$18.00**; price, with Russia oven..............................**$19.**

No. 15785. The **Acme** Process Cabinet Stove, No. 113, is preferred by some, as it has large capacity and takes up little floor space. No. 113 has two burners on top, one on step and one under oven. Beautifully decorated, strongly constructed. Main top, 27x17; shelf, 16x12; step top, 21x15; height to top, 36 inches; height over all, 63 inches; shipping weight, 222 lbs.; floor space, 27x24.
Price each...............**$21.00**

We can save you money on these Stoves, and you know it by the price we name. If you are afraid to trust your order with us, send it to any express company in Chicago with instructions not to turn it over to us unless they know us to be reliable.

OUR OWN SPECIAL GUARANTEED REMEDIES

Many Unreliable Drugs and Special Remedies are being offered by houses whose reliability is unknown by us or you. That there is merit in some there is no doubt, but that any amount of worthless remedies are being offered and sold to the public under as many glowing names we all know too well.

OUR SPECIAL REMEDIES are all reliable and can be depended upon to cure the diseases for which they are intended.

An Able Chemist and Registered Pharmacist is in charge of this department, a man whose long experience and almost world wide reputation is a guarantee for every preparation we offer.

Our 60c. Nerve and Brain Pills.

GUARANTEED THE HIGHEST GRADE ON THE MARKET.
SIX BOXES POSITIVELY GUARANTEED TO CURE any disease for which they are intended.

ONLY $3.00 for 6 boxes, when retail dealers sell inferior goods at $1.00 per box; $5.00 for six boxes.

BEWARE OF QUACK DOCTORS who advertise to scare men into paying money for remedies which have no merit.

OUR NERVE AND BRAIN PILLS are compounded from a prescription of one of the most noted German scientists and is the same as has been used in the German hospitals for years with marvelous success. Never before was sold at less than $1.00. Our price, 60 cents per box or six boxes, enough to cure any case of any nature, $3.00. This pill has a remarkable effect on both old and young. It cannot be equaled by any others as a cure for impotence, spermatorrhoea and all diseases arising from excesses and abuses of any kind. It will tone up the whole nervous system, no matter how much worn out, overworked or depressed you may be, and give you a new lease of life. It can be sent by mail, private and secure. Full and very explicit directions telling you how to treat yourself to get thoroughly well and strong again.
No. D 158 Per box, 60c; one-half d'z. boxes............$3.00

IRON PILLS FOR THE WEAK.

25 CENTS FOR A $1.00 REMEDY.
ONE DOZEN BOXES FOR $2.00 ~~~ **ALWAYS SOLD AT $10.00 PER DOZEN**

OUR GUARANTEE. We guarantee 6 boxes of this remedy to cure in every case. THE GREATEST REMEDY EVER KNOWN. First prescribed by an eminent French physician and found to produce results of another medicine. Our sale has been so large that we have, by buying in immense quantities, been able to reduce the price—formerly $1.00 per box, $10.00 per dozen—to 25 cents per box, $2.00 per dozen.

Order One Dozen Boxes at once is our advice for we can not guarantee to maintain this price after our present stock becomes exhausted.

The great blood builder. Cures pale and sallow complexions, suppression of the periods, rheumatism and all diseases arising from mental worry, overwork, early decay, etc. Full directions on circular around the box.
No. D 172 Price, 25c; 1oz. boxes...................$2.00

Our 50 Cent Cure to Stop the Drinking and Tobacco Habit.

The only positive Tobacco and Liquor Cure on the market.
DON'T PAY TWO PRICES for remedies that will do you no good. We guarantee this medicine to cure any case and to our knowledge it is the only remedy that will positively cure in every case.

We guarantee this to cure anyone of the habit of drinking alcoholic stimulants or the tobacco habit in any of its forms. It is the greatest temperance worker the world has ever known. It creates a desire for food instead of drink. It stops the craving for liquor or tobacco instantly and stimulates the entire system to healthy action. It quiets nervous excitement, improves the appetite and regulates digestion, regulates the bowels, repairs the waste caused by over indulgence in liquor or tobacco and makes one feel like a new man again. We will give special prices to any temperance society who would wish to give it a trial and test its merits. Treat yourself at home and become a new man.
No. D 124 Box containing 24 doses, 50c............$5.00
          Box containing 6 doses, $1.00; doz........9.10

ARE YOU ONE OF THEM? SCORES HAVE SENT US MONEY FOR GOODS WITH NO NAME OR ADDRESS OR OTHER MEANS OF IDENTIFICATION. WE ARE HOLDING THIS MONEY IN THE BANK AWAITING CLAIMS. BE SURE YOU MAKE NO SUCH MISTAKE.

Our Great Kidney and Liver Cure For 85 Cents.

ONE BOTTLE, 85 CENTS.   +   12 BOTTLES, $9.00.
Nothing to compare with it ever compounded.

~~~~~~**READ OF ITS MERITS**~~~~~~
FOR BRIGHT'S DISEASE it is known to cure when all other remedies fail.
IN FEMALE COMPLAINTS it has no equal. As a kidney, liver and bladder medicine it is simply wonderful and will effect a speedy cure when all other remedies have failed.

This is a scientific preparation of vegetable ingredients, highly esteemed for its soothing and healing qualities in all diseases of the kidneys, liver and bladder. It is one of the recognized remedies for Bright's disease and has performed some remarkable cures. It is very valuable in female complaints of urinary organs, change in life, irregularities, prolapsus, etc. Full directions accompany each bottle.
No. D 150 Pint bottle, 85c; per doz..............$9.00

Female Pills.

These pills are a combination of Pennyroyal, Tansy, Cottonroot Bark in a concentrated form, with other ingredients which increase the peculiar effect of these medicines. They are very powerful and require to be used cautiously, but if the very complete directions which can be found separately in each box will be followed closely, all will be well. Full treatment in each box.
No. D 153 Per box.............$0.35
          Per doz. boxes.........3.50
With useful information and instructions to ladies concerning their troubles.

OUR 25-CENT PILE REMEDY

We know of no other unfailing cure for piles in all its forms. We have sold many thousand boxes and do not know of a single case when a positive and permanent cure has not been effected. We do not mean to offer a remedy that has not been put to every test, hence our safety in guaranteeing every one of our special remedies.

This is a guaranteed cure for blind, bleeding or itching piles. If you have tried other remedies without getting relief, we advise you to send for a box of this. It never fails to give relief and a cure.
No. D 164 Box, 25c; doz. boxes, $2.00

ARSENIC COMPLEXION WAFERS FOR 40 CENTS.

D 162 Arsenic Complexion Wafers for 40 cents. Inferior preparations are sold by others as high as $1.50. These wafers are from the prescription of a famous French physician, and are perfectly harmless when used according to the directions on each box. They are an excellent remedy for rough and discolored skin. They clear the complexion and make the skin soft and smooth. They tone up the whole system and when used for a length of time will make thin persons plump and keep them so. There are many similar preparations on the market offered at retail as high as $1.50, but we reduce the price to 40 cents, based on the actual cost of material and labor with only our one small profit added.
Small box, 40c; per dozen.........$4.35
Large   "   79c;   " 8.00

wonderful," "greatest value," or "of highest quality." Everything
was guaranteed, seemingly forever.

Even by today's standards, the range of goods offered for sale by
the company in its early days is impressive. How must it have
seemed 70 or 80 years ago, when farmers and small-town dwellers
were largely dependent on one-room general stores? Within a few
pages in the 1908 Sears catalog, for instance, were such items as
precision drafting instruments, hammerless double-barrel shot-
guns (price: $8.95), a crank-operated Mississippi-brand washing
machine guaranteed to clean clothes better than anything on the
market "without toil or sweat to the housewife," and oil-painted
backgrounds suitable for the imposition of favorite family photographs.

Early Sears catalogs contained more than just descriptions of
goods that could be purchased. There were detailed freight-rate
tables and instructions on how to carry out the mail-order process,
which many potential customers undoubtedly found daunting.

There were letters extolling Sears's products and service, meant
to assure readers that the company's claims for its merchandise
were not mere hyperbole. One letter in the 1896 catalog read as
follows:

Gentlemen:

The watch I bought from you 16 months ago is a daisy. I have
always got the time. I call it The Regulator.

Sincerely,

James E. Bowman

Union City, Kentucky

And there were editorials setting down the policies of the new
mail-order house and combatting slurs against it by the retail
merchants of the day, who correctly saw in the mass-merchandis-
ing firms the end of the local general store as they knew it.

It is hard now to appreciate the depth of feeling behind the anti-
mail-order campaigns launched by turn-of-the-century American
merchants. These individuals held a good deal of power in their
communities by virtue of their sway over credit and newspaper
advertising, and they used it to organize catalog burnings in their

town squares and attacks against the catalog houses in the local press.

Personal slanders against the owners and officers of the mail-order firms were common. In the South, for instance, Sears Roebuck competitors began the rumor that Roebuck was a black man, in hopes of discouraging white patronage. So persistent was this rumor that as recently as 1978 the *Chicago Tribune's* "Action Line" column answered a query about it.

Some of the flavor of the attacks on the mail-order houses (but none of the bitterness) comes through in this rhyme from *The Emporia Gazette* in Kansas around 1900, quoted by Louis Asher in *Send No Money.*

THE GHOST

The evening was chill, and the frost it was hoar, when the shade of my grandmother stood in the door. She looked at me long with her luminous eyes, expressing reproach that she could not disguise. "It's mighty bad taste to come haunting," I said. "Go back to the boneyard and sleep with the dead."

"I wouldn't have left it," my grandma replied, "but I haven't been able to sleep when I tried. That gravestone you gave me is really a sin; it's painted like marble, but it is only tin. And it squawks and it groans in the murmuring breeze, in a sickening way that would make your blood freeze.

"O why did you send to Searsbuck and Rose for a slab for your granny, who'd turned up her toes? The home marble dealers were after the job, but you thought you could save fifty centimes, you slob. That bloomin' tin headstone has made me a fright, and now I shall haunt you six hours every night."

Richard Sears used his catalog to fight back, playing skillfully on farmers' age-old suspicions of middlemen. He did it bluntly, writing in his 1896 catalog, "It is natural for the retail dealer to keep you from sending your money away from home, if possible. By ordering from us, you take the profit from his pocket and put it in your own."

Or he could do it craftily. Witness this "economics lesson," titled "Our Compliments to the Retail Merchant," which he included in his catalog of 1902:

He (the retailer) fills an important place in commerce, in that he is a necessary agent for the distributing of all kinds of merchandise to the convenience of customers everywhere. Very rarely the country merchant who sells you dry goods, shoes, hardware and other merchandise overcharges you. As a rule, the merchant from whom you buy adds as little profit to the cost of the goods to him as he can possibly afford to add, for example: if a certain article in our catalog is quoted at $1 and your hardware merchant asks you $1.50 for the same article, we wish to say in behalf of your hardware dealer that this difference of 50 cents does not represent an excessive profit he is charging you; for by reason of his being compelled to buy from wholesale houses in small quantities, he is compelled to pay more for this article than we would pay. . . . His sales are necessarily small, his expenses necessarily large in proportion to the amount of business he does, and he must get his cost, his expenses and a fair profit out of the goods he sells.

Mr. Sears also was an early and highly-successful practitioner of the art of public relations. To induce farmers to deal with a far-away company about which they knew little, he had to establish a reputation for attentiveness to customer complaints—no small feat in light of his company's erratic early order-filling record. He did this in part by circulating stories to the effect that Sears Roebuck would exchange any piece of merchandise for any reason.

One story of the time, widely quoted by company historians, had a streetcar conductor Richard Sears had chanced to meet ruefully telling the mail-order magnate how he had inadvertently dropped and broken a watch he had bought at Sears Roebuck. Sears is said to have told the man to come to his office and select a new one. "I guarantee our watches not to fall out of people's pockets and break," he is reported to have said.

In another, Sears is said to have learned that a boy in Ohio had become crippled after a local doctor improperly set a leg the boy had broken in an accident involving his Sears bicycle. Sears brought the lad to Chicago and had his leg reset at his expense.

Such examples were compelling, and they lifted the new company's sales past those of its competitors. But supply was not always dependable, money for expansion was sometimes hard to obtain, and profits did not always keep pace. They hit a reef during the economic depression of 1907, which sparked an inevitable conflict between Sears, who wanted to increase advertising and sales no matter what the cost, and Rosenwald, who favored cutting expenses and waiting until business conditions improved.

The argument, which came to a head the next year, found Rosenwald with the support of the now-large concern's other officers. Sears had threatened to quit several times previously as a result of disputes with Rosenwald over business tactics, but this time he made good his threat and resigned as president in 1908.

Julius Rosenwald succeeded Sears as president and, later, as chairman. He died in 1932, having presided over the establishment of Sears, Roebuck & Co. as the nation's leading merchandiser. His son, Lessing, was chairman of the company from 1932 to 1938. Lessing's son, Julius II, is a director of the company, but not an executive. Edgar B. Stern, Jr., Lessing's nephew, also is a director.

Sears stayed on as chairman of the board for five years more, but the title was strictly ceremonial. By one account, he never attended a board meeting after his resignation as president, and he evinced little other interest in the company. In 1913, he sold his Sears Roebuck stock to Goldman, Sachs & Co., the New York investment banking house, for $10 million. When he died a year later in Waukesha, Wis., at age 50, his death certificate listed "apoplexy" as the cause. He left a wife, two sons, two daughters, and an estate worth about $25 million.

Printers Ink, the trade magazine of the advertising industry, wrote this as his obituary:

R. W. Sears was a mail-order man, had the mail-order viewpoint, knew how to use advertising space, knew the value of copy, knew the conditions surrounding mail-order publications, and he succeeded in a big way because he possessed those qualities to a greater degree than any other mail-order man who ever lived.

Those words are as true today as they were when they were written. Perhaps more than any man who succeeded in founding a landmark American company, Richard W. Sears was a specialist. He could do only one thing really well: sell merchandise to farmers. He did it so well that his name remains one of the most familiar in American business.

Richard Sears could sell things to farmers because, essentially, he was one himself. Despite the fact that he spent most of his adult years in Chicago and accumulated a great fortune, he left little mark there during his lifetime and none thereafter. In the latter regard he was quite unlike his partner, Rosenwald, whose philanthropic monuments—most notably the Museum of Science and Industry—are admired by Chicagoans who know nothing about his accomplishments in business.

The lure of the rural heartland remained strong for Sears throughout his life. Soon after entering his early partnership with Roebuck, he chucked his new mail-order business to trade in farm mortgages in Iowa. Since this activity left no outlet for his creative writing skills he quickly abandoned it, but once back in the saddle he took frequent trips through the rural Midwest, often stopping to chat with farmers along the way. He invariably expressed delight in finding back issues of his famous catalog in farmers' outhouses.

Indeed, his penchant for leaving his Chicago offices to travel around the countryside on missions of self-renewal weakened his position when the final showdown with Rosenwald came. Not only was he widely judged to be a poor executive—headstrong, impetuous, and committed to massive advertising campaigns in bad times as well as good ones—but he also was an absent one, and his absences cost him dearly.

His last years were spent in sad decline. A sort of exile, he traveled the United States and Europe in search of diversion for himself and medical aid for his perennially ailing wife. All the while, he bombarded his friends in the company with letters advising them in the most minute aspects of Sears, Roebuck affairs. But the newly-respected company had no further need for his flamboyant advertising prose, and his business advice was no more welcome coming from afar than it was when he was on hand to deliver it personally.

The $25 million that Sears left to his heirs was a truly regal sum in 1914, and it should have been enough to establish the Sears family as an important one in the Midwest for many years to come. It didn't work out that way.

Sears had few business interests and little expertise outside his own company; by most accounts he was a careless and even whimsical investor. The inventory of his estate, filed in September, 1914, in Lake County, Illinois, just north of Chicago, bears this out. Besides almost $2 million in cash, Sears left a clutter of parcels of farmland in his native Minnesota, timberland in Florida, and residential and commercial tracts in Chicago. He also is said to have had an interest in some property in California, and immediately before his death he reportedly played with the idea of selling it as home sites through a mail-order promotion patterned on his efforts with Sears, Roebuck and Co.

His estate also listed the ownership of a company that had defaulted on a loan he had made to it, as well as numerous and scattered municipal and railroad bonds. Most interestingly, almost half of the 48-page estate inventory was devoted to listing personal real-estate loans, ranging in size from $1,000 to $100,000 and totaling nearly $2 million, that he had made to 290 individuals and groups. Sears, it seemed, was a one-man mortgage bank. One can imagine the difficulty of his heirs in keeping track of and collecting those loans.

Sears's approach to buying land is related by Donald Gold, a retired banker in Redwood Falls, Minn., who was 86 years old in 1979. Gold's father, William, also was a banker, and he managed several of Sears's properties around Redwood Falls. As a young man, Gold often chauffeured his father and Sears when they visited Sears's holdings in the area.

"My dad and Richard Sears would be riding around, and they would come upon a particularly beautiful piece of farmland that would catch Mr. Sears's eye. He would ask my father to buy it for him—just like that. At times he wouldn't even ask who owned the place, what it might cost, or what could be grown there."

Managing such a diverse estate would have been difficult for an experienced businessman, and it was well beyond the capacities of Sears's wife, Anna. Although she lived to age 77—a full 31 years after the death of her husband—she was a frail woman for most of her adult life. And, like almost all women of that period, she had no training in business or in the management of large sums of money.

What began as a tangled collection of holdings soon became totally unwieldy. "I recall grandmother asking my father, who was a lawyer, to go through her business affairs and advise her on how to straighten them out," recalls Addison L. Gardner III, a Connecticut businessman whose mother, Sylvia, was the oldest child of Richard and Anna Sears. "He looked them over, and he declined. He said they were in such a state that putting them in order was more than he could handle."

Much of the land in Richard Sears's estate was sold at inopportune times or was worked until it was exhausted economically. Such was the fate of the family's timber holdings in south-central Florida, which once were so sizable that a town there carried the Sears name. The town remains on some maps, but it ceased to exist in the 1940s after the trees had been cut and carted away.

Some of the companies in which Richard Sears had an interest met a similar fate, those familiar with his estate say. In addition, some of his children knew more about spending money than about earning it. "Uncle Wesley (Richard Sears's youngest son) lived it up pretty well, and, goodness knows, so did my mother," says Joan Higgins, a daughter of Serena Griess, Richard Sears's youngest daughter.

If Sears had any vocational plans for his children, they have escaped his biographers. At the time of his death, the children ranged in age from 14 to 18 and were perhaps too young for him to have given serious thought to their careers. It is also possible that, wrapped up in his own projects as he was, Richard Sears never devoted much time to the subject.

O f   T H E   F O U R Sears children, only one made any sort of a mark on his own. He was Richard W. Sears II, the oldest son. He spent much of his life as an executive of the Emerson Typewriter Co., of Woodstock, Ill., a firm his father had acquired when it failed to repay a loan. The company is out of business now, but it prospered for many years and provided one noteworthy footnote to history: It manufactured the Woodstock brand typewriter that figured prominently in the famous Alger Hiss perjury trial of 1950.

(Emerson Typewriter Co. also was the scene of the last business collaboration between the elder Richard Sears and Alvah Roebuck. In 1909, when Richard Sears took over the company, he decided it needed a new model of typewriter to remain competitive. He brought in the mechanically-talented Roebuck to devise one. Roebuck was installed as company president, and he came up with a new model. Roebuck stayed with Emerson Typewriter Co. until Sears died and Anna Sears replaced him with her brother.)

Richard W. Sears II died in 1949 at age 49, leaving no children.

Of the four children of Richard and Anna Sears, only one lived past the age of 50. Their second son, Wesley, was a broker on the Chicago Board of Trade; he died at the age of 46 of a liver ailment, a complication of alcoholism. A daughter, Mrs. Griess, died at age 42 from a surgical infection. Sylvia, their oldest child, died in 1969 at age 73.

Tragedy and early death stalked the Sears family into the next generation. Wesley's first son, Wesley Jr., has been a life-long invalid as a result of a brain injury sustained at birth. His second son, Richard, was killed in an automobile accident at the age of 12. Carroll Sears, the fellow who had all the trouble with his bill for the do-it-yourself garage kit ordered from Sears Roebuck, is Wesley's son by adoption.

Mrs. Griess, whose husband was in the leather-goods business, had three daughters. One, Anne Gibson, died of cancer in London in her early 40s. Another, Mrs. Gioia Bonomini, was suffocated by burglars who invaded her home in Anaheim, Calif., in January 1975. (Two boys, aged 15 and 16, were convicted and imprisoned for the crime.) Joan Higgins, Mrs. Griess's remaining daughter, is in her mid-50s. An artist and former landscape architect, and the widow of an advertising executive, she lives and works in New York City.

Mrs. Gardner's two children are Addison, who lives in Greenwich, Conn., and owns an oil-and-gas exploration firm, and Alexander, a private investor with homes in Connecticut and Arizona.

All of Sears's grandchildren received inheritances from his estate, but the early years of waste and mismanagement—coupled with inheritance taxes—took a heavy toll. None of the grandchildren will be specific about the amounts of money that came down to them, but they say they were not overly large, and it is doubtful that more than a few million dollars remains from Richard Sears's $25 million estate. "My inheritance was enough to retire on, but not enough to raise a family," says Addison Gardner, the father of four.

All of Richard Sears's grandchildren were born after his death, so none has any direct memory of him. "He was the fellow with the mustache, whose portrait hung in the living room," says Addison Gardner of his grandfather. (That portrait later was given to Sears, Roebuck & Co., and it hangs in the company's boardroom. Copies of it are distributed as Richard Sears's "official" portrait. It is one of the few paintings or photographs of him extant; he apparently had neither the time nor the inclination to pose for photographers.)

"The only story I know about him came from Grandmother Sears," says Joan Higgins, a slim, vivacious woman. "She told us he trained his dog to eat food off his fork without touching the fork with its mouth. We kids drove our mother crazy trying to teach our dog to do that."

Neither the Gardner brothers nor Mrs. Higgins carried the Sears name, so their descent rested lightly on them. They said that many of their friends were not aware of it, and they never have been especially eager to bring it up. "It's not the sort of subject that comes up in normal conversation," says Addison Gardner. "Besides, I'm half afraid that if the word got around, the price of everything would go up for me."

Mr. Gardner, a large man of conservative dress and demeanor, is an economics graduate of Harvard University. As a young man he considered applying for a job at Sears Roebuck but decided against it. "I didn't want to go under the colors of my grandfather," he said. "I thought that succeeding in that situation might be twice as hard as somewhere else."

Before he went into business for himself in 1964 (his company searches for oil and gas, mostly in West Virginia and Ohio), he was a marketing executive with Jewel Foods in Chicago; earlier he worked for Lever Brothers and Johnson & Johnson Co. in New York.

For Carroll Sears, though, things are different. "Once people know who I am—and I always tell them if they ask—it kind of throws them," he says. "I guess they do not expect that (kind of background) from a guy like me."

Carroll Sears is one of those individuals who seem strangely out of sync with his time and place. Adopted as an infant by Wesley Sears, he grew up in the affluent Chicago suburbs of Lake Forest, Lake Bluff, and Grayslake, attended private primary and secondary schools, and mingled with other boys and girls of considerable wealth and social status.

But book learning was not for him, and neither was the social whirl. He dropped out of little Lincoln College in downstate Illinois after two years and became, first, a ditch-digger for an electric utility in the South and, later, a $125-a-week machinist for a tool company in Chicago. His friends then were his fellow-workers, and even later, when he left manual work for his inheritance and a more leisurely life, his best friend was a fireman in the suburb where he lived.

Likewise, in his tinkerings and his many collections, he evinces a strong preference for the past, when, he believes, "they made things to last."

"We are living in a throwaway society, and it burns me up no end," he says. "The other day, my washer went on the blink, and the repairman came out to fix it. A 15-cent switch had stopped working, but he said he could not get that part alone. He wanted me to pay $80 for a whole new motor. Can you beat that?"

Carroll Sears has spent the years since his "retirement" at age 25 collecting and repairing antique autos, of which his pride is a yellow 1930 Essex coup. "That's my baby," he says. "I restored it totally. I have had it eight years and drive it regularly, and I have never had a problem with it."

He also collects other replicas of motoring's past, such as old oil cans, gasoline-station advertising signs, and the globes off the tops of old-time gas pumps. He has more than 500 gas-pump globes stored in his basement—one of the largest such collections in the United States, he says.

He also collects miniature autos, porcelain figures, Christmas commemorative plates, Oriental objects of art, and radios and phonographs built in the 1920s and 1930s. To house and maintain his collections, he built a 3,200-square-foot workshop and storage building on his estate, which he hopes one day to turn into a private museum.

"It's funny about collections: once I get into something it's hard for me to stop," he says. "Even things like miniature cars and gas-pump globes have a lot of history behind them once you start to dig, and once I have a few I always want more."

He also spends a lot of time with his children, something he thinks most people don't do enough. He and his wife, Darlene, whom he met through their shared interest in antique cars, have two young sons, Richard Warren Sears III ("Ricky") and Tommy. He also has three sons and a daughter by a previous marriage.

When home life and collecting things grow wearisome, Carroll Sears takes a job as a clerk in a large hardware store near his home. The job, he explains, provides extra money for his hobbies and gives him a chance to swap shop talk with the store's customers about projects they are carrying out. He likes the "atmosphere" that he associates with tools and people who use them knowledgeably.

His personal ambitions seem to stretch no further. He has considered the idea of opening a restaurant with an antique-car motif, but he admits that the chances of his actually doing it were small. "I have always enjoyed taking things apart to see what makes them work," he says. "Since I can afford it, that's mostly what I do."

Since his experience with the garage-kit bill, Carroll Sears has come to know a few Sears officials. One of them is Arthur Wood, a company director who previously was chairman. (Mr. Wood was not a relative of General Robert E. Wood, who headed Sears, Roebuck & Co. between 1928 and 1954, and who was given most credit for turning it from a catalog house into the nation's largest retailer.)

Carroll Sears's relationship with Arthur Wood centered, not surprisingly, on antique cars. "He had a '41 Cadillac—a real beauty," Carroll says. "I replaced his master cylinder for him."

But the enormous company his grandfather created remains very much a thing apart for him and his family. "Sometimes, when I take my boys to Sears to shop, one of them will say, 'Look, Dad, that's our store,' " he says. "I tell them that's our name, but it's not our store."

III

The Guggenheims

SITTING CROSS-LEGGED on the floor of the sparsely-furnished studio apartment that serves as his office in Longwood, Fla., William Guggenheim III, one of the few living Guggenheim scions still carrying the name, recalls some of the jobs he has held. He has, he says, been a securities analyst, sex-manual author, owner of a store that sold paper dresses, volunteer fire fighter, and activities coordinator at a school for mentally-retarded children.

But a few years ago—on May 12, 1974, to be exact—Guggenheim began receiving messages from beyond the grave. As might be expected, this changed his life. The messages led Guggenheim to what he calls his true vocation—mystic counseling. "I feel," he says, "as though I have a calling." Having a private income allows him to pursue that calling.

As a mystic counselor, Bill Guggenheim reviews, collects, and catalogues books and tapes on spiritual subjects; attends conferences on such topics as thanatology, the study of death; and corresponds regularly with about 250 other seekers after eternal truth. Guggenheim can, and does, do these things without pay because he and his family live comfortably off the income from his inheritance.

"The money has indulged some of the grosser parts of Bill," says his wife, Judy, who grew up in a working-class family. "But it has also protected the refinements. I don't think he would have reached his current spiritual awareness if he had to compete aggressively to make a living."

Mrs. Guggenheim concedes, however, that despite the high value she and her husband place on his work, it might not look all that important to others. "A lot of people probably think he lives the life of a country gentleman and doesn't do anything very serious," she says resignedly.

Indeed, the peculiarity of Guggenheim's activities might also suggest that he is one of those wealthy eccentrics—with private fortunes that free them from ordinary concerns and conventions—who have either entertained or appalled us over the years: Howard Hughes and his obsessive need for privacy, asbestos heir Tommy Manville and his 13 marriages to 11 women.

Stephen Birmingham, author of several best-selling books about the rich, says he has observed that eccentric behavior commonly emerges in the third or fourth generations of wealthy American families.

Birmingham explains that the founding fathers of great fortunes struggle and scheme to make their millions, and their sons and daughters usually strive to consolidate (or legitimize) those gains and to secure a place for themselves in "Society." It's the following generations that tend to go awry. "They don't have to do anything —it's all been done for them," he says. So, their seemingly aberrant behavior often stems from the feeling that they can't or won't compete with the achievements of the past generations.

Their antics can also be earnest, albeit sometimes misplaced, attempts to create a personality apart from the collective family identity. Further, Birmingham suggests, many of the members of the younger generations fear that people "are only interested in them for their money." The peculiarities may simply be a form of self-protection.

Regardless of the reasons for doing what they do, however, individuals who are considered eccentric add color and texture to the fabric of a family, and their escapades make splendid tales. The Guggenheims, who once controlled some 80 percent of the world's

metal-mining industry and amassed one of the nation's largest
fortunes, are particularly rich in such lore.

ACCORDING TO FAMILY legend, M. Robert Guggen-
heim, the first grandson of the family founder, Meyer, announced
very early in life: "Every wealthy family supports at least one
gentleman in leisure. I have elected to assume that position in
mine."

Colonel Bob, as he was called after a stint in the army during
which he specialized in organizing parties for the officers, lived in
an extremely opulent manner. He had been forced to attend the
Columbia School of Mines, but pedigree rather than grades got
him through. Young Bob's subsequent work in the family business
was so poor that his father and uncles thought it advisable to give
him a $1 million trust fund that would allow him to pursue his
leisurely goals rather than continue to embarrass the Guggenheim
name in the business world.

This delighted Bob. He married four times, once converting to
Catholicism from Judaism to do so. He maintained two estates, a
stable of some 20 thoroughbred horses, a kennel of prize-winning
schipperkes and Bedlington terriers, and a 180-foot yacht complete with wood-burning fireplace in the living room and a dining
room that comfortably accommodated 12 people. The yacht, the
estates, the dogs, the horses were all named the Italianized "Fi-
renze" in honor of Colonel Bob's mother, Florence, whom he
adored and unfailingly called every Sunday at 1 p.m., regardless of
where in the world he was.

The colonel reached his highest level of distinction when, as U.S.
ambassador to Portugal during the Eisenhower administration, he
flipped a spoon down the dress of one of the ladies at a state dinner
. . . and retrieved it. Colonel Bob resigned his position for "personal reasons" a few days later.

Meyer Guggenheim, the man whose business acumen made it
possible for Colonel Bob and Bill to pursue their interests, was, as
would be expected, a totally different sort from them. He was, in
fact, a prototype of the tough, hard-working, single-minded men

who founded U.S. industry as it is known today. For them, the joy of money lay far more in accumulating it than in the comforts it brought.

In 1848, 20-year-old Meyer immigrated to the U.S. from Switzerland with his father, stepmother, four sisters, three stepbrothers, and four stepsisters. The family settled outside Philadelphia.

The Guggenheim clan, like so many other 19th-century Jewish immigrants to the U.S., was fleeing the oppressive anti-Semitism of Europe. Jews there were often forced to live in ghettos separate from the other citizens in the city; there were severe restrictions on the size of their homes and the jobs they could hold.

The Guggenheims had been tailors in a small Swiss village called Lengnau, where the family had been prominent in the Jewish community for over 200 years. But, also like many other immigrants, they started their new life in America as door-to-door peddlers. Meyer Guggenheim was a good deal more clever and enterprising than most, though. He soon figured out that while he and his 56-year-old father did most of the work, trudging through city and countryside with heavy packs on their backs, the manufacturers of the goods they sold made most of the money. So Meyer hired a chemist to determine the formula of one of the more popular items he sold, stove polish. He modified the ingredients slightly and put his family to work making it.

Later Meyer used the same approach with an early form of instant coffee. Other products followed. Within six years, the young entrepreneur had earned enough to quit peddling and open a small grocery store. There was also enough money for him to marry his stepsister, Barbara, with whom he had fallen in love during their voyage to America.

Encouraged by his earlier successes, Meyer tried his hand at other business ventures. During the Civil War, he speculated in clothes and foodstuffs to supply the Union army. He imported herbs and spices, lace and embroidery from Switzerland. He also began to dabble in the stock market. Once, gambling on a merger rumor, Meyer invested $84,000 in an ailing railroad. He later happily sold his interest to financier Jay Gould for nearly $500,000.

Meyer did so well that barely 20 years after he arrived in this country as a penniless immigrant he could afford to own and staff a large, luxurious home in the most fashionable section of Philadelphia and to send his children to fine, prestigious schools abroad.

A few years later, in 1881, when he was 53 years old and already financially secure, Meyer Guggenheim made a small investment that changed his life and the destiny of what was to become his dynasty: he paid $5,000 for a one-third interest in the A.Y. and the Minnie, two lead and silver mines named after the prospectors who had discovered them in Leadville, Colo.

Meyer knew nothing about mining at the time. He had gone into the deal primarily to help an old acquaintance who was in debt. But shortly after Meyer invested in the mines, they flooded and his partners wanted out.

Meyer, dressed in the standard frock coat and formal hat worn by Eastern gentlemen of his day, visited the rough western mining town of Leadville for a firsthand look. He took along a load of dry goods to sell so the trip wouldn't be a total loss. After inspecting the mines, mainly by dropping stones down the shaft and listening to the water splash, Meyer decided they could be saved and bought out his partners. He also sold all the goods he had taken along.

The cost of the project totaled more than $50,000 by some estimates, but once the mines were pumped dry the site proved to have one of the richest ore bodies in the area—large quantities of pure native silver, lead ore thick with the metal, and huge copper deposits as well. Meyer recouped his original investment in less than a year. As shafts were drilled deeper into the deposit, the profits soared to as much as $750,000 a year.

Once Meyer had a chance to examine the new business he was in, he came to much the same conclusion he had as a peddler: he would make more money processing his own metals than paying someone else to do it. So he went into the smelting business.

First, he bought interests in an existing smelter; then he decided to build one in Pueblo, Colo., already an important smelting town. The smelter, which introduced a cheaper copper-refining process, soaked up so much money at first that Meyer's newly-acquired wealth seemed threatened. But, over his sons' worried objections, Meyer stuck with the project, and eventually the Pueblo smelter began to contribute handsomely to the growing Guggenheim fortune.

When the McKinley Tariff Act of 1890 made it too expensive to import Mexican ores for the smelter, an undaunted Meyer sent his son Solomon to negotiate with the Mexican government for the construction of two in that country. By 1895, the family had become one of the major industrial powers in Mexico.

The future obviously lay in mining. Meyer sold his other businesses. He and his sons formed Guggenheim Exploration Co., which, under the direction of mining engineer John Hays Hammond, eventually discovered and developed copper and silver mines in Nevada, Utah, New Mexico, and Chile, gold in Alaska, tin in Bolivia, and diamonds in Africa. These operations led to the formation of such giant corporations as Kennecott Copper Corp. and Anaconda Co., now a unit of Atlantic Richfield Co. Not long after Meyer Guggenheim's death in 1905 at age 77, his sons dominated the world's metal markets and were worth an estimated $2 billion.

Meyer and Barbara Guggenheim had 11 children, including eight sons—a fine start for a dynasty. The Guggenheim daughters were educated at fancy finishing schools in Paris. They were expected to marry well, which they did. Jeanette, the oldest girl, died while giving birth to her first child. Cora Guggenheim married Louis F. Rothschild, who would later found the investment-banking house, L. F. Rothschild. Rose married Albert Loeb, nephew of Solomon Loeb, one of the founders of the investment firm of Kuhn Loeb & Co. Her oldest son, Harold, became a writer and editor of a magazine that published the early works of John Dos Passos, Gertrude Stein, e.e. cummings, and Virginia Woolf. He was also, for a time, a companion of F. Scott Fitzgerald and Ernest Hemingway, who would eventually betray their friendship by unflatteringly portraying Harold as the character Robert Cohn in his first novel, *The Sun Also Rises*. Some people suggested that the caricature revealed Hemingway as anti-Semitic. But the more conventional wisdom held that Hemingway was simply angry that Loeb, at the time, was a better sportsman, writer, and lady's man than he.

Meyer Guggenheim loved his daughters, and it pleased him that they married well, but he provided them with relatively modest inheritances. The major focus of his attention, and the chief beneficiaries of his fortune, were his sons—Isaac, Daniel, Murry, Solomon, Benjamin, Simon, and William. (The eighth son, Robert, Simon's twin, died in a childhood accident.)

Meyer was convinced that the chief boon to his business was having a large number of sons who could share the vast amount of work required to build and maintain the Guggenheim empire. Accordingly, he emphasized family togetherness. Friday night dinners were mandatory for the brothers and their wives. Grandchildren old enough to sit at the family table, particularly the boys, were often quizzed about family matters as closely as about school subjects. And, over the objections of the older brothers, Meyer insisted that each son be given an equal partnership as soon as he was old enough to join the family business and to contribute his talents to its advancement.

According to family legend, Meyer once gathered his sons in his office and handed each of them a stick. He told them to break the sticks, and they did. Next, he handed them a bundle of seven sticks tied together and told them to break this. None of the sons could do so. The moral, Meyer told his sons: "Singly, the sticks are easily broken; together, they can't be. So it is with you. Together you are invincible. Singly each of you may be easily broken. Stay together, my sons, and the world will be yours. Break up, and you will lose everything."

In 1888, Meyer moved his family to New York. Neither he nor Barbara was eager to leave Philadelphia, but Meyer wanted to be closer to the country's financial center. He also wanted his children to have the social advantages New York offered. Philadelphia was a reasonably tolerant city, but its reverence for the old families whose ancestors had fought in the Revolutionary War precluded newcomers, particularly Jews such as the Guggenheims, from gaining social prominence or influence.

New York's Gentile society didn't totally accept Jews. "The Jews did business with the Gentiles during the day," social historian Birmingham says, "but there was that five o'clock shadow that descended." Although Jews were free to live anywhere they could afford, some hotels and restaurants refused to serve them. They were excluded from select clubs, and their children were barred from certain schools.

Still, there were many wealthy Jewish families in New York City —investment bankers like the Seligmans and Loebs, retail magnates like the Strausses who owned R.H. Macy & Co.—and they had created a society of their own. It was separate from that of the Morgans, Vanderbilts, and Whitneys, but it wielded similar influence and was respected.

The Guggenheims weren't instantly accepted into New York's Jewish society. They were considered crude. Their money came from mining, a dirty business, not as refined as finance or retailing. Barbara Guggenheim spoke English with a strong accent, and she dressed unfashionably. Meyer, the snobbish claimed, had made his money simply by dumb luck. They were called derisively "The Googs." But gradually—perhaps because their vast wealth made it impossible to ignore them—the family was accepted. Marriages were arranged. Partnerships were formed.

F IVE OF MEYER'S SONS (the older ones, who had grown up before their father was prosperous) continued to work together after his death. Unlike their father, they didn't produce enough male heirs to carry on the business after them.

Isaac, the oldest, was probably the most conservative of the brothers. Although he wanted the role badly and considered it his birthright, he was never strong enough to assume leadership of the family. Instead, he had to content himself with functioning as the company's treasurer, which he did ably.

Isaac had three daughters, and only one of them produced a son. Out of vanity he persuaded that boy to change his name legally to Isaac Guggenheim III and made him his principal heir. But after

Isaac died and the inheritance was secure, the boy changed his name back to William I. Spiegelberg Jr.

Daniel Guggenheim, the second son, was most like his father in appearance and attitude. Daniel, known to his business associates as Mr. Dan, was a short man, and behind his back people often joked about his small size and large ambition. But Daniel Guggenheim's business judgment and courage were widely respected.

Perhaps Dan's greatest moment was in turning a potential takeover threat into his largest business coup. When American Smelting & Refining Co. (later to become Asarco Inc.) approached the Guggenheims for a merger, they declined. But the potential competition and the constant threat of a possible takeover bothered Mr. Dan. As soon as he could, he took the offensive. When some crucial American Smelting operations went on strike, he stepped up his production and flooded the market with metal, which depressed the price. He knew that the struck company would suffer even more from the lower prices.

Pinching the purse of American Smelting didn't satisfy him. As the company's stock began to fall, principally because of the lower metal prices he had instigated, Mr. Dan began to acquire American Smelting shares. Then he allowed the company to purchase its stock back, at a huge profit to him. In addition it had to consent to having Daniel Guggenheim and four of his brothers move onto the American Smelting board.

American Smelting tried to shake the Guggenheims, even taking its case to the courts. But after each encounter, the brothers appeared to settle more securely into their board seats. Finally, the American Smelting management ceded total control to them.

Dan Guggenheim was a complex man with a wide variety of interests. Despite his own family-bred disposition toward male supremacy, he and his wife, Florence, who was more than a foot taller than he, supported women's rights causes. Although he wasn't religious, they also supported a number of Jewish philanthropies as well as the Catholic Writers' Guild. But, after business, Daniel Guggenheim's most consuming passion was his interest in

Meyer and Barbara Guggenheim and their family in 1889. From left, William (standing), Simon, Issac, Cora (front row), Carrie (Mrs. Isaac), Meyer, Solomon, Leonie (Mrs. Murry, standing), Barbara, Murry, Jeannette (front row), Florence (Mrs. Daniel), Daniel, Benjamin (standing), and Rose. *Credit: Nassau County Museum*

Daniel, Meyer's second son, who engineered the Guggenheim
takeover of American Smelting & Refining Co. *Credit: Wide
World Photo*

Daniel's son, "Colonel Bob" Guggenheim, second from left, with
Portuguese government officials following his appointment as
U.S. Ambassador to Portugal. *Credit: Wide World Photo*

Solomon, right, inspects a model of the New York art museum that bears his name. With him are Frank Lloyd Wright and Baroness Rebay, who fired Solomon's enthusiasm for modern art. *Credit: Wide World Photo*

Solomon's neice, Peggy, also a noted patron of modern art, cruises in her private gondola on a canal in Venice where she lived for many years prior to her death in 1979. *Credit: Wide World Photo*

Daniel's older son, Harry, with Col. Charles A. Lindbergh following a flight from New York to Washington. *Credit: Wide World
Photo*

Here he is pictured with author John Steinbeck, signed by Harry
as a columnist for Newsday. *Credit: Wide World Photo*

Meyer's youngest son, William lived out his final years estranged from his wife and family in this New York City mansion.

William spent much of his fortune throwing lavish parties here and courting show girls, including the two shown here whom he named to inherit part of his $1 million estate. According to news reports of the day, there were four "show girls" who were named in the will. *Credit: Wide World Photo*

Simon, the fifth of the brothers, was a U.S. Senator from Colorado, where the Guggenheims had mining interests. *Credit: Wide World Photo*

Simon's younger son, George, committed suicide at age 32. His older brother, John Simon, had died of pneumonia during his senior year at preparatory school. *Credit: Wide World Photo*

Meyer's third son, Murry, was the family's statistical expert, though one of his investments resulted in a $60 million loss to the company. *Credit: Wide World Photo*

the then-embryonic field of aviation; over the years, he gave some $6 million to fund research in that area.

Although Colonel Bob was no doubt a disappointment to his father, Daniel, his younger brother Harry must have compensated for Bob's failings. In contrast to Bob's self-indulgent life-style, Harry adopted this for his credo: "Inherited wealth should be used for the progress of man. People who make a business of pleasure are seldom happy."

Harry followed in his father's footsteps and easily became the pre-eminent Guggenheim of his generation. He was appointed ambassador to Cuba during the Hoover administration; he filled this position ably and with considerably more wisdom and decorum than his brother showed in Portugal.

Later, with his third wife, newspaper woman Alicia Patterson, Harry turned *Newsday* into one of the country's fastest-growing and most profitable newspapers. Despite a circulation in New York's suburban Long Island, *Newsday* surpassed many major city newspapers in quality. Harry also guided the various family businesses, foundations, and personal affairs. Harry produced only daughters.

Meyer's third son, Murry, was the family's mathematical wizard. He liked, understood, and knew how to use statistics. Murry was a quiet man who, despite his wealth, was extremely frugal. He was usually the most reluctant of the brothers to go along with any new venture, especially one that required a large investment. Ironically, the one time in his business career that Murry decided to be adventurous resulted in the company's largest single loss—some $60 million on a Chilean nitrate project. Although Murry had one son, Edmond, the younger Guggenheim retired early from the family business to devote his energies to golf. Edmond married three times and had one daughter.

Solomon is probably the best known of the original Guggenheim brothers. He was considered the most stylish, the most generous, and the most affable. Men on Wall Street trusted and liked Solomon Guggenheim. In his late 60s, Solomon fell in love with a redheaded German baroness, Hilla Rebay von Ehrenwiesen, who would help make him famous. Hilla, 30 years younger than Solomon, was a painter. She introduced him to modern art and urged him to collect works by Kandinsky, Leger, and Chagall, among others.

As Solomon's collection grew, the baroness pressed him to build a museum to house the works. The museum, one of the most controversial ever built and now a New York City landmark, was designed by the celebrated architect Frank Lloyd Wright. It opened in 1959, about 10 years after Solomon's death; he bequeathed $2 million for the construction and an additional $6 million for its endowment.

Solomon also had three daughters. The middle girl, Gertrude, was born a hunchback; she never married. Her two sisters both married Englishmen, one of whom was an earl and a descendant of Mary, Queen of Scots.

Simon Guggenheim, the fifth of the brothers, was perhaps the first to understand fully and exploit the political power that money can bring. In 1903, at age 36, Simon literally—and proudly—bought himself a seat in the U.S. Senate. At that time Senators were named by the state legislatures, and a number of Colorado legislators showed they were grateful for Simon's financial support. The Senator from Colorado, known as "the most conservative man in the Senate," rarely sponsored any significant legislation. But he hosted fine dinner parties, and he carefully safeguarded the Guggenheim mining interests.

Simon did produce two sons. The older, John Simon, had been one of the more promising members of his generation, but he died of pneumonia during his senior year at the Phillips Exeter Academy in New Hampshire. George, the younger, unable to live up to his family's high expectations and burdened with guilt for being a homosexual, shot himself at 32.

Heirless, Simon sought some way to carry on the name of his branch of the family and to honor the memory of his sons, particularly that of John. The result was the John Simon Guggenheim Memorial Foundation, whose fellowships have sponsored the works of composer Aaron Copland, writers Thomas Wolfe and

Katherine Anne Porter, economists Paul Samuelson and John Kenneth Galbraith, and political scientist Henry Kissinger, among others.

The five brothers—Isaac, Daniel, Murry, Solomon, and Simon —sought to live their father's parable of the bundled sticks. They all worked together in one large office, furnished with six equal-sized desks and portraits of all five. Called the Partners' Room, it still exists at 120 Broadway in New York City. Its sole occupant now is Solomon's grandson, Peter O. Lawson-Johnston, who oversees the family affairs, which have shrunk considerably since the heyday of Meyer and his sons.

Guggenheim management of the companies they helped launch was short-lived, primarily, as Meyer feared, because of the paucity of male heirs to carry on the businesses. Taxes took a big share of the family fortune, although the brothers attempted to use trusts to delay the bite for a generation or two. The large philanthropies also ate up a good deal of the money. In addition, the Guggenheims, even the frugal Murry, liked to live well. Most of the brothers built lavish estates complete with mansions of 20 to 30 rooms, private golf courses and formal gardens, all staffed by scores of servants.

The youngest brothers, Benjamin and William, were probably the most profligate. Both left the family business early, before the heavy expansion into international mining. While their brothers were building an even greater fortune, Ben and Will were exhausting theirs.

Ben, father of Peggy Guggenheim, the art collector, died at age 47 on the *Titanic*. Some say his death was his finest moment. Although Ben was the first Guggenheim to attend college, he didn't like it and dropped out to work at the family's Leadville mines. But there, Ben spent more time socializing with the town's available women than supervising the mines. The family brought him home, and in 1895 he performed the familiar duty of marrying Florette Seligman, a niece of Joseph Seligman, the country's wealthiest Jewish banker and a valuable relative for the Guggenheims to have.

Six years later, disagreeing with his brothers' expansionistic plans, Ben retired as an active partner in the family business and settled down to enjoy his share of the wealth they had already accumulated. It amounted to a tidy income of about $250,000 a year.

The money allowed Ben to pursue his favorite pleasures—fine clothes, women, and travel. On April 14, 1912, Ben, his valet, and a woman companion were making the maiden voyage on the *Titanic*. When the ship began to sink, family legend has it, Ben declined a seat in a lifeboat. Instead, he and his servant, Giglio, dressed in their finest evening clothes, honorably helped women and children to safety, and then went down with the ship.

When the brothers began to settle Ben's estate, they discovered that he had gone through some $8 million in bad business ventures and extravagant living. Although he had squandered his money, his daughter, Peggy, never particularly suffered. Her uncles took care of her, and she eventually came into a sizable fortune from her mother's side of the family as well. In a sense, she carried on her father's tradition of high living.

Shortly after she came into her fortune in her early 20s, she set out for Europe. She first married Laurence Vail, whom she later described as the "King of Bohemia." She also later described the beatings he administered to her; they eventually were divorced. A string of other courtships and marriages followed, including a secretive year-long affair with playwright Samuel Beckett.

Along the way, she also developed a love for art—and artists. She opened a gallery in London and started to build up a great collection of contemporary art. Her artist paramours included Yves Tanguy and Max Ernst, a German refugee. As World War II approached, she had her art collection sent from Europe to the U.S. for safekeeping; she and Max Ernst followed in 1941. They later married, but it lasted only a few years.

Peggy Guggenheim opened a New York gallery and became a patron to several artists, including Jackson Pollock. But not long after the war she returned to Europe and lived out her days in Venice, in an 18th-century stone palazzo. She installed an art museum in the garden and basement, and at her death in 1979 her collection was valued at $30 million. It was left to the museum in New York named after her uncle, Solomon R. Guggenheim—but the collection was to remain in Venice.

If Peggy and her father were eccentric, her Uncle William wasn't exactly conservative. William Guggenheim (the grandfather of Floridian Bill Guggenheim) was the youngest of the brothers. He retired from the family business when he was only 33 and thereafter severed his ties with the family. The other members of the family thoroughly disapproved of his flamboyant manner of living. For a while, he even changed his name to Gatenby Williams.

M EYER GUGGENHEIM HAD never been religious. Shellfish, a forbidden food under Orthodox Jewish dietary laws, was one of his favorite dishes. He sent his children to the Catholic schools in Philadelphia because he thought they did a better job than the Hebrew ones there did. Still, Meyer took pride in being a Jew, particularly one who had escaped the European ghettos and through sheer pluck and hard work had become a prosperous and powerful man in the U.S. The Guggenheims belonged to Temple Emanu-El, the reformed synagogue on New York's fashionable Fifth Avenue, where most of the city's wealthy Jewish families worshipped. They observed the holy days, and Meyer expected his children to marry Jews.

Accordingly, when the brothers discovered that William had eloped with Grace B. Herbert, a Gentile divorcee, they quickly arranged a divorce. Later on, of course, nearly all of their own children would marry Gentiles, and many would convert to some form of Christianity; but the family wasn't yet ready for that. The Guggenheims paid Grace Herbert to divorce Will, and Meyer himself went to court when she tried unsuccessfully to wheedle more money from them. The family found a suitable girl for Will to marry—Aimee Steinberger, a friend of the Guggenheim girls.

The marriage wasn't a happy one. Ironically, Aimee widened the breach between Will and his family when she urged him to sue his brothers for a share in the burgeoning profits from their international operations. Will lost the case. The marriage did, however, produce a son, William Jr.

William Sr. passed the final years of his life, separated from Aimee and from his family, living in a four-story mansion on New York's Riverside Drive. There, according to John Davis, author of the book, *The Guggenheims: An American Epic,* the rooms were named after the metals that made his fortune—Salon d'Or, Chambre de Cuivre, Bureau de Plomb. Will threw lavish parties and courted chorus girls. The combination drained his wealth, once estimated at more than $10 million. When he died in 1941 at the age of 72, he left his entire estate, valued at a mere $1 million, to four showgirls, including Miss America of 1929.

Aimee Guggenheim challenged the will on the grounds that Will was batty. She won. That money and an additional $1 million trust fund passed on to William Guggenheim Jr., a sickly man who had been born with a defective heart. William Jr. lived long enough to marry Elizabeth Newell, a direct descendant of one of the original Dutch families that settled Manhattan, and to produce a son, William III. William Jr. died at age 39 in 1941, when his son was just eight.

Trust arrangements prevented William Jr.'s money from passing on to Elizabeth Guggenheim and her son. Instead, it reverted to Grandmother Aimee. So Bill and his mother moved from their spacious Long Island estate, complete with a full staff including a gardener, to a comfortable, but far smaller, apartment in Manhattan where they were served by one maid who also cooked.

His father's early death and his grandfather's estrangement from the family meant that Bill grew up without knowing much about his kin. Among the things he didn't learn until his teens was that his forebears were Jewish; he was raised an Episcopalian and served as an acolyte.

It wasn't until he was 16 years old that Bill met a Guggenheim aside from his parents. That was cousin Harry, then head of the family. Harry stuck a $100 bill in Bill's pocket and told him there would always be a job for him at 120 Broadway. Later, when he was in his 20s, Bill was introduced to his cousin Peggy at a reception held in the museum of their great-uncle, Solomon, but the meeting was brief. "It was obvious," he recalls, "that she wasn't very interested in me." The only other contacts he has made with his Guggenheim relatives have been through calls he placed to Peter Lawson-Johnston and Roger Strauss, Dan Guggenheim's publisher grandson, when he tried to persuade them to invest money in various ventures. Neither was interested.

The dominant relative in young Bill's life was his grandmother Aimee. He says he was always aware that his financial future depended on pleasing her. She provided his allowance, which, he says, averaged an extravagant $150 a week. Bill Guggenheim says he saved most of the money, but he also treated himself regularly to taxicabs and box seats at baseball games.

For a period after his mother's second marriage, Bill Guggenheim recalls, the money stopped. He says he carried groceries for neighbors and caddied for his stepfather to earn spending money.

Young Bill attended the exclusive Browning School in New York City, which was started by John D. Rockefeller in 1888 when his own son reached school age. Teachers remember Bill Guggenheim as an honor student who did particularly well in math and history but who didn't participate in too many school activities. "Billy wasn't much of an athlete," says one. "He was a quiet boy who never had much to say. He had a sense of humor, but he wasn't a pill."

Despite some concern that "he wasn't well-rounded enough," Yale University, his first choice, accepted Bill Guggenheim for the class of 1960. He planned to study engineering, but switched to literature and then to history. Eventually, he dropped out. Grandmother Aimee had died, and when Bill reached his majority he came into a $1 million trust fund and an additional $400,000. The income from that money, which he places at "more than $50,000 a year but less than $100,000" supports him today. "I knew," he says looking back on his decision to leave school, "that I had enough money so that I could live without working and so didn't need the degree."

Bill Guggenheim tried photography school. He worked in a radio station. He sold the security systems that his stepfather's company marketed. Nothing held his interest long. Finally, in 1961, he married Grace Azro Embury, an heiress to the Upjohn pharmaceutical fortune. They bought a farm in New Jersey, hired a couple to look after them, and began a family. Guggenheim took a job with his brother-in-law's brokerage firm, Correau Smith, a small concern that has since been acquired by Janney Montgomery Scott Inc.

The work appealed to him . . . for a while. "I enjoyed making charts and wearing three-piece suits," he says now. But the enthusiasm waned, and after a few years Guggenheim quit because the job didn't make him any richer than he was already.

The Guggenheims divorced soon after that. Bill moved back to Manhattan, where he opened a store called Indispensable Disposables, which purveyed paper dresses priced between $5 and $150. He did all right for a while, clearing about $1,000 a week, but he packed it in as the paper-dress fad cooled. "I was lonely and I needed something to do, but I was very serious," he says, adding that he had hoped to open franchise stores around the country.

On the night he closed his store, Guggenheim proposed to Judy Arnold, the sister of his college roommate. She accepted, and they toasted their engagement in the shop's storeroom with paper cups of champagne.

For about a year and a half after they were married, Guggenheim spent most of his time writing and finding a publisher for his book, *The Love Game,* which he describes as "a system to help people communicate their sexual preferences, fantasies and so on" to their sex partners. Despite its subject matter, the book wasn't pornographic, he says. "It was worded so gently that no one could complain," he avers. "There was nothing in it that was far out." Nonetheless, the Guggenheims confess they never played the game themselves. "I played the game in my mind one thousand times, and we had friends who played and reported back to us," Guggenheim sheepishly explains. After a cross-country promotion tour, he says, the book sold 25,000 copies, which at $2.95 each barely covered the printing costs.

Then came stints at the school for the mentally-retarded, as an aide in an anti-drug-abuse program for teen-agers, and as a full-time volunteer fireman in Creekskill, N.J. "I guess you might say my work history is rather chopped up," Guggenheim admits. "If I didn't have the money, I couldn't have done it."

His life changed in May, 1974, when he started getting what he calls messages from the dead. Guggenheim is a bit hazy about the form these messages take, but they are nonetheless very real to him. "I do not hear words, either inside or outside myself," he says. "I receive only impressions or 'thought forms,' that is, thoughts by themselves as if by telepathy. The easiest way to understand this is to see me as a translator or transcriber."

What the messages tell him is that there is a God and that there is life after death. He has written them down in the form of stories, parables, poems and essays, and they now fill over 1,000 typewritten pages. He calls it the Book of Circles.

The messages from beyond led Bill Guggenheim into the study of various religions and philosophies, and also of psychic phenomena. The theology that developed, which he calls "mystical Christianity," is short on ritual and dogma and long on brotherhood. "The difference between me and most others who are involved in religion is that they will claim that the church down the street doesn't have as much truth as they do," he says. "I don't say that. I also don't think that revelations stopped 2,000 years ago. I think we can all receive them."

Revelations caused some changes in the way Bill and Judy Guggenheim live. They became vegetarians. They added *New Age,* a monthly magazine that covers spiritual subjects, to their subscriptions. The Guggenheims made new friends who shared their interests and met with them regularly. Bill Guggenheim, who says he once believed that "sales people were humanoids who were activated at 9 a.m. and shut off at 5 p.m., their only purpose being to serve you," began chatting with sales people, offering to send them tapes and books he had discovered. The Guggenheims even sold Judy's $3,300 engagement ring and gave the money to a spiritual cause.

In the first flush of their new-found spirtuality, the Guggenheims got a bit carried away. They became what Bill calls "phony holy." He explains: "That's when you eat Oreos all week but serve natural whole-grain cookies to your guests on Friday nights." Now the family eats meat again, including Big Macs. "My only ritual is smoking cigarets," says Guggenheim, a chain smoker.

Bill and Judy and their children live simply in Longwood, Fla., a suburb of Orlando, to which they were directed by one of Judy's unearthly communications. Bill has two daughters, Maire and Jaenet, from his first marriage. He and Judy have three sons—William, Christopher, and Jonathan, who was named after the character in one of Guggenheim's favorite books, *Jonathan Livingston Seagull.* The boys are the only males bearing the name Guggenheim in their generation.

Willie, the oldest, knows that there is a museum in New York that has the same name as his, and he and his father have talked a little about his heritage. "I've told Willie that people might treat him special because of his name but that he's not to take it seriously," Guggenheim says.

Meanwhile, the Guggenheims continue to live modestly. Their home is a simply-furnished, four-bedroom house that they bought for $62,000. The sign on the door just says "Bill and Judy." Judy Guggenheim uses a Sears food processor instead of a more expensive model, and she buys her sheets at white sales. After Jonathan was born, she hired a woman to come in and help her part time, but she does her own cooking. Bill Guggenheim frequently baby-sits. The children attend integrated public schools.

"They say he's rich, but he sure doesn't act like it," says daughter Jaenet. "He's cheap."

Still, the money and the name are there when they want them. And the Guggenheims ruefully admit that they can't be totally ignored. "People who grow up with money have a manner about them," Bill says. "It affects the way they walk, they talk, they order in restaurants." Even Judy Guggenheim, whose own mother always worked to support her family, admits that she occasionally indulges in some of the privileges of money. Two years ago she took her mother to Europe. They flew coach but "stayed in the best rooms in the finest hotels and ate at only the best restaurants," she recalls.

Sometimes, Guggenheim concedes, he does feel guilty that he doesn't have to work. But he says the feeling usually passes quickly.

"When I was 19 years old," he recalls, "I spent $200 to take some vocational tests at NYU. The results showed I was best suited to be a gentleman farmer. Now, I consider myself a farmer of gentlemen. Of course, I can't say this isn't just another of my phases, but it's been five years now and I feel absolutely comfortable and natural."

IV

The Astors

J OHN JACOB ASTOR, the shrewd and industrious German immigrant youth who, in the late 18th and early 19th centuries, built a record American fortune by trading furs with the Indians and then investing his profits in Manhattan real estate, dreamed of founding a House of Astor—an American dynasty to rank with the great families of Europe.

For a good while, his descendants' steadily increasing wealth and social position took that American dream well along the way to reality. But today, almost 200 years after John Jacob's arrival in the New World, the American Astors have almost vanished from view. Ironically, however, a branch of the family that abandoned the United States 90 years ago to live in England has flourished. An Astor dynasty has indeed been established—but it is a British, not an American, one.

In the 19th century, an American dynasty of Astors certainly seemed to be in the making. John Jacob's son grew so rich husbanding the family's property that he became known as "The Landlord of New York." Two of his sons, in turn, moved high up the social ladder and occupied ornate twin mansions on Fifth Avenue. The wife of one of them established herself as "The Mrs. Astor," for more than a quarter of a century the reigning queen of eastern society's elite Four Hundred.

Society chronicler Cleveland Amory links the Astors with the Vanderbilts and Whitneys as the "three dominant families, on a national scale, in the history of American society"—dominant to the point where they were irreverently lumped together as "the Astorbilts."

But near the turn of the century, personal problems began afflicting the family in America, and the 20th century saw the rise of the British Astors. One of John Jacob's great-grandsons left America in 1890 for England, took up English citizenship, eventually became a baron and then a viscount. His children and their children and grandchildren went to Eton and Oxford, served Britain with great distinction in peace and in the two World Wars, and long controlled two of Britain's greatest newspapers, the *Times* and the *Observer*.

One of that emigre's sons married a dynamic, magnetic American divorcee who, as Nancy Astor, became one of the world's most famous women, a ranking hostess who made the historic Cliveden country estate that her husband had received from his father into the fashionable center for England's political and literary establishment, and who was the first woman to sit in the British Parliament.

The emigre's other son later became a baron in his own right for his philanthropic and publishing activities; he lived at Hever Castle, which he received from his father, and where Henry VIII had wooed and won Anne Boleyn. One or more Astors sat in the House of Commons almost without a break from 1910 to 1974, and at one time five members of the family were in Parliament.

All of this was made possible by the wealth that came down from old John Jacob. But today, while most of the Astors are either remarkably well-off or at least comfortable enough, they certainly are no longer the richest family around.

Though the family name survives in New York City through the landmark Waldorf-Astoria Hotel and the sprawling Astoria section of the borough of Queens, the vast U.S. landholdings that built the family fortune have practically all been sold and the proceeds spent or reinvested in other types of assets. Most of the American Astors' wealth has wound up in a charitable foundation set up by the late Vincent Astor, the last titular head of the American family.

And natural increase in the numbers of British Astors, stiff income and inheritance taxes there, and generous gifts to worthy causes seem to have slimmed down their formidable resources.

H OW DID IT all begin? Some family members trace the family back to Spanish counts named D'Astorga, who fought the Moors and then emigrated first to France and later to Germany, but in fact this appears dubious history. What is unchallengeable is that the first John Jacob Astor was born in 1763 in Waldorf, a small village near Heidelberg, the son of a relatively poor, frequently drunk village butcher; that he left school at 14 to work in the family butcher shop; that he quickly became restless there and decided to leave Waldorf, as two older brothers had done, one going to London and the other to New York; and that at the age of 16 he did indeed leave Germany, heading for America.

The continuation of the Revolutionary War, however, forced him to stop over for several years in London, where he stayed with his brother George, who sold musical instruments. Soon after the war ended, having saved enough for steerage passage, he set sail for the U.S.—a voyage that, due to winter gales, took four months. He finally landed in Baltimore and made his way directly to New York. When John Jacob Astor reached there, a youth of 20 in 1784, he is said to have had "one good suit of Sunday clothes, seven flutes, and five pounds sterling of money."

Brother Henry was there, having done well as a butcher selling to the British Army of Occupation, but John Jacob had had enough of the butcher business back in Germany. He briefly tried peddling cake as a baker's apprentice and selling musical instruments made by his brother in London, but then he went to work as an odd-job helper in a firm trading with and buying furs from the Indians. Some sources say that en route to the U.S., a shipboard conversation with a fur trader had fired the young man's imagination in that direction, as a business in which a quick fortune could be made; more likely, though, the fact was simply that when he was looking around for a more rewarding job than peddling, the fur firm opening was the one he found.

Whatever work he was doing around the store—beating the furs, packing them, running errands—he always found time to quiz the trappers about their travels, and he soon learned the business well enough to persuade the owner to let him go off on his own on fur-buying trips in upstate New York.

In 1786 the energetic and ambitious young man set up the fur-trade business for himself. To do this, he used money he had saved from his salary; the dowry acquired in his marriage to Sarah Todd, a young woman with valuable family connections and a keen business mind; loans from his brother Henry; and the help of a friendly banker, William Backhouse. The business quickly prospered. The firm's trading area spread from New York on up into Canada and west to some of the Great Lakes area, and it employed a growing number of trappers and agents.

Over the next two decades, John Jacob made several canny decisions. He bought his own ships to carry the furs across the Atlantic for sale in England, thus eliminating one middleman. He increased his profits by using the money received from selling the furs in England to buy woolens, cutlery, and other British items to carry back for sale in the U.S. A little later, in the early 1800s, he entered the trade with the Orient, his ships taking furs there and bringing back tea and silks.

Though he had only a small store on Water Street when he started his business (he and Sarah lived frugally in rooms over the store), by 1800 he had become so prosperous that he was able to move his combined salesroom-office-residence to a house at the corner of Broadway and Vesey Street, then a quite fashionable neighborhood. The invaluable Sarah was busy not only producing a stream of children but taking a major role in managing the business.

In 1808, an enlarged Astor operation was incorporated as American Fur Trading Company. When the slaughter of the fur animals depleted the supply in the East, American Fur gradually expanded westward. Soon the company built a near-monopoly in the fur-rich areas beyond the Mississippi.

There is continuing debate about the extent to which Astor,

personally in his early trading ventures and later in his supervision of his corporate agents, swindled the Indians with whom they traded, and the extent to which they illegally supplied them with whisky (a common fur-trading practice which made it possible to cheat the natives more easily).

Gustavus Myers, in his *History of the Great American Fortunes,* declares that the Astor firm's exploitation of the natives "was one of the most deliberate, cruel and appalling that has ever taken place in any country." Friendly family historians, however, suggest the firm was near-exemplary in its dealings. The fairest judgment seems to be that Astor and his company might not have been the worst offenders on this score.

In his efforts to build a western fur-trading empire, Astor's one notable failure was his attempt to establish himself in the Pacific Northwest. An expedition he organized did indeed settle Astoria, at the mouth of the Columbia River in Oregon, but it was taken over by British forces when the War of 1812 started. (The settlement wasn't a complete failure for the U.S., even if it was for John Jacob Astor; its American origin was part of the case the U.S. later made to get the Northwest lands back from the British.)

Though his fur trading, shipping and other merchant ventures showed his great drive and shrewdness, John Jacob's greatest genius may have been in investing, for he used all his fur and shipping profits, and his loans from banker William Backhouse, to buy New York real estate. Whatever money he could lay his hands on he invested in Manhattan farmland, always just a little beyond the existing settlements. Then he sat back and waited until the city's commercial development, new immigrants, and inevitable urban expansion made the land many times more valuable.

Land, says Gustavus Myers, was always "a prolific breeder of wealth. . . . A more formidable system for the foundation and amplification of listing fortunes has not existed." For no one was that more true than for John Jacob Astor.

He bought his first lots in 1789, just a few years after starting in business, and he never stopped buying after that. In just three years, between 1803 and 1806, he invested nearly $300,000 in Manhattan real estate, according to an estimate by biographer Harvey O'Connor.

Astor didn't believe in selling land, and he didn't believe in building on it himself, except for an occasional conspicuous structure like his Astor House hotel. Instead, he rented the land, usually for 21 years, to someone who would build an office building or stores or houses on it. Astor would require the tenant to pay rent, maintain the building, and pay the taxes—and then, at the end of the lease, John Jacob would take it all over, buildings included. He invested in mortgages and pitilessly foreclosed when times were bad. And all the rental income and other real-estate profits provided money for buying still more land—in the Bronx, up the Hudson, in Wisconsin and Missouri and Iowa, but always chiefly in Manhattan.

The result was well-described by the late Michael Astor, a member of the British branch, in a fascinating autobiography called *Tribal Feelings.* "John Jacob," he wrote, "established the fortune. All the family had to do after that was sit tight (metaphorically speaking) and their wealth increased as the wealth of New York increased."

By 1835, the heavy-faced, stout John Jacob, still speaking with a thick German accent and writing in a nearly-illegible scrawl, was by far the richest man in America. (He cunningly had gotten out of the fur trade, selling the American Fur Trading Company to one of his lieutenants in 1834, just before the trade collapsed and the company with it.) He built a pretentious home on Broadway near Prince Street, and adorned it with costly works of art acquired on his frequent trips to Europe. When he died in 1848 at the age of 84, his estate was worth about $20 million, at a time when only a few Americans had assets of even $1 million or $2 million.

His fortune, Gustavus Myers wrote, "was the colossus of the times, an object of awe to all wealth-strivers." *Harper's Magazine* editorialized that "in the art of prospering in business, he had no equal. To get all that he could and to keep nearly all that he got— those were the laws of his being."

His older son, John Jacob II, was imbecilic after a childhood fall, and John Jacob Astor's will provided for his care and comfort. But most of the family fortune went to John Jacob's next son, William Backhouse Astor, named after the long-time family friend and helper.

In his frequent trips to Europe late in life, John Jacob had become impressed with a European practice that he believed had helped build family fortunes there: primogeniture, under which most of a dead man's property went to the eldest son. While that wasn't quite the U.S. system, John Jacob came as close to it as he could, setting a pattern that his descendants on both sides of the Atlantic tried to follow.

Younger sons, daughters, and grandchildren received comfortable but not huge marriage settlements or inheritances, frequently only a life-interest in property. But the bulk went to the eldest competent son, or perhaps the two older sons. (The primogeniture pattern established by John Jacob Astor ultimately contributed—in one of many ironies in the family story—to the decline of the American Astors, since Vincent Astor, the last American Astor to inherit great resources under this doctrine, had no children of his own to whom to bequeath the money.)

William Backhouse Astor, the son who at age 56 inherited most of the original John Jacob's wealth, already had a small fortune of his own from land speculation and banking. A heavy-set man, careless in dress and appearance, basically antisocial, he wasn't a notably bold or inventive businessman. But he was methodical and hard-working, a good man to safeguard existing assets. Of him, his father is reported to have said, "William will never make money, but he will keep what he has," and a biographer referred to him as "the richest and least attractive young man of his time."

He married into an old New York family to advance up the social ladder, and he continued to invest in land and buildings so carefully that he in time acquired the title of "Landlord of New York." When he died at the age of 83 in 1875, his estate was put at more than $40 million, having more than doubled in a quarter of a century.

Following the principles of his father, he left small amounts to daughters and grandchildren, but most of his wealth went to his two older sons, John Jacob III and William B. Jr. The former, a cold imperious man almost as businesslike as his father and grand-father, concentrated on real-estate investments but also dabbled in coal, banking, transportation, and other enterprises. His broth-er, William B. Jr., was a more sociable man who disliked business and (according to Astor biographer Harvey O'Connor) preferred to live off his income at his Hudson Valley estate in spring and fall, on his yacht in summer, and at his Florida home in winter.

It was William B. Jr. who married the well-connected Caroline Webster Schermerhorn and then left her much to her own devices to raise their children and carve out her place in society as "The Mrs. Astor." Their richly furnished Fifth Avenue home—John Jacob III and his socially-prominent wife had one next door—was the site of huge dinner parties and fabulous balls. It had a spacious ballroom and picture gallery, immense dining room covered with antique tapestries, and a wide marble staircase. Attendance at Mrs. Astor's dinners and dances there and at her Newport, R.I., home determined acceptance into fashionable society from about 1880 until her death in 1908.

The minister of one fashionable New York City church report-edly declared that "not to have received an invitation to an Astor ball, not to have dined at Mrs. Astor's" was the equivalent of being banished from polite upper-class society. The queen lived so grandly, in fact, that a common phrase of the time for someone ostentatiously overdressed was that he or she looked like "Mrs. Astor's pet horse."

Cleveland Amory, in *Who Killed Society?*, says that many date the passing of the Old Order to her death, since no one since has had her autocratic authority.

When John Jacob III died in 1890, just 15 years after his father, his wealth was estimated at over $100 million. Something between $75 million and $100 million went to his only son, William Waldorf. And the increase in land values was such that even the unambi-tious William B. Jr. left an estate of $30 million to $50 million when he died two years later.

"No other family," says biographer Lucy Kavaler, "had ever

owned so much of a modern city—owned it in the most literal sense, too. Countless blocks, thousands of residences, scores of commercial buildings, miles of waterfront property, acres of vacant lots, hotels—all, all belonged to the Astors."

But then the American Astor story made a turn for the worse. John Jacob IV, the only son and chief heir of William B. Jr., was a shy man who preferred tinkering with cars and machinery to real estate or other business. Divorced by his beautiful society wife, he shocked New York society by setting up housekeeping with, and eventually marrying, an 18-year-old Brooklyn girl, younger than his son by his first marriage. The shock waves were such that he and his new bride went off to Europe to let things simmer down in New York. After a year wandering through Europe, they set out to return to the U.S.—aboard the *Titanic.*

Though Mrs. Astor, five months pregnant at the time with John Jacob VI, was saved, John Jacob IV drowned in the disaster. His son by his first marriage, 20-year-old William Vincent Astor (he later dropped the William), inherited most of his father's estate, receiving some $68 million.

Vincent loved racing cars and yachting and smart international society. In fact, the fast-paced social life and many marriages of Vincent, his sister Alice, and his half-brother John Jacob VI, led Cleveland Amory to declare that they "rather well proved that by six generations, an American family is about ready to start all over again."

A little unfair, perhaps, for Vincent Astor did work at trying to preserve and enlarge the family wealth. He sold off a great many old slum properties in New York City and invested in newer buildings there and on Long Island. He remodeled the St. Regis Hotel, which he had inherited, and made it into a Manhattan gathering place for the international set. He bankrolled a news magazine, *Today,* that was later merged into *Newsweek,* and he was *Newsweek's* largest stockholder for an extended time.

At his death, he was involved in plans for ambitious real-estate projects in Manhattan, Cleveland, and elsewhere in the U.S. He was an early supporter of the political career of his cousin, Franklin

D. Roosevelt, and was for a time quite close to the President, frequently taking him for cruises on his luxurious yacht, the Nourmahal. Ultimately, he broke with F.D.R. when the President began his soak-the-rich rhetoric.

But the American Astors were slipping down, comparatively, on the financial scale—even with rising real-estate and common-stock values. One estimate in the mid-1950s put Vincent Astor's worth at about $125 million, mostly in real estate—and while that certainly was no small sum, there were by then at least 15 other men and women outranking him: Rockefellers, Mellons, Fords, and oil millionaires like Getty and Hunt.

Though married three times, he never had any children, and in his old age he began to think deeply about giving much of his wealth to charity. In 1948, he created the Vincent Astor Foundation to support cultural and community projects in New York City, and when he died in 1959, almost all the property that hadn't already gone to the foundation was sold, with half the proceeds going directly to the foundation and the other half set aside to produce income for his widow, Brooke Astor; that, too, presumably will go to the foundation on her death. As far as can be told, the American Astors now own very little American property other than their own homes.

The foundation, with current assets of about $50 million and annual grants of between $5 million and $10 million, is really the most significant instance of Astor philanthropy in the U.S., for by and large, considering their great wealth, the American Astors were not particularly charitable or philanthropic. Though many Americans believe the Astors founded and financed the New York Public Library, the original John Jacob actually endowed something called the Astor Library, and ultimately this had to be merged into the New York Public Library when his immediate descendants gave it only token financial support. Nor did the American Astors do much for any other worthy cause until the Vincent Astor Foundation came along.

Since the family wealth had been derived from investments in New York City, the foundation appropriately concentrates on projects that "contribute significantly to making New York a better place in which to live"—projects ranging from the Public Library, Metropolitan Museum, Bronx Zoo and educational station WNET to neighborhood activities for teen-agers and old folks and special programs for both disturbed children and gifted children.

But however good the cause, the fact is that most of the American Astor wealth now is in Foundation hands and no longer in the hands of Astor family members. "Vincent's childlessness was the one blow of fate that has changed the American Astor family irrevocably," observes biographer Kavaler.

Vincent's sister, Alice, who was brought up by her mother in England and inherited about $5 million on her father's death, died in 1956, much of her money spent as a patroness of ballet companies, writers and painters. She had become a friend of Aldous Huxley and a searcher for mystical experiences. She had four children by three of her four husbands; they live in the United States and England.

John Jacob VI, the posthumous son of the man who died on the *Titanic,* got about $5 million when he came of age in 1933 and spent much of it on fast cars, fast living, and three wives—acquiring a playboy image in the process. He was extremely bitter that he hadn't received a bigger inheritance from his father and that his wealthy half-brother, Vincent, gave him only token help later. After a while, he and Vincent broke off relations completely.

As just plain John Astor, or, more usually, Jack Astor, he lives now in Miami Beach. "The American Astors," he remarked to Mrs. Kavaler, "are now just ordinary millionaires, like thousands of others." A few years ago, though, the biographer estimated his pretax income was still $250,000 a year.

A son by his first wife has worked as a security analyst and raiser of venture capital for new enterprises, and he and his family studiously avoid any attention or publicity. Jacqueline, a daughter by Jack Astor's second wife, lives in Manhattan and, appropriately enough, works in the New York real-estate operation of Sotheby's.

"People say the British Astors are a branch of the family," Mrs.

Kavaler quotes Jack Astor as remarking. "That is no longer true. Today, they are the trunk and we are the branch."

B A C K I N T H E latter part of the 19th century, as noted, the good fortune of the American Astors began to reverse. The other unhappy development, besides the *Titanic* death of John Jacob IV, was the experience of his first cousin, William Waldorf Astor, the heir of John Jacob III.

An ambitious but strangely introverted and sensitive man, he was educated privately in Germany and Italy and then studied and practiced real-estate law for a while; but he was bored with the law and uncomfortable with business.

His grandson, Michael Astor, wrote on the subject:

"William Waldorf's predicament was heightened by the fact that his family had become practically a dynasty, and his name in New York had a hierarchical ring. In a society which was still coagulating and searching for its identity, to the man in the street the Astor name did not conform to any popular image of what an American was like.

"Added to which, William Waldorf was by temperament extremely remote. As a young man, he never went to college; he was never exposed to the rough and tumble that is met with either in a large family or at a boarding school. He was an only child, educated privately until he went to Columbia Law School. He was taught by tutors; he was sent to Europe to acquire a conventional appreciation of the arts, and he learned not baseball or football or even tennis but, again with tutors, riding, boxing and fencing.

"The mood of his country was still a pioneer mood, noisy, friendly, combative and competitive. America was looking to the future, convinced of the greatness of her destiny. The pace of life in New York was fast and its music raucous, and he did not take to it all. And yet he did make an effort to break new ground and take part in the corporate life of the nation. He made an attempt to move away from his moorings, to navigate nearer to the mainstream of events. But due to his circumstances, and due to the fact that he lacked the imagination and the flexibility to surmount them, instead of navigating he practically capsized. His journey led him in an unexpected direction, away from the very thing that he set out to find, into a life even more solitary than the one he abandoned."

What William Waldorf did, at the age of 29, was to enter politics. He ran for and was elected to the New York State Legislature and seemed briefly to have found his niche. But then he lost two races for the U.S. Congress, the first in an overwhelmingly Democratic district and the second in a more Republican district where he expected to win but lost largely because of his opponent's slashing attacks on the Astor family wealth.

Brief service as President Arthur's Ambassador to Italy strengthened his already-formed fondness for European culture and the life-style of Europe's upper classes. He was, said Michael Astor, "an American lineal aristocrat," who envied the way the leisured class was accepted in England and the rest of Europe, and who regarded Europe as a place for people who wanted "to enjoy, in an untroubled way, the privileges of wealth." Harvey O'Connor says William Waldorf might have been "the most anti-democratic man in America . . . (with) a brittle belief in the prerogatives and privileges of wealth." When William returned to New York from Italy, he felt more out of place than ever, with few friends and few enterprises to interest him.

Some accounts suggest that his unhappiness over his political defeats was re-enforced by other factors. He had built an elegant new Manhattan hotel, only to have his cousin build an equally elegant one next door. He went to Newport to help his wife establish a place in high society, only to find his aunt Caroline refusing to share the stage.

Whatever the fundamental reasons, it was clear that his sights were turning eastward across the Atlantic. His father had lived part of the last winter of his life in England and had related how pleasant life there was. In 1890, seven months after his father's death, William Waldorf Astor left New York with his wife and children for England, angrily declaring that "America is not a fit place for a gentleman to live."

There have always been American expatriates of one sort or another, people who left the U.S. in search of something different. Rich men have had vacation homes on the Riviera or in the English countryside, seeking to enjoy the older culture and often more tranquil ways of Europe; John Paul Getty, the late oil billionaire who lived out his later years in England, was a notable recent example.

Rich American women have become ranking hostesses in Europe, or have been great art patrons, subsidizing painters and writers in Venice and Rome, Paris and London. Writers and painters and poets from the U.S. have long been attracted by the charm of Chelsea or the free and easy life of the Left Bank in Paris.

At the turn of the century, a steady procession of young American heiresses toured Europe in search of titled husbands—and often found them, especially since titled families were frequently impoverished and looking for rich young American heiresses to bail them out of their financial troubles.

In 1895, for example, Consuelo Vanderbilt became the Duchess of Marlborough, and poured millions of her father's dollars into rebuilding the magnificent house and grounds at Blenheim. Anna Gould married Count Boni de Castellane and later the Duke of Talleyrand. The daughter of Levi Z. Leiter, the partner of Marshall Field, married Lord Curzon, later Viceroy to India. Author Gustavus Myers estimated that by 1910, the marriage of about 500 American women to European men had transferred some $200 million from America to the Old World.

Nonetheless, it was almost unique for a major branch of a wealthy American family to transplant itself—husband, wife, children—to another country, take up permanent foreign residence and renounce U.S. citizenship. And if the Astors haven't become more British than the British, as several cynics have suggested, they certainly have become every bit as British.

THE ASTORS
MALE LINE OF DESCENT

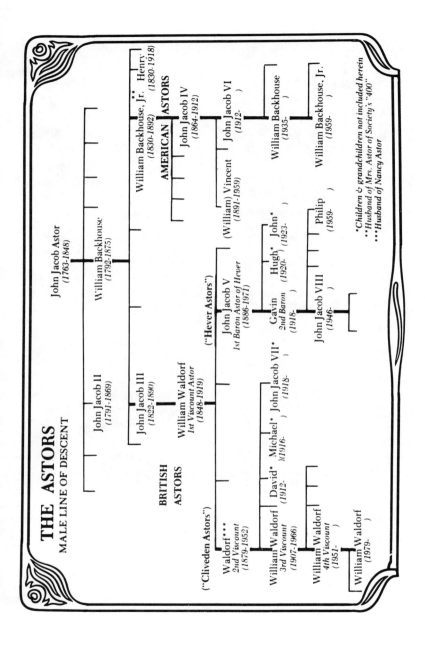

John Jacob Astor
(1763-1848)

John Jacob II
(1791-1869)

William Backhouse
(1792-1875)

John Jacob III
(1822-1890)

William Backhouse, Jr.**
(1830-1892)

Henry
(1830-1918)

AMERICAN ASTORS

John Jacob IV
(1864-1912)

BRITISH ASTORS

William Waldorf
1st Viscount Astor
(1848-1919)

(William) Vincent
(1891-1959)

John Jacob VI
(1912-   )

William Backhouse
(1935-   )

William Backhouse, Jr.
(1959-   )

("Hever Astors")

John Jacob V
1st Baron Astor of Hever
(1886-1971)

("Cliveden Astors")

Waldorf***
2nd Viscount
(1879-1952)

Gavin
2nd Baron
(1918-   )

Hugh*
(1920-   )

John*
(1923-   )

Philip
(1959-   )

William Waldorf
3rd Viscount
(1907-1966)

David*
(1912-   )

Michael*
(1916-   )

John Jacob VII*
(1918-   )

John Jacob VIII
(1946-   )

William Waldorf
4th Viscount
(1951-   )

William Waldorf
(1979-   )

*Children & grandchildren not included herein
**Husband of Mrs. Astor of Society's "400"
***Husband of Nancy Astor

John Jacob Astor, shrewd founder of the dynasty who built an American fortune by trading furs, and investing in Manhattan real estate. *Credit S.W. Newbery.*

William Waldorf Astor, the first Viscount, who transplanted his family to England in 1890. *Credit: S.W. Newbery*

In 1895 William Waldorf Astor purchased Cliveden, and proceeded to spend a small fortune remodeling it.

John Jacob Astor V, Lord Astor of Hever, left England for France in order to protect his estate from inheritance tax. He did this primarily to keep Hever Castle in the family. *Credit: Scott*

Nancy Lady Astor, beautiful divorcee from Virginia and wife of Waldorf Astor (son of William Waldorf). She made Cliveden into a gathering point for the political and literary great of England in the years around World War I. She was the first woman to sit in the British Parliament.
Credit: Sargent

The coat of arms designed for William Waldorf Astor, a mix of American symbolism and traditional heraldry.

The coat of arms of John Jacob Astor V, who became Lord Astor of Hever. The figure represents the god of healing because of his interest in a hospital, and the other represents Mercury, the messenger of the gods, because of his interest in the *Times*.

As board chairman of England's most prestigious newspaper, the *Times,* Gavin Astor, Lord Astor of Hever, brought in an injection of money to help it meet competition from magazines and television. In the process he reduced family ownership from 100% to 15%. *Credit: B. Astor*

W ILLIAM WALDORF ASTOR, the emigre, bought the *Pall Mall Gazette,* and changed it, literally overnight, from a liberal to a conservative paper. Much later, he bought the far more influential *Sunday Observer.*

In 1895, he purchased from the Duke of Westminster the Italianate villa known as Cliveden on 400 acres high above the Thames, near Maidenhead. For the next decade, he remodeled the palatial house, overhauled its huge gardens and terraces, installed the Roman, Greek, and Italian statuary he had bought on the Continent, including the entire marble balustrade from Rome's Villa Borghese.

In 1899, he became a British citizen. He bought a magnificent house in central London, and fishing and shooting estates in northern England and Scotland. In 1903, he purchased Hever Castle in Kent in southeastern England—not really a castle but rather a 13th-century moated manor house once owned by a Sir Thomas Bullen, whose daughter, Anne, changed the spelling of her name to Boleyn, married Henry VIII, became Queen of England and mother of Elizabeth I, and eventually was beheaded at the Tower of London for having failed to produce a royal son.

Again. William Waldorf undertook extensive renovation. For many years, hundreds of workmen labored to restore and redecorate the castle, to build connecting Tudor-style cottages to accommodate guests and servants, to excavate a huge 35-acre lake and divert the Eden River through it, to lay out huge formal gardens and a loggia with a colonnaded piazza.

But William Waldorf also became increasingly moody and eccentric as he grew older, and to a large extent withdrew from society. One commentator referred to him as "Waldorf by name and walled-off by nature." Nevertheless, his ownership of the *Observer* and his substantial charitable contributions and gifts to the Conservative Party and to the war effort won him a baronetcy in 1916 and made him a viscount a year later.

Critics at the time referred to him as the first American to spend his way into the House of Lords. In the biographical book *Tribal*

Feeling, Grandson Michael Astor wrote that William Waldorf received his titles "for political and public services, an ambiguous phrase which is still employed in the bestowal of honors," and which, the author noted, usually means handsome contributions to good causes, including the treasury of the political party in power. "William Waldorf had qualified on both scores," he declared, but "there was plenty of precedent for purchasing a title."

And while William Waldorf had turned his back on America, he didn't forget the source of the family fortune. The coat of arms he adopted includes such traditional heraldic devices as falcons and a gloved fist, but the shield is flanked on one side by an American Indian in war bonnet and on the other by a Daniel Boone-type fur trapper. (The "Ad Astra" motto was apparently a deliberate play on the family name.)

His older son, Waldorf, a modest and conscientious young man, initially had conformed to the traditional prescription for wealthy young Englishmen: he had gone to Eton and Oxford, went in for riding and horse-racing, and joined the right clubs. But all that changed in 1906 when he married Nancy Langhorne, a lively divorcee from Virginia, one of five beautiful and well-publicized sisters. (Coincidentally, Waldorf and Nancy were both born on the same day—May 19, 1879—and the recent centenary of their birth was observed in England by a series of newspaper articles and TV documentaries.)

While William Waldorf would have preferred a rich or titled English lady as his senior daughter-in-law, Waldorf was still the first-born son. So William gave the young couple Cliveden as a wedding present. A few years later, he gave Waldorf control of the *Observer,* too. Shortly before his death in 1919, William Waldorf, by then a viscount, similarly gave Hever Castle to his younger son, John (as John Jacob V preferred to be known). There was also a daughter, Pauline, who married a commoner but whose daughter later became sister-in-law to Queen Elizabeth.

Biographer Harvey O'Connor estimates the viscount's estate was worth about $100 million at his death, but British and American inheritance taxes bit deeply into that.

"William Waldorf had striven to create roots," Michael Astor commented, "and his children, not he, would reap the benefits."

Nancy Astor had meanwhile proceeded to make Cliveden into an exciting though frequently turbulent place—the glittering gathering-point for the political and literary great of England in the years before and after World War I: Lloyd George and Balfour, Curzon and Churchill, Henry James and Shaw and O'Casey.

Waldorf reluctantly moved to the House of Lords when he became the second Viscount Astor on his father's death. He had been elected to the House of Commons in 1910, was looking forward to a long political career there as a mild social reformer, and was the first person to try, repeatedly but unsuccessfully, to give up his title. And Nancy was elected to his seat in the Commons, becoming the first woman to sit in the British Parliament. (She was not, however, the first woman elected to Parliament, as frequently is reported; another woman had been elected earlier but, a Sinn Feiner, had refused to take the seat.)

Nancy not only was a staunch champion of temperance and of the rights of women and children but also was known for her sharp tongue and quick wit. She once described herself thus: "My vigor, vitality and cheek repel me. I am the kind of woman I would run from." Usually, she came out the best in parliamentary and other give-and-take, but in one of the most famous Nancy Astor tales, she wound up second-best—an exchange with Winston Churchill, who frequently referred to her as "the American Virago."

"Winston," Lady Astor is reported to have said on one occasion when he was making some remarks of which she strongly disapproved, "if I were your wife, I'd put poison in your coffee."

To which he is said to have replied, "And madame, if I were your husband, I would drink it."

Waldorf and Nancy Astor had five children. The oldest, another William Waldorf who was known as Bill and eventually became the third viscount, served as a Member of Parliament for a number of years. The next son, David, went into journalism and for 27 years was the active, working editor of the *Observer;* now retired, he still serves as a director of the paper, occasionally writes articles about foreign affairs, and raises money for a group trying to develop small-scale technology for both industrial and underdeveloped nations.

Michael Astor, another son, the author of the autobiography quoted herein, both painted and wrote with professional skill; he, too, was a Member of Parliament for several years after World War II. John Jacob Astor VII—or Jakey, as all his family and friends call him—had a distinguished World War II career, was a Member of Parliament for eight years in the 1950s, and long headed the Agricultural Research Council, a semi-official group that decides which kinds of experimental farming should receive government financial support; he was eventually knighted for this service, and so technically is Sir John. Between Bill and his three brothers was a sister, Nancy Phyllis, whose husband was long a Member of Parliament and later became the Earl of Ancaster; she died in 1975.

Each of the brothers married two or three times, and had several sons and daughters by their various wives. Their sister was married only once, and had one daughter and one son, the latter now dead.

Eventually, Cliveden lost some of its glitter. In the mid-1930s, the "Cliveden Set" was roundly attacked as a government-press clique trying to persuade Britain to appease Hitler. More recently, under the third viscount, it was linked to the Profumo scandal. A key figure in that scandal, osteopath Stephen Ward, had treated Bill Astor after a bad horseback fall and in return was frequently allowed to use a cottage at Cliveden. It was there in 1956 that War Minister John Profumo saw and was attracted to Mr. Ward's friend, Christine Keeler, a call girl also carrying on an affair with a Soviet diplomat alleged to be a spy.

"Cliveden, the pride of them all, was touched by the hot breath of scandal," Mrs. Kavaler has written. Many of the Astors believe that the scandal's strain on Bill hastened his death in 1966 at the age of 59.

The present Viscount Astor is Bill's son, another William Waldorf, a slim, dark 28-year-old who in 1966 at the age of 14 technically became the head of the Cliveden Astors, the senior branch of the British family.

In 1942, the second viscount had given Cliveden to the National Trust, the organization that preserves historic houses and estates, with an endowment to maintain it. The Trust always gives the donor's family the first right to rent the donated property, and the Astors remained at Cliveden as tenants until the death of the third viscount. Now it is rented to Stanford University for one of Stanford's overseas student centers, in keeping with the Astor family's desire that it be used "to bring about a better understanding between English-speaking peoples."

THE HEVER BRANCH of the British Astors has always seemed to lead a less chaotic, more settled life than the Cliveden Astors. They have been active in banking and insurance and generally have seemed more typical of the wealthy titled class in Britain. Some of the Cliveden Astors reluctantly admit that this difference may arise from the fact that the wife of John Astor was a typical British lady, the daughter of the Earl of Minto, rather than, as Michael Astor described his mother, "a Virginia hot rodder."

John Astor, the first head of the Hever Astors and brother of the second viscount, had a career supremely typical of that of the wealthy or titled Britisher: like his brother, educated at Eton and Oxford; an Olympic medallist in racquets; a distinguished war record, being twice wounded and losing a leg in the process; a Member of Parliament for 23 years. It was he who, starting in the early 1920s, gradually acquired ownership of Britain's most prestigious paper, the *Times*. And it was for owning the *Times* and his dedicated work for, and huge gifts to, Middlesex Hospital that John Astor was in 1956 made a baron in his own right, with the title of Lord Astor of Hever.

Although the Astor branch in the U.S., where the fortune was originally made, long tended to be aloof from public affairs and rather niggardly in the support of charitable and other worthy causes, the British branch has been public-spirited, philanthropic, and involved in public life to a degree unusual even for many long-established British families. That's how they won two peerages in two generations.

"We were," says Sir John, or Jakey, of the Cliveden Astors, "brought up to believe that if you were fortunate enough to be rich, there was an obligation to give a part of your time to public life—a very English point of view."

When the other John Astor became Lord Astor of Hever, he took a coat of arms very similar to that taken by his father, except that instead of a gold background on the shield, there were horizontal black lines against a white background, to suggest the printed page. And instead of the Indian and the fur-trapper, the Hever Astor shield was flanked by Aesculapius and Mercury—the god of healing and the messenger of the gods, to indicate John Astor's twin interests of Middlesex Hospital and the *Times*.

An unexpected change in British tax laws in 1962 made real estate owned outside of Britain subject for the first time to British inheritance taxes, and Lord Astor, then 76, realized that if he died a British resident, most of his wealth would be subject to a near-confiscatory 80 percent tax, and Hever Castle would have to be sold.

As a booklet written by his son Gavin, the present Lord Astor of Hever, puts it: He would have been "vulnerable to the payment of crippling British death duties if he were to die a resident of the United Kingdom. So, in order to protect his family's American inheritance from the grasp of the British government, he decided to leave the country to which he had been brought as a boy of seven and to which he had devoted a lifetime of service."

What he did was to take up residence in southern France, in a large house on substantial grounds near Cannes. "It is my firm hope," he said on leaving England, "that as a result, my descendants will be enabled to continue to uphold the family traditions and responsibilities as I have always tried to do."

His then 82-year-old sister, Pauline, left England at about the same time, to take up residence in the Channel Island of Guernsey, a noted tax haven. Their brother, the second viscount, had already died when the new law was passed, and his share of the property in family trusts in America had passed on to his children; for complex tax-law reasons, this made the 1962 changes less of a problem for the Cliveden Astors.

It was after the 1962 tax-law change that the American trustees of the British Astor holdings began selling off their U.S. properties, since these no longer carried any tax advantages for their owners, and they sold steadily all through the 1960s, according to persons familiar with the situation. The Astors won't discuss this, or tell what assets they might have acquired with the money raised from the sales; one British tax lawyer speculates that a large portion must have gone into tax-exempt British bonds.

The present Lord Astor of Hever, a cousin and contemporary of the present viscount's father, took over Hever Castle in 1962 when his father left England, and succeeded to the title when his father died in 1971. (The French property was to be sold.) He had inherited his father's shares in the *Times* in 1954, at which time it was a 90 percent interest, and he acquired the remaining 10 percent in 1962. From 1959 on, he was board chairman of the *Times* and worked diligently at the job. It was he who ultimately brought in the Thomson Organization to take it over in 1966.

"The *Times* needed the injection of more money than I was able to provide," says Lord Astor, a tweedy, ruddy-faced, very British-looking man of 61. "We were jogging along jolly well, but we had to look to the future. And with the competition ahead from glossy magazines and television, it seemed to me that it needed to be part of a larger organization."

The *Times* and *Sunday Times* were merged into a new company, 85 percent owned by the Thomson group and 15 percent by Lord Astor and his children. He remains a director of the new company but spends far more of his time in various public activities. As Lord Lieutenant of Kent, for example, he represents the Royal Family at an endless round of local luncheons, fairs, teas and similar ceremonies.

In 1962, Lord Astor and his wife, the daughter of Field Marshal Earl Haig, set up Hever Castle and its surrounding 4,000 acres as a commercial enterprise, with the castle open to the public for an admission fee from early spring to late fall and with the best land farmed commercially and the fishing and shooting rights rented out. "With the present impact of taxation," an official Hever Castle brochure says, "the only way such a heritage can be maintained and held together intact is by inviting the public to share in its appreciation and upkeep."

In this way, the family not only realizes income from farming and admission fees and sales in the refreshment stand and souvenir shop, but can also charge off many maintenance expenses to the corporation. Lord and Lady Astor, with their children grown and gone, rarely stay in the castle except at Christmas and other family occasions when their five children gather together. Instead, they use one of the self-contained apartments in the Tudor village attached to the Castle.

"It is easier to live in this smaller apartment," Lord Astor explains, "nearer the heating plant, nearer the garage. It would be much more inconvenient and much more expensive and extravagant to live in the castle."

Lord Astor's two brothers, Hugh and John, have been active in real-estate, banking, and insurance enterprises, but recently have been cutting back the pace of their activity. Each has several children.

Naturally, both the Cliveden Astors and the Hever Astors are reluctant to talk about their wealth. And since much of it is in trusts and other difficult-to-penetrate forms, it's impossible to know just how much they retain of the $200 million-plus that a family biographer estimated the American and British Astors together were worth in 1900.

Certainly great wealth is still there. Lord Astor of Hever and the older Cliveden and Hever Astors, in their late 50s and 60s, travel widely without appearing to worry about costs, belong to the best clubs, have social secretaries, drive Daimlers or BMWs or Mercedeses. Several have shooting and fishing preserves in Scotland.

But some of their sons and daughters—and there are about 30 of them, cousins and contemporaries of the young viscount—appear to be beginning to feel some financial pressures. And both older and younger Astors are clearly concerned about just how the next generation will make out, given the steep British tax rates and the growing abundance of offspring to be provided for. (In this respect, at least, their fate doesn't appear too different from the fate of many similarly wealthy families that stayed in America.)

"I suppose you would say we are rich," concedes Lord Astor of Hever, "but there are lots of British families far richer than we."

Some wealthy families, notes David Astor, the former editor of the *Observer,* keep on in business, adding to their wealth, but the Cliveden Astors haven't. His mother, Nancy, used to say, he recalls, "that we hadn't produced any wastrels, but then, neither had we produced anyone that made a lot more money. Certainly, there are many people now much richer than we, and that will be even more true in my children's generation."

Astor, a shy, heavy-set man of 67, lives in a large, comfortably furnished but certainly not elegant house in northwest London— Beatle Paul McCartney and wife Lynda are "very pleasant" next-door neighbors—and has a "not very grand" weekend home in Berkshire. "We're steadily contracting," he says, referring not only to himself but to the entire family. "You'd see that if you could see the way we lived in our youth compared to the way we live today. Our wealth has steadily eroded. You try to shelter it, of course, to pass things to your children in your lifetime. But that is becoming increasingly difficult."

He himself, for example, couldn't find enough family funds to keep on bankrolling the *Observer* and had to turn to Atlantic Richfield to keep it afloat. As noted, Lord Astor of Hever didn't feel wealthy enough to give the *Times* all the financial support he thought it needed and had to call in the Thomson organization. Sir John Astor wasn't rich enough, his accountant told him, to keep up the racing stable he so dearly loved.

And even though serious application to some sort of enterprise has long been a well-established trait of the British Astors, quite a few of the younger ones seem to think not merely that they really *ought* to work as a matter of form, but that they *must* work as a matter of financial necessity—for their children's sake, if not for their own.

The new generation includes a psychotherapist and a civil engineer, a teacher and a professional photographer of children, an interior decorator and a doctor's wife, a law student and an art historian. Several actively operate farms, perhaps a throwback to the original John Jacob's fondness for land, but more likely because farming is one activity that still gets preferential tax treatment in Britain.

"There is no question that my children are not going to be able to sit around and live off their inheritance," declares the present viscount. He himself operates a large farm in England and another in Scotland, and is trying to build two small businesses—one making kitchen cupboards and the other manufacturing and repairing farm machinery. Obviously, his inherited wealth enables him to tackle these projects, but he insists that "it isn't just that I can't conceive of sitting around in the country doing nothing. If I stopped work now, I would definitely have to cut down the way I live."

One of the viscount's cousins, a younger David Astor, who is the son of Michael Astor, lives on and operates a 400-acre farm, runs an antiquarian bookshop, and works for the National Theatre as a lobbyist seeking greater government financial aid.

The family fortune, he believes, "is petering out at exactly the right time," since British tax laws make it so difficult to pass on wealth. "There are a lot of us around, and we have to start working, and it's about time we did," he adds; he winds up with the philosophical thought that "this way, anyhow, I'll have a much more interesting and varied life."

The London residences of the Astors, even of the senior family members, are for the most part small town houses or flats, rather than imposing mansions. And while their country homes range from the modest to the quite large and comfortable, only a couple could be called truly baronial. Taxes and maintenance costs make large estates like Hever the exception not only for Astors but for Britons generally nowadays. "The large English country home and estate has now clearly vanished," Michael Astor observed, "except as a spectacle for sightseers who today are usually invited to view the corpse, now that the spirit has left it."

Few Astors, in either the older or younger generations, have very many live-in servants, and most seem to have none. The viscount, for example, has a small servantless flat in London (close to the specialty shop his wife owned before their marriage and which she continues to operate), and a medium-sized house for his growing family in the country, where the staff consists of a nanny for his infant son, a cleaning "daily," and a gardener who doubles as a handyman.

It could be a mistake to assume that lack of servants, smaller homes, and other apparent cutbacks indicate seriously-shrinking fortunes for the Astors or for any other of Britain's wealthier families. Even the very rich, some observers suggest, simply find it more sensible, more becoming, and even far easier to live less ostentatiously and less lavishly these days.

"There is a great deal of wealth around Britain, but not out there in public gaze," asserts Lady Marina Vaizey, an American art expert married to a ranking British economist. "The Astors and other well-to-do people simply blend into the landscape here—like the pheasants."

Nonetheless, the Astors' present way of life does indeed—as the older David Astor has remarked—seem a far cry from the golden days at Cliveden before World War I: 20 indoor servants, 40 to 50 gardeners, 10 to 12 stablemen, a superb racing stable, all 46 bedrooms frequently occupied by famous guests. Even in the 1920s, Hever Castle had 30 or more full-time servants. Now Lord Astor and his wife make do with three.

The older British Astors travel to the U.S. fairly often, and the viscount and most of the other younger members of the family have also traveled there from time to time. A few have gone to school in the U.S. or even worked there for a while.

Almost all, old and young, say that while they are completely British, they do feel quite at ease in the U.S. "Father and Mother were proud of their American connections and taught us to be proud of them, too," says the elder David Astor. The viscount believes that "because my generation is so well-established here (in England), we can look back on our American heritage in a much easier way than our parents. Previous generations, I think, were trying so desperately not to be rich Americans trying to be English."

He himself goes three or four times a year to the States, finds Americans "much more friendly than English people are," and particularly likes the Midwest and South. He is thinking of buying a farm in the Midwest, with several associates. But he can't abide New York, because "everyone there wants to know what your salary is, everyone is going to a psychiatrist, and no one has time to laugh."

Sir John calls himself "pretty near a Civil War buff," and he has visited most of the major Civil War battlefields. He feels at home in America, he says, but is always aware that "I was born British, I am British, I feel British."

And this feeling of being very British makes it hard for the British Astors to speculate just how their lives might be different if old William Waldorf had never quit the United States.

Several believe that in all likelihood the U.S. tax laws would have treated them more kindly than British tax laws have. "We'd probably be a lot wealthier," says the old David Astor, while his nephew David similarly contends that "I would be much better off financially if I lived in America." Sir John notes another possible difference. "I doubt we'd have had the public life in America that we've had here," he says. But most of the British Astors simply shrug off the question of differences and say they have never thought much about it, one way or the other.

There isn't much contact between the two branches of the British family, but this appears to arise from geographical separation and differences in interests and tastes rather than from any family feud or ill-will. They still come together for a family wedding, for a 60th birthday celebration, or other milestone occasions. The Cliveden Astors, for similar reasons, don't see much of each other, either. The senior Hever Astors, who have been linked in a number of business enterprises, seem generally to continue to keep in relatively close touch with each other.

What does the Astor name mean to Britons in general? Ironically, despite the outstanding record of the British Astors and the rather meager contributions of recent American Astors, the name may still mean more in America, where it continues to connote unusual wealth and status. This is probably due in good part to such conspicuous reminders as New York's Waldorf-Astoria Hotel.

"I don't think the British have ever had the American respect for wealth alone," says British social commentator Thomas Pakenham. "And there isn't any sort of respect for inherited title or position anymore. The monarchy in Britain was once the apex of a substantial pyramid. Now it's completely isolated. There's no longer any broad belief that people of title or wealth have special rights—or for that matter, special obligations—simply because of what they inherited. That attitude may still exist in the particular locality where they live, but not broadly."

Lady Vaizey believes that "generally speaking, the name doesn't mean much to the average Briton. Some may think of wealth, and some may remember Nancy as a rather eccentric person, but neither group is very large." The viscount finds more familiarity with the name in the United States than he does in Britain.

Says Lord Astor of Hever: "I would hope it means a family that has come over from America, gotten itself deeply involved in the public life of this country, and contributed something to this country."

V

The McCormicks

BEFORE BROOKS MCCORMICK stepped down as chairman of International Harvester Co. in 1979, he could look up from his desk and see on his office wall a picture of a Chicago factory as it had looked more than a century earlier. The factory dated back to 1847, when Cyrus Hall McCormick took his reaper from Virginia to Chicago and built the McCormick Reaper Works, near where the Chicago River joins Lake Michigan. Since that time International Harvester, the multibillion-dollar concern that grew out of the revolutionary invention, has made its headquarters in a succession of buildings on the very same spot. When 62-year-old Brooks McCormick, a great-grandnephew of Cyrus Hall McCormick, phased himself out of the company's management, International Harvester was without a McCormick at or near the helm for the first time in its long history.

International Harvester and its predecessor companies have been in business since 1831, when Cyrus McCormick demonstrated the first successful mechanical reaper of grain. For nearly 150 years after that a McCormick either headed the company or waited in the wings to do so. It is a record of family management that few American corporations can match.

One of the few that comes close, oddly enough, is Deere & Co., Harvester's chief rival in the farm-equipment industry. Leadership of Deere has been handed down to succeeding generations of sons-in-law since 1837, when John Deere invented a plow that would slice cleanly through the Midwest's thick black soil. The latest in the line is William A. Hewitt, a great-great-grandson-in-law of the inventor. The company has prospered under the succession arrangement.

The McCormicks's longevity in the International Harvester Co., however, isn't the only noteworthy aspect of what is surely one of America's great industrial families. A look at the McCormicks on the eve of the sesquicentennial anniversary of the machine that carried them to fortune and fame reveals a family rich in tradition and achievement—and rich in oddities and ironies as well. Generations of McCormicks have helped industrialize America, entertained it, scandalized it, preached to it, and—in diverse ways—profited from it. Along the way, they have formed marital and business alliances with other families of the American industrial aristocracy, including the Rockefellers, the Medills, and the Deerings.

One irony, in fact, is how Brooks McCormick went to International Harvester. While he is a latter-day relative of the company's founder, his own family came into the company by a circuitous route of marriage. Brooks McCormick is descended not from Cyrus Hall McCormick but from one of Cyrus's younger brothers—William Sanderson McCormick. William's widow sold her interest in the budding concern to Cyrus shortly after William died in 1865. Years later, Brooks's father was married to Marion Deering of the Deering Harvester Co. family. And in 1902, Deering Harvester was one of the four companies that merged with the McCormick Harvesting Machine Co. to form International Harvester. "My father came into the company as a representative of the Deering side, so you might say I came in through the back door," Brooks says of the odd bit of circumstance. "It was really an accident of history."

Another McCormick irony is that while Cyrus McCormick is credited with inventing the reaper, brother William's descendants —not his—have since achieved the greatest prominence in business. Besides Brooks McCormick, William's line includes William McCormick Blair, who founded the Chicago brokerage and investment-banking house of William Blair & Co. Two more generations of Blairs, including his sons Edward McCormick and Bowen, have followed William in the firm.

One of William Sanderson McCormick's grandsons was publisher Robert R. McCormick, who made the *Chicago Tribune* one of the nation's staunchest (and loudest) voices of Republican conservatism before he died in 1955. His relatives are still among the owners of the closely-held Tribune Co., one of the nation's largest publishing concerns. Among its holdings, besides the *Chicago Tribune,* are the New York *Daily News* and the *Orlando Tribune* in Florida.

While Robert McCormick was preaching conservatism from the pages of his newspaper, a great-granddaughter of Cyrus McCormick bought *The New Republic,* one of the country's best-known liberal journals. She was Anne Blaine "Nancy" Harrison. When she met and married Gilbert Harrison, she was a union organizer and lobbyist—notwithstanding the fact that labor strife at the McCormick Harvesting Machinery Works had helped spark the bloody Haymarket Square labor riot in Chicago in 1886. The Harrisons published *The New Republic* for 20 years before selling the magazine in 1974.

Gilbert Harrison has written a biography of Anita McCormick Blaine, Nancy's strong-willed grandmother who imbued her with the liberal politics that were sheer anathema to the rest of the family. Anita Blaine was not only a supporter of Franklin Roosevelt, unusual for a McCormick, but she also provided considerable financial support to the abortive 1948 presidential bid of the liberal Henry Wallace, who had been Agriculture Secretary and Vice-President under Roosevelt.

Nancy Harrison died of cancer in 1977, at age 58. The Harrisons' four children are among the few living descendants of Cyrus Hall McCormick, even though the inventor himself had five children. His other living descendants, members of the family of Mrs. Anita Oser, live in Europe. They are descended from the 1895 marriage of Harold F. McCormick to Edith Rockefeller. (Harold was a son of Cyrus Hall McCormick and Edith was a daughter of John D. Rockefeller; their marriage ended in divorce.)

While the line of Cyrus Hall McCormick has dwindled in numbers, that of his youngest brother, Leander James McCormick, has multiplied and prospered, despite its one-time ostracism from the rest of the family. Leander didn't get along with Cyrus's sons, who took over the McCormicks' company after Cyrus died in 1884. The sons solved the problem by buying out their Uncle Leander, but the parting was bitter. Leander maintained that his and Cyrus's father, Robert McCormick, really invented the reaper, and that Cyrus, as the eldest son, merely took out the patent and took his place as head of the family company.

Leander's descendants have continued to profess that belief. Among their proudest possessions are dozens of documents purporting to prove that Robert McCormick invented the reaper patented by Cyrus. The bitterness has largely left the dispute over the years, but the issue of who really invented the reaper is still alive and kicking any time the McCormicks talk about the machine that launched their family saga.

F AMILY RECORDS INDICATE that the McCormicks got their start in the New World sometime around 1735, when Thomas McCormick emigrated from County Londonderry, in Northern Ireland. Thomas settled in Pennsylvania's Cumberland County, but his grandson, Robert McCormick, was born in Rockbridge County in western Virginia in 1780. There the McCormicks raised livestock and grew wheat on their farm, called Walnut Grove, and young Robert tinkered continually in the farm's blacksmith shop. While generations of McCormicks have fought over who invented the reaper, there isn't any doubt about who was the first family member to try. By International Harvester's account, Robert's first attempt came in 1816, when his son Cyrus was seven years old. But Robert apparently had no more luck than the many others who were trying at that time to develop a machine to speed up the harvesting of grain.

Robert returned to his reaper project off and on for the next 15 years, and no doubt young Cyrus pitched in to help his father somewhere along the line. Whatever Cyrus did, it's certain that the reaper didn't just leap full-blown out of his 22-year-old brain in 1831; instead, he certainly built on the work of his father. But on a hot July day of that year, Cyrus demonstrated a successful reaper to onlookers in a field near Steele's Tavern, Va. The young man reportedly strode behind the machine while a family slave, Jo Anderson, raked the cut grain onto the reaper's platform. Even after that successful demonstration, however, Cyrus apparently wasn't sure just what he had. He didn't even get a patent for his machine until three years later, and he didn't start to seek a market for the reaper until 1840, nine years after that day at Steele's Tavern.

About all most Americans know about the reaper is that Cyrus McCormick is credited with inventing it. But it is hard to overstate the machine's significance. The early reaper combined wheels, blades, knives, and mechanical fingers on a horse-drawn platform. It required two men to operate it, but they could harvest in a day as much wheat as five men could by hand. Later refinements, of course, increased its efficiency considerably. In 1830, 91 percent of the 13 million Americans lived on farms, and the production of food and fiber required a lot of hard labor. Fifty years later, the Industrial Revolution was well underway, and a major reason was that inventions like the reaper and the cotton gin freed men from the fields to work in factories. The reaper also freed the farmers of the northern American prairies to fight the Civil War, helping to assure the Union's manpower advantage.

"The reaper is to the North what slavery is to the South," said Secretary of War Stanton in 1862. "By taking the place of regiments of young men in the Western harvest fields, it releases them to do battle for the Union at the front and at the same time keeps up the supply of bread for the nation's armies." Without the reaper, he added, "the Union would be dismembered."

The reaper didn't make the McCormicks wealthy overnight. Competition from models by other inventors was an early drawback, and it wasn't until the 1840s that Cyrus was able to prove the superiority of the McCormick machine. Cyrus spent years trying to perfect his first reaper; meanwhile he built an iron furnace and entered into a partnership with his father to manufacture iron. The iron business failed in 1841, leaving the McCormicks with debts of $18,000. Only then did Cyrus start to manufacture reapers at the family's Walnut Grove farm.

Cyrus began to travel throughout Virginia to promote his machine, managing to sell seven reapers in 1842. The next year he sold 29 of the machines, and in 1844 he sold 50 for $100 apiece. In 1846, the year when old Robert McCormick died, Cyrus sold 190 reapers, and enough of them went to Ohio, Indiana, and Illinois to convince him that the machine's future lay not in Virginia but in the West. So the next year, 1847, Cyrus McCormick moved the business to Chicago, and, with local businessman C. M. Gray, he built his factory at the mouth of the Chicago River. Gray soon sold his half of the business to two other men, W. E. Jones and Chicago pioneer William B. Ogden; but in 1849 the McCormicks bought them out for $65,000. The McCormicks' reaper business was now purely a family affair, with Cyrus firmly in charge.

The family business, however, didn't keep Cyrus in Chicago much. Instead, he traveled around the world to promote his machine and to defend his patents in endless rounds of litigation, while brothers William and Leander minded the store in Chicago. One of Cyrus's most important early decisions was to let farmers buy their machines on credit and pledge to complete their payments with part of the proceeds from future crops. In the early 1850s the reaper sold for $125. Farmers were asked to pay $35 down in cash, plus the cost of freight from Chicago. The balance was due the next Dec. 1, with 6 percent interest owed from July 1. The payment system was an early form of installment buying, and 125 years later Brooks McCormick could proudly note that "we still use that system in our company today."

The Civil War meant an explosion of profits for the McCormicks, but it also troubled the brothers. They weren't in favor of the South's secession; but they had been slave owners in Virginia, and they wanted the South's position on the issue respected. The McCormicks' stand wasn't appreciated by some Chicagoans, notably the editors of the *Chicago Tribune*—the paper that their descendants would one day run. When Cyrus ran for Congress in 1864, the *Tribune* rose to the challenge. It charged in an editorial that Cyrus didn't invent the reaper but "pirated the invention of a poor New York mechanic named Obed Hussey," who in fact had tried to develop a machine of his own. Cyrus went down to defeat at the hands of John Wentworth.

On May 13, 1884, Cyrus Hall McCormick died a wealthy man of 75 in his house on Rush Street, on Chicago's North Side. It was the end of a full life, for Cyrus had seen his company grow to become one of the nation's biggest businesses. By that time, his brother William's family had been out of the company for nearly 20 years. When William died in 1865, his four children were youngsters, so neither of the two boys was old enough to take their father's place in the company. William's widow sold her interest to Cyrus.

But Leander McCormick was still in business with Cyrus, and that meant trouble. There had long been tension between Cyrus and Leander, and Cyrus's death shattered the uneasy peace within the family. Leander soon clashed openly with the company's new president, 25-year-old Cyrus H. McCormick Jr. Among other things, Leander wanted a more prominent position in the company for his own son, Robert Hall McCormick II. But young Cyrus, with strong support from his mother, Nettie, resisted and then bought out his uncle for $3,250,000. By 1885, the McCormicks' company was in the hands of Cyrus's family alone, and the inventor's descendants would lead the company for another 65 years.

International Harvester Co. was formed in 1902, when two major farm-equipment makers combined with three smaller ones. The two dominant concerns were McCormick Harvesting Machine Co. and Deering Harvester Co., a rival founded in 1869 by William Deering. The others were Milwaukee Harvester Co.; Wardner, Bushnell & Glessner Co.; and Plano Manufacturing Co. The Deerings placed on the new company's board of directors a grandson-in-law of William Deering, Chauncey McCormick. Chauncey's grandfather was William Sanderson McCormick, whose early death had removed his family from company affairs.

Cyrus McCormick Jr. became the first president of International Harvester, and in December, 1918, he was succeeded by his younger brother, Harold F. McCormick. Harold held the post until 1922, when it was turned over to Alexander Legge, the first non-family member to get the position. A succession of presidents from outside the family followed, but young Cyrus and Harold were always present—as chairman of the board and chairman of the company's executive committee.

Harold F. McCormick was constantly in the public eye, largely because of his tumultuous private life. Harold was 23 years old in 1895 when he married John D. Rockefeller's daughter, Edith, in a widely-heralded union of two of the wealthiest clans in America. Following the wedding and honeymoon, Harold whisked his bride off to the unlikely destination of Council Bluffs, Iowa; Harold's first full-time job with the company his father founded was as head of its sales branch there. Three years later, he returned to Chicago to become a vice-president of Harvester, but then his marriage began to sour. The first child of Harold and Edith, John Rockefeller McCormick, died in early childhood. The couple had three other children—Fowler, Muriel, and Mathilde—but Edith never really recovered from the loss of her first-born. After years of separation, the couple was divorced in 1921, and Harold went on to two more well-publicized marriages. The first was to Polish opera star Ganna Walska, whom he later divorced. In 1938 he was married to Adah Wilson, who had been his nurse. Harold died three years later, still chairman of Harvester; his son Fowler became president of the company that year.

Fowler McCormick was colorful and controversial in his personal and business affairs, as befitted the son of Harold McCormick. Fowler never knew his paternal grandfather, for Cyrus McCormick had died 14 years before Fowler was born. But Grandfather Rockefeller was still alive, and young Fowler was one of his favorites. The grandson of two of the world's richest men went to Groton School and Princeton University, and then spent four years deciding what to do with his life. At first Fowler steered clear of both Standard Oil and International Harvester. Instead, he traveled, started his own brokerage firm, and delved into self-analysis in

Zurich, Switzerland, with psychologist C. G. Jung, whom he met through his mother. Finally, in 1925, the prince entered his father's kingdom when he started loading pig iron at Harvester's Milwaukee plant for 25 cents an hour. He was learning the family business from the bottom up, but the top wasn't very far away. By 1934 Fowler was a vice-president, and in 1941 he was named president.

Along the way Fowler's personal life made sensational headlines. At age 32, in 1931, Fowler was married to Anne "Fifi" Stillman, the 51-year-old mother of one of his Princeton classmates. Her divorce from her banker husband had come only after long and bitter court proceedings. Then, in the 1940s, Fowler fought a prolonged and successful court battle to have two adopted children taken away from his sister, Muriel McCormick Hubbard, on the grounds that she wasn't a fit mother. Both Fowler's marriage (which lasted until Mrs. McCormick died in 1969 at age 89) and the child-custody battle chagrined members of the family, but Fowler McCormick had his way.

In business, Fowler stood out in his day as a pioneer of nondiscriminatory hiring. In 1946, Harvester opened a plant in Louisville, Ky., and placed an ad in a local newspaper saying that "It will be the company's definite policy to offer Negroes equal economic opportunity to the greatest degree possible." That was a controversial position at the time and widely criticized in the South, but Harvester proclaimed the same policy two years later when it opened a plant in Memphis, Tenn. The company later stuck to its stand in the face of wildcat strikes by some white workers.

Fowler McCormick was named Harvester's chairman and chief executive in 1946, but five years later he abruptly resigned after clashing with John L. McCaffrey, the company's president. McCormick and McCaffrey had been friends since 1931, when McCaffrey was McCormick's boss at Harvester's Grand Island, Neb., sales branch. But in the early months of 1951 the two men were quarreling, and McCormick took the matter to the company's directors. He was shocked when, after talking with McCaffrey, the board decided to back the No. 2 executive. On May 28, Harvester's directors took the chief executive's post from McCormick and handed it to McCaffrey, leaving Fowler with the title of chairman but with no power. "There was a feeling that McCormick was indecisive and wasn't serious enough about profits," one company executive recalls. McCormick was, however, decisive enough to quit promptly as chairman (although he stayed on the board). Angry and hurt, he later told an interviewer, "I do not believe that my record justified the demotion that the directors decided upon, and it was a demotion—there is no point in concealing it. What happened to change the attitude of these men with whom I had been closely associated in a personal and business way for 20 or 30 years, I do not know."

Fowler McCormick's sudden departure meant the end of a 120-year era during which a McCormick had always held one of the top executive positions in the company that Cyrus McCormick had started. But when Fowler left, Brooks McCormick was already well on his way to restoring the family's leadership. Brooks had been hired out of Yale University by Fowler in 1940. With his father a McCormick and his mother a Deering, his hiring might have seemed more or less automatic, but Brooks recalls that he was "grateful that Fowler had agreed to take me on." The only other place where Brooks had applied for a job was at Tribune Tower, which stands just a few hundred feet north of International Harvester's headquarters in Chicago. But there, publisher Robert McCormick had given his young cousin a brisk rebuff.

After the usual entrance-level jobs, Brooks was put in charge of the company's operations in Britain. He became executive vice-president in 1957, president in 1968, and chief executive officer in 1971. "I clawed my way to the top," is Brooks's jesting response when asked how his family ties had helped his career. But, of course, Brooks's co-workers and superiors at Harvester were well-aware that he was destined to rise in the company. "I felt honored that they would place him under my direction," says Harald Reishus, who was Brooks's boss in the late 1940s and who later retired as a vice-president. "Brooks never flaunted his background, and nobody ever held him in awe, but I felt that in time he would be running the company."

By the time Brooks McCormick reached the top, however, International Harvester itself was near the bottom. The company's business had long since expanded to include trucks and construction machinery as well as farm equipment, but Harvester was a bumbling giant, rapidly losing ground to aggressive competitors like Caterpillar Tractor Co. and Deere & Co. Harvester's construction-machinery business made decent profits only in boom times, when Caterpillar's production schedules couldn't meet the industry demand for machines, and Deere had snatched sales leadership in the farm-equipment industry away from Harvester in the 1960s. Harvester was a bigger company than Deere, with higher overall sales, but Deere was earning more money—indicating that Harvester was burdened with too many employes. "The whole company was a mess," says one Harvester observer, and a host of statistics support that assessment. In 1971, the year Brooks took over, Harvester's earnings had declined for the fifth straight year. The company's net income was just $1.65 a share, and Harvester paid out nearly all of that—$1.60 a share—in dividends to shareholders. Hardly anything was left over for modernizing old plants and developing new and better machines to sell. Even Brooks admits, "It was a question of how long the company would survive."

Brooks moved to set things straight. He disposed of Harvester's marginal steel-making business, discontinued several lines of trucks, and reoriented the company's upper echelons and its marketing staff, among other moves. The actions paid off with higher earnings; in Brooks's last year as chief executive, the fiscal year ending in October, 1978, Harvester earned nearly $7 a share, more than four times its earnings when his tenure started. But more needed to be done, and the most pressing need was to pare Harvester's bloated work force.

"Brooks, with his patrician mind, couldn't bring himself to fire all those people," explains one close observer of Harvester affairs. To do that, he conducted a spectacular executive raid on one of the nation's biggest and most glamorous companies, Xerox Corp., hiring its president, Archie R. McCardell, to become Harvester's president. McCardell quickly trimmed some 2,000 persons from

Harvester's worldwide payroll of 90,000, at the same time increasing its production schedules. In 1979 McCardell, who already had been named chief executive of the company, became chairman too, and Brooks stepped aside to become chairman of Harvester's executive committee, the final step in his plan to phase himself out of the company's management in preparation for retirement. "I have been part of a team that made some significant steps in revitalizing the company," Brooks says. Commented one analyst who had watched the company's progress, "He laid the groundwork for straightening things out."

How did the McCormicks manage to hold onto the reins of International Harvester for nearly a century and a half? After all, they outlasted a slew of other founding families in their companies, including the du Ponts, the Searses, the Maytags, the Swifts, the Pillsburys, the Pullmans, and the Armours. Obviously, the factors that militate against continuing family operation of big companies are numerous. Death and taxes almost always result in families selling off stock in the companies their forebears founded—and losing their influence over company affairs due to the simple arithmetic of ownership.

Then there are the inevitable battles between generations; they are often waged over entire lifetimes, especially where strong, entrepreneurial spirits are involved. Sons sometimes aren't anxious to follow in their fathers' footsteps for personal reasons, and fathers sometimes return those sentiments. There is also the enduring notion that it is somehow shameful to employ one's family name and position to succeed. The younger generations of wealthy families frequently have a sense of guilt about inheriting great wealth, and along with it a position at or near the top of a major corporation. Many members of succeeding generations feel a need to demonstrate their competence to others and to themselves, and that need often leads them away from the family company.

Against all those factors, luck certainly worked in the McCormicks' favor. It was natural for Cyrus Hall McCormick to be succeeded by two of his sons, and not unexpected that his grandson Fowler would head the company. But the generation after Fowler produced no males to carry on the family name in the company; indeed, Cyrus McCormick's grandchildren produced few children at all. Meanwhile, plenty of William Sanderson McCormick's descendants were around, and one of them just happened to be a Deering with the McCormick name—Brooks McCormick.

In his tenure as chairman of Harvester, Brooks's office was nearly a small-scale company museum. His desk was one that had belonged to his great-grandfather, William Deering. The walls were filled with early company mementoes, including advertising for McCormick reapers and medals won by company machines at farm-equipment expositions. His bookshelf contained such volumes as *Cyrus Hall McCormick,* by William T. Hutchinson, and *McCormick of Chicago,* Frank C. Waldrop's biography of publisher Robert McCormick of the *Chicago Tribune.* Also on the shelves were books on Chicago and Illinois history, which Brooks's ancestors did so much to shape even though none had held public office. (Brooks's wife, Hope, was an Illinois state representative from 1965 to 1967, and she went on to hold various Republican Party offices. But politics by and large hasn't been a successful McCormick field of endeavor. Cyrus Hall McCormick wasn't the only family member to be rejected by the voters.) "I'm very proud of my antecedents," Brooks explained about the mementoes. "I have always felt I grew up in the shadows of some very interesting men and women."

Ironically, though, Brooks McCormick himself helped to prevent the McCormick presence at International Harvester from lasting even longer. His two sons and two daughters weren't in the company as he prepared for his retirement, and Brooks wanted it just that way. He made that clear in 1971, when his son Mark, who had worked for three summers at Harvester, asked for a full-time job after receiving his M.B.A. degree from the University of Chicago.

"I told him that I didn't think nepotism was in order in this day and age," Brooks recalls, even though he himself had asked for jobs at two McCormick concerns—Harvester and the *Tribune.* "I said that for his own benefit, and for the good of the company, he should seek employment elsewhere. It was a hard thing to say to the young man, but I haven't regretted it." (Mark, for his part, went to live in New York, and there he described himself as "self-employed, doing a lot of different things." He would not talk about the time his father refused to hire him.) Brooks knew full-well that his decision was likely to end his family's direct involvement in International Harvester. He says, "It looks like I'm the last of the Mohicans."

T HE DESCENDANTS OF William Sanderson McCormick might not have reaped the full benefits of the family company because of William's early death, but many of them managed to make up for that disadvantage by marrying well. After all, it was the marriage of William's grandson, Chauncey McCormick, to Marion Deering that propelled their son Brooks into International Harvester. William's son, Robert Sanderson McCormick, married Katherine Medill, whose father owned the *Chicago Tribune,* and their two sons, J. Medill and Robert R., eventually became publishers of that newspaper. Less well-known is the marriage of William's daughter, Ruby, to Edward Tyler Blair, whose father had accumulated his own fortune by peddling hardware. Edward's father, William Blair, started his hardware business in Chicago in 1842, five years before Cyrus McCormick brought his reaper to town. William Blair was in the right place at the right time, for the growing city needed his goods. His modest hardware store became a large wholesale business, and William built a big house on Michigan Avenue, on the site of what eventually became the Pick-Congress Hotel.

Edward and Ruby Blair settled in a red brick house on the northeast corner of Superior Street and Cass Street (since renamed Wabash Avenue) on Chicago's near North Side—an area that housed so many of their McCormick relatives that it was then dubbed "McCormickville." On May 2, 1884, just 11 days before Cyrus McCormick died, they had a son whom they named William McCormick Blair. William Blair isn't one of the most famous McCormicks, but he is one of the more remarkable members of the clan, partly because of his longevity and partly because in midlife he went through an experience that few McCormicks have ever remotely known—going broke. Later he recovered his financial health in grand style. At the time he celebrated his 95th birthday, in 1979, he was continuing to visit the LaSalle Street office of his Chicago-based investment firm once or twice a week. The oldest living McCormick—Brooks terms him the McCormicks' *pater-familias*—he was still maintaining the grand and gracious style of living that he had known in his Victorian-era boyhood.

"We were the poor McCormicks," Blair says of his early days, "because our company interest was sold when our parents were very young." But poor for a McCormick didn't exactly mean poverty. It simply meant that his branch of the family wasn't as extravagantly wealthy as the rich cousins descended from Uncle Cyrus. The Blairs had enough money that young William's father didn't have to work for a living. Edward Blair did work in the family hardware business for a few years, until he decided that he preferred the life of a gentleman writer. He didn't write much. His only bona fide book was *Henry of Navarre and the Religious Wars of France*—which didn't sell enough to support the Blairs for a week. But as a result of Edward's research in France, William lived much of his early life there. The Edward Blairs were among the first tenants of the Ritz Hotel in Paris; they also lived in the town of Pau and traveled extensively. One of William's clearest boyhood memories was setting himself ablaze while staying with a family in Versailles. (He accidentally stuck his elbow in a candle but wasn't badly burned.) Young William did spend time in the U.S., however. The family's summers often were spent in Bar Harbor, Maine, where the Blairs had their horses and bicycles shipped to enjoy on their vacation. "You might say we commuted between the United States and France," said William Blair of the family's life around the turn of the century.

His formal education was strictly American, and strictly McCormick. It included Groton School and Yale University. Groton and an Ivy League university, usually Princeton or Yale, have long been standard fare for members of the family. At Yale William played freshman football and rowed on the crew, but his sports

Cyrus McCormick, who patented the first mechanical reaper which allowed two men to harvest as much wheat in a day as it took five men by hand. Eleven years after its invention he sold seven reapers. The next year he sold 29, and then the new company was off and running. Photo was made around 1869 by Matthew Brady.

Some family members feel that Cyrus took claim for inventing the reaper when his father Robert, pictured right, had actually done most of the work.

FAMILY CREST

Nettie Fowler McCormick, wife of Cyrus.

Cyrus McCormick Jr., the inventor's son, who bought out Leander McCormick for $3.25 million. By 1885 he had the company firmly under the control of his father's family.

Harold F. McCormick, younger brother of Cyrus Jr., active in running International Harvester from 1918 until his death in 1941.

Fowler McCormick, who lead International Harvester for 10 years beginning in the year his father, Harold, died. He was a pioneer in giving equal employment opportunities to minorities.

William McCormick Blair shunned the idea of working in International Harvester. Instead he entered the securities business, went broke in 1932, then went on to found William Blair & Co. in 1935. Photo by Fabian Bachrach.

A model of the first reaper.

Cyrus McCormick's demonstration of the first reaper in 1831. Cyrus is walking behind the machine while Jo Anderson, a family slave, rakes the wheat off the platform. Painting is by N.C. Wyeth, who painted it for International Harvester's centennial celebration.

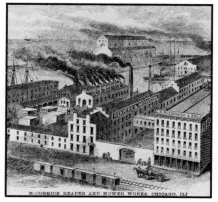

The McCormick reaper works near Chicago's lakefront, about 1861.

International Harvester's first tractor, built in 1906.

The "auto wagon", built in 1909. International Harvester regards this as one of its first trucks.

International Harvester's first cotton picker, photographed in 1942 with Fowler McCormick at the wheel.

career ended with a bout of pneumonia in his junior year. As a senior he coached the freshman football team, and one of his proudest college memories was watching his freshmen defeat Yale's varsity squad.

After college, William Blair was faced with a decision that has confronted McCormicks ever since the reaper revolutionized American agriculture: How does a young heir spend his life? "I did a lot of thinking about what I could do," he recalls, and he quickly ruled out his father's advice that work wasn't for gentlemen. He also rejected a career at International Harvester. "I just didn't want to get involved in business with the family," he says. "I guess I wanted to make my own way." He wanted to return to his home town of Chicago, and so it was that William started his working life as a messenger at the Northern Trust Co. there. Within a few years he worked his way up to the post of receiving teller, and "learned bookkeeping and the importance of accuracy and punctuality." (Being punctual, he later concluded, could be a waste of time, because "when you're prompt you spend a lot of time waiting for other people who aren't.") From the Northern Trust he went to work in the Chicago office of Lee, Higginson & Co., a respected Wall Street investment-banking concern.

In 1910 William Blair started making his solo auto trips, a practice that would develop into cross-country sojourns and continue for more than six decades, providing a rich source of family lore. Every year he would select a destination—perhaps Florida, Maine, California, or the Groton School in Connecticut—and plot a general course and timetable. On his day of departure he would rise at 2:30 a.m. and summon the servants. They would fill his lunch "bucket" with such fare as watercress sandwiches, fresh fruit, and chocolates, for he did not like to interrupt his driving by eating at restaurants. When all was ready—usually by about 3 a.m.—he would hop into his car and venture out onto America's roads and highways, alone and happy.

"It was my way of relaxing, and a great relief from the phone," Blair says of those journeys. "I was entirely detached from everything." Even in the days before interstate highways, he would travel 800 miles a day (his record was 1,200 miles), nearly always starting each day's driving before dawn. Early one morning, in fact, he was almost arrested for vagrancy in Phoenix, while he was hanging around a gas station waiting for it to open so he could fill his tank and start the day. The trips had only one rule: At the end of each day's driving, whether he was staying with friends or at a motel, Blair was to phone his wife.

The first of Blair's touring cars was a 1910 Marion. It met an untimely end, though, when Blair donated it to the government in 1917 "to help win the war." Just over a decade later, in 1928, he bought a new apple-green Rolls Royce Flying Cloud. "It was a great car to travel in because it was so well built," he said, and he eventually drove the car in all 48 states. The Flying Cloud was Blair's traveling companion until 1960, when he bought a new Rolls. He donated the old car to the Museum of Science and Industry in Chicago. Because he wouldn't allow anyone else to drive the car, he delivered it to the museum himself, and it is still on display.

Blair's annual solo trips continued until 1974, when he was 90 years old. And it wasn't his age that put a stop to the tours. Instead, it was the Arab oil embargo, which caused a shortage of fuel. "I didn't like waiting in line for gas," he says. So he printed a flyer, complete with pictures of the Marion, the Flying Cloud, and the new Rolls Royce, and sent it to the friends he had visited on his trips.

The flyer said, "I have motored throughout the United States, visiting friends and drawing inspiration from viewing our magnificent country. Now the Arabs have grounded me. But this card with pictures of the cars I have used in my travels is a warning that I'll be around again before too long, most anxious to see you." That wasn't to be, however, for age finally put a stop to the trips. Blair sold his car in 1977 for $25,000 and distributed $5,000 apiece to his grandchildren, so each of them could buy a car.

In the earlier years of those annual tours, Blair was still on the job at the investment firm of Lee, Higginson & Co., eventually becoming a partner. Both Blair and the firm were riding high until a chain of events in 1932 profoundly affected both.

On March 12 of that year, Ivar Kreuger, a Swede who had built his family's match factory into a multibillion-dollar financial empire, committed suicide in his Paris apartment. Within a few days of his suicide, "the Match King," as he was known, was exposed as a cheat and a fraud—and Lee Higginson was carried down along with his reputation. A decade earlier, the firm's Eastern partners had been duped by Kreuger. The firm acted as investment banker to the Kreuger operations, offering their securities to the American public and buying a considerable amount of them for Lee Higginson's own holdings. So the firm's reputation and financial position were shattered by the disclosures. Although Blair wasn't directly involved with the Match King, his money went down the drain along with Lee Higginson.

Blair wasn't left penniless. His wife, the former Helen Bowen, had inherited wealth of her own. But Blair had lost all his invested capital. He stayed with Lee Higginson for a short time, while the firm was being reorganized into a much smaller concern. And then on Jan. 8, 1935, he started William Blair & Co., a regional investment-banking concern with the same name that his grandfather's hardware company had had before the family sold it.

The birth of William Blair & Co. wasn't without considerable pain. First, Blair had to borrow $50,000 from his friends to get started—no easy thing for a man who had been used to having lots of money. The new firm promptly backed two unsuccessful securities offerings, and within two months Mr. Blair's borrowed $50,000 was gone. He then went back to his friends for another $50,000. Blair wanted his company to become "the most important Chicago investment banker," and if it wasn't that it certainly became one of the most important. At age 95 Blair saw one of his grandsons become a partner, the third generation of Blairs in the firm, and the founder himself still paid close attention to business affairs. "I hope to be a partner until the day I kick the bucket," he said at the time.

Indeed, William Blair prided himself on being the businessman of his family. In his adult years he handled the financial affairs of his father, his two sisters, and his younger brother, Seymour. Seymour Blair "was an eccentric, and never had a business thought in his life," William Blair recalled. In 1976, at age 87, Seymour was killed when he lost control of his motorcycle on a street in Acapulco, Mexico. He was wearing only his bathing suit at the time, and his body remained in the local morgue for several days before he was finally identified.

With the Great Depression and the collapse of Lee Higginson, the William Blairs rented out their city house on posh Astor Street on Chicago's North Side, generating extra income at a time when they needed it. But through thick and thin, the family has held onto its 200-acre Crab Tree Farm estate in Lake Bluff, Ill., 35 miles north of Chicago. There, in his 90s, William Blair would ride a three-wheeled Schwinn bicycle on summer mornings for his daily exercise, and would show the estate to visitors by piloting an electric golf cart through the tall oaks and maples, and through the meadows, pastures, and plowed fields. Sitting on a high cliff over-looking Lake Michigan, Crab Tree Farm bespeaks old money. The estate contains a lakefront house for William Blair and one for his son Edward, in addition to a number of farm buildings and servants' quarters. A huge indoor tennis court was built in 1928 and dedicated with a circus-theme party to which the guests came dressed as clowns, lion-tamers, and trapeze artists. The actual tennis court, with its huge skylight roof, was attached to what amounted to a small house, with a sitting room, two bedrooms with bathrooms (one for the men to dress in and another for the women), and a kitchenette. The walls of the rooms were decorated with Currier and Ives prints, all favorites of Blair's. The walls of the tennis court itself were covered with ivy. On one side stood the high judge's chair and on the other was a life-sized cigar-store Indian who watched over the proceedings.

At Crab Tree Farm the Blairs had the attention of butlers, cooks, gardeners, chauffeurs—and, of course, the farm manager and his assistants. The farm had a small herd of Hereford cattle and some land set aside for field crops, so even though it was a country

retreat, the name "farm" wasn't entirely misleading. In recent
years, the Blairs haven't used International Harvester equipment
on the farm, choosing Massey-Ferguson tractors instead. Blair
found that his farm hands were simply having too much trouble
getting Harvester equipment serviced and repaired, so he
switched.

William McCormick Blair enjoyed life. "Not every minute of it,"
he said, "but overall." Among his friends and acquaintances were
the great names of Chicago society and business, including the
Potter Palmers of the Palmer House hotel, the Swifts and Armours
of the meat-packing business, and the Marshall Fields of retailing
and publishing. History had unfolded in his Chicago home on
Astor Street. Illinois Gov. Adlai Stevenson was staying there on
the night that the Democratic convention, meeting in Chicago,
nominated him for President in 1952. (Blair was a staunch Republican, but his son, William Jr., was an aide to Gov. Stevenson.
Later, President Kennedy named William Jr., an attorney, ambassador to Denmark, and President Johnson later named him ambassador to the Philippines.) The William Blairs' marriage lasted
62 years, until Helen Bowen Blair died in 1972. At age 95, there was
one thing he was sure of: "Cyrus invented it," he said. "The family
fought over that for years, but I never entered into it."

T HE M C C O R M I C K N A M E has pretty much passed from its
former prominent and frequent public display in Chicago. But the
McCormick Building still stands at 332 South Michigan Avenue,
just a few blocks south of Tribune Tower and International Harvester headquarters. The McCormick Building was built by the
descendants of Leander J. McCormick in 1912, at a time when their
branch of the family couldn't talk to the other McCormicks without starting a shouting match over who really invented the reaper.
But it is one of those odd twists of McCormick history that Leander's unhappy ouster from the family company—an event that
spawned the family feud over the reaper's true origin—was the
very thing that would make his descendants the closest knit of the
McCormick branches. Not only did the turn of events provide his

family with a cause that its members have continued to defend, but it also helped to give them a business of their own. Room 1950 of the McCormick Building still houses the offices of the Leander J. McCormick estate, which consists of family real-estate holdings whose proceeds are regularly dispensed to several dozen McCormicks.

Leander, the youngest son of Robert McCormick, was born in 1819, 10 years after Cyrus, in whose shadow he lived most of his life. He followed Cyrus from Virginia to Chicago when Cyrus moved his reaper business there, and, along with brother William, Leander oversaw the company's manufacturing operations while Cyrus took to the road. When William was dying in 1865, he is reported to have urged his brothers "to forbear one another in love" and not to quarrel over money. The two men did manage to put up with each other, although just barely, until Cyrus died.

Leander couldn't, however, forbear being a junior partner to his nephew, Cyrus Jr. Tension between the two men mounted sharply after old Cyrus's death, and Cyrus Jr. offered to buy his uncle out. After painstaking negotiations, they agreed on the $3.25 million selling price, $600,000 to be paid in cash and the rest in five yearly installments. Leander didn't let the money sit idle. He lived 16 years after Cyrus's death, and before he died in 1900 he had amassed considerable real-estate holdings in Chicago's rapidly growing downtown. One of the properties Leander bought, in fact, was the land where the McCormick Building still stands.

The children and grandchildren of Leander found themselves at odds with their other McCormick cousins, so it was perhaps to compensate for that and to prove their true family colors that they clung rigidly to their McCormick heritage. Leander's daughter, Henrietta, married an Englishman named Frederick Goodhart, and the couple named their first son Leander McCormick Goodhart. But Henrietta convinced her husband that they should hyphenate their last names, and that made their son's full name Leander McCormick McCormick-Goodhart. (He eventually had a career in the British Foreign Office, including a stint at the British embassy in Washington.) Various males in the line have borne the name Leander, and some females the name Leandra. The most prevalent of the family's names, however, has been Robert. Leander McCormick named his eldest son Robert Hall McCormick II, after a brother who had died in childhood, and the name was passed down for three more generations. Within the family, Robert Hall McCormick II was known as "R. Hall," and his son was called Bob. The fourth in the line was also called Bob, and his son, in turn, is known as Rob. Perhaps because the family was running out of nicknames, young Rob McCormick broke the string in 1972 when he named his son Jeffrey. But Rob later had second thoughts. "Maybe now I wish I had named him Roberts," Rob said when Jeff was seven years old. "But you go through changes in how you feel about that. At the time I just felt it wasn't important. And besides, I didn't like the times when people had called me 'Junior.' "

A family's owning of a business doesn't always help assure that its members will stick together. The descendants of Cyrus Hall McCormick have drifted farther and farther apart over the years, even as their numbers have dwindled. Sometimes a family business aggravates fraternal strife, as was the case with Leander's disputes with Cyrus and his sons. The real-estate business founded by Leander, however, has been a glue that has helped hold his descendants together, mainly because of the way the business is set up. There aren't any shares of stock that can be publicly traded. Instead, the business is a joint ownership among all of Leander's heirs, each heir owning an allotted portion of each piece of property. So if Leander's trust wanted to sell a building, for example, all the beneficiaries of the trust would have to agree to the transaction. The arrangement has been unwieldy at times, and eventually a new setup no doubt will replace it, but "it has forced us to get along with each other," one member of the family says.

Of course, Leander's heirs could have placed their holdings under the management of professional outsiders and simply sat back to collect their money, having little to do with one another. But the heirs were determined not to let that happen, and they got help from Ross J. Beatty, the husband of one of Leander McCormick's great-granddaughters. When he took over as manager of the family real-estate business in 1945, he insisted on certain conditions. One of them was that the family members were to pay attention to their business and meet every year to review its status and make major decisions. The heirs of Leander do just that every April. This annual meeting doubles as a family reunion, at which cousins from the United States, England, and France gather for both business and pleasure. Beatty retired from his management post in 1978, but by that time the tradition of family cooperation on business matters was well-established. The business was turned over to a management committee of nine family members. Day-to-day affairs were put in the hands of Draper & Kramer Inc., the Chicago real-estate concern where, conveniently enough, young Rob McCormick was employed as a broker.

The outer portion of the office of Leander J. McCormick's estate is a typical business office with its collection of desks, tables, chairs, and couches. But the back rooms are what amounts to a family museum. There, the McCormicks keep artifacts covering more than a century of family history. Among the prized possessions is a bronze casting of the hand and forearm of Leander, made in 1899, the year before he died. Leander's own desk sits there too, and there is a bust of his son, R. Hall. The rooms also contain a picture of R. Hall's house on the corner of Rush and Erie Streets in Chicago, since supplanted by a restaurant, and an enormous painting of his yacht sailing off the coast of Maine. Amid a few old pieces of furniture with the stuffing sticking out, there are dozens of other pictures of the succeeding generations of McCormicks. Prospective tenants for the McCormick Building are sometimes shown the estate's artifacts to indicate that when they rent rooms in the building they aren't just renting office space, they are renting a bit of history.

The offices hold only two pictures of members of other branches of the McCormick clan. One is a picture of the late Robert R. McCormick of the *Chicago Tribune.* The other, oddly enough, is a portrait of Cyrus Hall McCormick. Leander's estate came across the portrait of Cyrus when it was offered to Ross Beatty, who felt he was hardly in a position to refuse it. Whoever offered it to Beatty doubtless didn't know that Cyrus was relatively without honor among the family of his brother Leander.

Actually, Leander's heirs do pay Cyrus some grudging homage. "Cyrus was a developer, a business genius, a promoter, and a hell of a bright guy," says Robert Hall McCormick IV. "If it wasn't for Cyrus, the machine might have just stayed on the farm in Virginia. But Cyrus was simply not a mechanic, and he was not the inventor of the reaper."

It is not hard to envision how the McCormick family feud over who invented the reaper got started. Robert McCormick, the father of Cyrus, William, and Leander, did a lot of work on developing a machine, and even Cyrus's heirs always admitted that Robert was partly responsible for Cyrus's success. But it was Cyrus who patented the reaper. He kept both his brothers in the role of junior partners, and retained the bulk of the reaper's profits for himself and his family. This angered Leander, and the easiest way for him to press his claim to more responsibility and more money was to maintain that, after all, his own father had invented the machine that his brother was cashing in on. Even before Cyrus died, Leander started collecting "eyewitness proof" that his father, Robert, really invented the reaper, and he continued collecting documents for years. The originals are still stored in the office of Leander's estate, in an old metal filing cabinet standing in the corner of a small bedroom for out-of-town McCormicks visiting Chicago. A typical piece of "proof" is a letter to Leander from Henry Schultz of Greenville, Va., dated Sept. 27, 1894. The letter reads:

> Dear Sir,
>
> I am nearly 72 years old, remember your father well, and always heard it said that he invented the Reaper, and was frequently in his shop and saw him and yourself at work. I never recollect of seeing C. H. McCormick in the shop or any where else. I understand that he, C. H. McCormick, helped to make some improvements on it just before he went to Chicago. I also remember having heard my father say that he, Robert McCormick, worked on it in his father's lifetime, and your grandfather

would tell him, Ah, Robert, it is no use to try to make a machine
to cut wheat, that would be the Devil's work.

Respectively yours,
(signed) Henry Schultz

Some of the documents are letters from McCormicks who, like
Leander, felt that Cyrus had shortchanged them. Mary Caroline
McCormick Shields, sister of Cyrus and Leander, wrote, "Ma
persuaded father to give the invention of the reaper to Brother
Cyrus, and it took a good deal of persuasion, too. Ma said, 'Cyrus
has promised me that if the reaper is made a success all the children
shall be interested in it, and I know he will do it.'. . . As long as Ma
lived she repeated to me when she had the opportunity, and to
sister Amanda, the promise Cyrus had made her. . . ."

In 1910, a decade after Leander's death, Leander's son R. Hall
and nephew James Hall Shields collected all the "evidence" and
published it in booklet form. The title: *Robert McCormick: Inventor.* Years later, in 1955, Robert Hall McCormick III would follow
in his father's footsteps by commissioning a book to prove his
family's case. It was entitled *The McCormick Reaper Legend.*

Leander himself did more than just collect documents. Before
he died, he commissioned small-scale models of the various inventions that he attributed to his father. Replicas of those original
models still hold an honored place in the boardroom of the Leander
J. McCormick estate. The inscription on one reads: "Original
reaper invented and constructed in 1831 by Robert McCormick of
Rockbridge County, Virginia. This machine embodied the essential features of all future machines." Another model is of a later
version of the reaper, and its inscription says, "The Old Reliable.
This was the original reaper of Robert McCormick improved and
perfected. It shows the raker's stand added by Leander J. McCormick."

It has mattered not a bit to Leander's heirs that the 1834 reaper
patent on file at the U.S. Patent Office is in the name of Cyrus Hall
McCormick. They have steadfastly maintained that only the tradition of the times and family expediency caused Cyrus to take out
the patent on the machine that his father developed. And they

have homed in on what they have seen as *prima facie* evidence that Cyrus *couldn't* have invented the reaper. "Cyrus was only 22 years old in 1831, and he couldn't have invented the reaper at that early age," Ross Beatty says.

International Harvester, naturally, has expressed a different view over the years, and the company has often resorted to just as much overkill as the descendants of Leander and other disgruntled McCormicks. In 1931, the 100th anniversary of the reaper's invention, Harvester published a 68-page booklet on the machine. The booklet stated, "Cyrus must have started on his own machines as soon as he saw the admitted evidence of his father's failure. Between May and July (of 1831) he conceived of his own new principles, built one or more models, and developed a machine which cut grain successfully.. . . Tall, square-shouldered, high of brow, purposeful, wise before his time, determined, feeling the power of destiny within him, he strode behind the machine which was laying the foundation for all mechanized agriculture." Twenty-six years later, in 1957, Fowler McCormick, by then deposed as Harvester's chairman but still on its board, made the same case somewhat more modestly. He said, "Although full value must be given to Robert McCormick's contribution to the final result, and although it must be recognized that Cyrus was continuing the work of his father and that he built upon it, it would not seem possible to say that Robert McCormick invented the reaper, for the reason that his machine never passed the test of cutting grain satisfactorily in the field."

Generations of Leander's descendants can remember standing up in their fifth-grade classrooms to dispute the history-book version of who invented the reaper. But the bitterness has largely dissipated over time. Still, Leander's heirs remain serious about their contention. It's not that they have anything to gain financially; any hope of that is long gone. Besides, Leander invested his money from the reaper company wisely, and generations of his heirs have "lived very, very well" because of it, as one of them puts it. Still, Leander's descendants kept sticking to their story "because of some sort of pride, I suppose," says Robert Hall McCormick IV, Leander's great-grandson. There is also tradition, for the story of how Robert McCormick invented the reaper is handed down from generation to generation. "I remember when I was a kid my grandfather telling me that Cyrus didn't do it," Rob McCormick says. "And when I bring my son (Jeff) up to our office, I show him his last name on the wall, and then I tell him that his great-great-great-great-grandfather, Robert McCormick, invented the reaper."

O N F E B. 4, 1 9 7 7, Mark McCormick Miller quit his reporter's job on the *Chicago Tribune* just a few months shy of his 30th birthday. His relatives still owned the Tribune Co., but young Miller's departure left the paper's news staff without a McCormick. That circumstance might change in the future, of course, if other family members develop an inclination to journalism. Still, the event at least temporarily ended an era. Mark Miller's grandfather, J. Medill McCormick, had joined the paper as a reporter in 1900. Later, after Medill McCormick left for a career in politics, his younger brother, Robert Rutherford McCormick, brought the *Tribune* to national prominence as the most strident voice of Midwestern conservatism.

Robert R. McCormick became one of the clan's most famous members, but he owed his position to the fact that his mother was a Medill. The "poor" branch of the McCormick family married into the *Chicago Tribune*. William Sanderson McCormick's eldest son, Robert Sanderson, was married to Katherine Medill in 1876. She was a daughter of Joseph Medill, who had bought into the *Tribune* in 1855. Robert S. McCormick became the U.S. ambassador to Austria, Russia, and France, and as a result of those assignments his sons did much of their growing up in Europe. The experience was said to have left young Robert with his profound distaste for anything European—an attitude that he would later trumpet from the pages of the *Tribune*.

Much has been written about Robert R. McCormick because so much about the man was controversial—even his military title. To the world and to his newspaper staff he was "Col. McCormick," or simply "the Colonel." He had attained the rank in World War I (having started out as a major in the Illinois National Guard). After the war he changed the name of the Wheaton, Ill., estate, some 25 miles west of Chicago, from Red Oak Farm to Cantigny, to recall his participation in that famous Allied victory. Later, however, Col. McCormick's political enemies scornfully charged that he hadn't ventured very close to much actual shooting, and even friendly observers conceded there was considerable doubt about whether he had really fought at Cantigny.

As the *Tribune's* publisher, however, Col. McCormick rarely shied away from a fight. One of his most famous publishing battles started in 1916, when the *Tribune* began an attack on Henry Ford with a story headlined "Flivver Patriotism," which told of the pacifist Ford's plans not to rehire Ford workers who enlisted in the armed forces. The *Tribune* followed the story with an editorial calling Ford an "anarchist," and saying that the "deluded human being" didn't deserve the benefits of government. Ford sued for libel. When the trial began three years later, he made something of a fool of himself on the witness stand by declaring that "history is bunk" and by guessing, under questioning from the *Tribune's* lawyers, that Benedict Arnold was a writer of some sort. Still, Ford won the decision, getting an award of six cents.

Later, Col. McCormick's *Tribune* expressed horror at the New Deal. It also took a stridently isolationist stand on the eve of World War II, calling for the United States to steer clear of "the problems of Europe." In 1942, shortly after Marshall Field III had started the *Chicago Sun* as an alternative to the McCormick view in Chicago, the Colonel unleashed his full fury against his new rival. The *Tribune* editorialized, "Field is of age to volunteer. He cried for war before it came. . . . The term to fit him and all the herd of hysterical effeminates is coward."

Within the family Robert McCormick was known as "Bertie." "All the McCormicks are crazy except me," he once said, although some of his relatives maintained just the opposite. His major family opponent was Anita McCormick Blaine, the liberal daughter of Cyrus, who spoke out publicly against her cousin when she saw fit. (The Colonel, however, attended Anita's 80th birthday party at her Chicago home in 1946.) Of course, Col. McCormick had his staunch admirers within the family, and still other family members simply reacted to him with amusement. McCormicks have continued to relish telling stories about him. Robert Hall McCormick IV, for example, recalled being invited to Col. McCormick's office on the night of the Roosevelt-Landon election in 1936. The Colonel, of course, had loudly supported Landon, and when the will of the electorate was becoming obvious, he received an anonymous telegram saying, "Now you know what you can do with the Tribune Tower." The Colonel handed the message to Cousin Bob, who was standing nearby, and stomped away.

Col. McCormick died childless in 1955, and his brand of personal journalism has since faded from the newspaper. In 1977 the paper went so far as to drop the slogan "World's Greatest Newspaper" from its page-one nameplate. The action was fine with some McCormicks, who maintained that the paper's greatness had ended when Bertie died. The Colonel's Cantigny estate now is a public museum, as he wished. There, children can still cavort on the World War I tanks that dot the huge lawn.

B Y 1 9 7 9, 1 4 8 years after Cyrus McCormick invented the reaper, the McCormick clan had grown so large that members of the younger generations had never met or even heard of some of their cousins. That isn't unusual, of course. Families tend to drift apart as the years pass and the members of succeeding generations have thinner and thinner blood ties to one another. Most Americans don't know about their ancestors beyond their great-grandparents, and sometimes not even beyond their grandparents. The members of the fourth and fifth generations after Cyrus and his brothers probably wouldn't otherwise be aware of their distant relatives, but when a family gets rich and famous, and goes down in the history books, genealogy gets to be a more serious business. Even that interest, though, fades with time. International Harvester compiled a huge, table-sized McCormick family tree in 1932, but the company hasn't updated it since, so most of the young McCormicks aren't on it.

Joan Claybrook, a great-great-granddaughter of Leander Mc-Cormick, doesn't appear on that chart. She became one of the more famous of her generation of McCormicks, although few people realized she was a member of the family. She worked for consumer advocate Ralph Nader, until President Jimmy Carter named her as head of the National Highway Traffic Safety Administration. From that regulatory post she waged a continual war with makers of cars and other motor vehicles—including International Harvester Co., which makes trucks. After she took her government post, she helped young Matthew McCormick, her first cousin, get a job on the Nader staff.

Meanwhile, her brother, Warren Buckler III, was an editorial writer for the respected *Louisville Times.* Another cousin, Anne Austin, lived in Chicago and worked as an artist for a local television station, producing drawings of courtroom scenes and other news events. Other Leander-branch cousins were accountants, stockbrokers, farmers, and art collectors, both in the U.S. and abroad.

The four children of Gilbert and Nancy Blaine Harrison are the only descendants of Cyrus McCormick living in the U.S. They had never met the Osers, Cyrus's descendants in Europe. David Blaine Harrison, the eldest child, is an attorney. One of his brothers is Joel McCormick Harrison, the only one of the four children with Mc-Cormick in his name.

Edward Blair, grandson of William McCormick Blair, was made a partner in William Blair & Co. in 1978. He became the third generation of Blairs to be a partner in the firm.

As the reaper's 150th anniversary approached, there was no longer a single center of McCormick wealth, the way McCormick Harvesting Machine Co. used to be. Nobody can tabulate the extent of the holdings of the many McCormicks. International Harvester's 30 million common shares are widely held among the public; as a percentage of the total, McCormick holdings are min-uscule. Different branches of the family, of course, had considerable stakes in Tribune Co. and William Blair & Co. Leander's descendants were the sole beneficiaries of his estate, with its real-estate holdings. The heirs of Leander aren't saying how large those holdings are, but with office buildings in Chicago's Loop, a shopping center in New Orleans, and a ski resort in Colorado, the estate of Leander J. McCormick certainly has a value in the tens of millions of dollars.

While Leander's estate has held his descendants together over the years, the older generation wonders how long that will last. "We intend to try to keep this a family business," says Robert H. McCormick IV, "but it will be difficult. All the cousins of my generation knew each other well because of the business. But now there is a tendency of the younger people to say, 'Give me my marbles, I want to play somewhere else.' I'm trying very hard to keep them interested and involved. Keeping the business together means keeping the family together."

Even within the closest of the family's clans, then, there is concern about the McCormicks' future as a family. One of them says, "It's remarkable that we've stayed together this long."

VI

The du Ponts

P IERRE SAMUEL DU PONT didn't always dream of leaving France for America. He had, after all, risen to some prominence in his homeland. The son of a struggling watchmaker, Pierre gained attention in the court of Louis XVI by developing a series of economic treatises, and he became an influential member of the National Assembly.

Unfortunately for him, however, his firm belief in the merits of a constitutional monarchy wasn't especially popular with either the monarchy or the anarchists at the time of the French Revolution. He was imprisoned several times, and only twists of fate enabled him to escape the guillotine.

Those experiences undoubtedly led to his decision in 1799 to seek a new life in the New World. So at age 60 he cleaned up his affairs, raised a few hundred thousand francs, and prepared to form a company—Du Pont de Nemours Pere, Fils et Cie.

Before leaving France, Pierre made his two sons, Eleuthere Irenee, 28, and Victor, 32, stand by their mother's grave and swear to remain united forever. Legend has it that he blessed them with the words, "May each generation of your descendants strive unceasingly to make the next generation better than its own."

The voyage, on a decrepit ship called the *American Eagle,* took three months, and when land was finally sighted, it was far north of their New York destination—at Newport, R.I. The time: Jan. 1, 1800. The rest is history.

Sailing in the New World at first wasn't any smoother than sailing to it. Most of their early ventures failed, Victor went bankrupt in New York, and all three du Ponts had to return to France at times to seek more capital. Indeed, it was by chance that Irenee, as he was called, ultimately got into the gunpowder business that became the basis for the family's fortune.

Yet the handsome, debonair Victor and the birthmarked, conscientious Irenee did their utmost from the start to satisfy their father's wish for family unity and improvement. And so did their sons and their sons' sons. The family built Du Pont Co. of Wilmington, Del., into one of the largest industrial corporations in the U.S. Du Ponts also had a hand in making General Motors Corp. the colossus that it became.

Today, however, the descendants of Pierre Samuel du Pont have become too numerous to tally precisely. The best guess is that there are about 1,700 of them. They have become scattered through most of the states of the U.S. and at least 10 foreign countries, including, of course, France.

While family members still own about 35 percent of the stock of the company their ancestors created, they no longer have a hand in top management. The last du Pont stepped out as chairman in 1971, and only three family members now work at the chemical company full time—none above the middle-management level.

Having lost that common tie at the company, the du Ponts also have just about ceased to be a family with common interests and concerns. Even in the rolling countryside north of Wilmington, where some 120 members of the clan still own estates or homes, the du Ponts have gone their separate ways. Pierre S. du Pont IV is governor of Delaware, John E. du Pont collects seashells and runs his own natural-history museum, Robert Brett Lunger races cars, and Robert R. M. Carpenter Jr. owns the Philadelphia Phillies baseball team.

Family members around Wilmington periodically update a genealogy volume that traces their six main branches, and they have managed to keep alive their tradition of New Year's Day "calling," in which du Pont males shower candy, flowers, and other gifts upon their assembled female kin. But the annual event also serves to point out how weak their links have become: The du Ponts who attend have resorted to wearing name tags to identify themselves.

"There's still a bond of heritage holding us together," says Gov. du Pont, who religiously attends the New Year's gatherings, "but I don't feel it as strongly as my father did, and my children don't feel it as strongly as I do. I think that's too bad, although I suppose it's inevitable."

Historians agree. They note that what is happening to the du Ponts has already happened to such other "founding families" of American industry and finance as the Vanderbilts, Armours, and Morgans, and they say it is what happens eventually to all of them.

One reason is the sheer weight of natural increase, which spreads the families geographically and financially. Another reason is that wealth provides its holders with the freedom to pursue many career or leisure options. Still another is that public ownership, an ultimate step for almost all American companies that grow large, creates impersonal competitive pressures that descendants of their founders either can't or won't satisfy.

Scions of the men who formed important American corporations "often face a no-win situation," says John Gates, author of *The du Pont Family,* published in 1979. "If they don't make it, they're considered hopeless. If they do, their co-workers say it's because of their name."

That notion, familiar to some present-day du Ponts, has led several to quit the company in recent years. Henry E. I. du Pont, who worked in the company's mechanical-testing laboratory, believes his name was a hindrance to him there. "When I started training young kids and they wound up being my boss, I said bye, bye to that," he says.

Other du Ponts have been daunted by the size of the family concern, which employs about 132,000 persons in more than 30 countries and has annual revenues of more than $12.5 billion. "It has become so vast that you might as well be working for IBM," says Alfred du Pont Dent, a stockbroker near Wilmington. He says that his brother and several cousins resigned from the company when they realized "they were just knocking their heads against a wall."

The disinclination of most du Ponts to involve themselves in the company has broader corporate consequences. In 1977 Christiana Securities, the family holding company that owned 28 percent of Du Pont Co.'s common stock, was merged into the chemical company, and Christiana's Du Pont Co. shares were distributed among family members. The step was taken partly because of a lack of du Ponts willing and able to run Christiana. "There was worry about what could happen when people who don't know the business have that kind of power over a block of stock," says Irving S. Shapiro, Du Pont Co.'s chairman.

Similarly, a three-for-one split of the corporation's common shares in 1979 was widely viewed as a prelude to decreased family ownership—the reasoning being that more shares outstanding will lower the stock's price and make it easier for family members to sell their shares.

The remarkable thing about the du Ponts, however, isn't that they finally seem to have bowed out of their company, but that they stayed in it for so long. Family management of the concern stretched over almost 170 years, or seven generations. "I can't think of any other family in which so many collateral branches were involved in the family business," says Joseph Wall, professor of history at the State University of New York.

In the beginning, of course, the du Ponts had little choice but to stick together. French-speaking immigrants in an English-speaking land, they clung to one another in their community in the narrow valley of Delaware's Brandywine Creek. "I like to tell people my family lived almost like Communists during their first hundred years here," says Anthony du Pont, of Verdes, California.

Actually, Pierre du Pont and his sons had hoped to set up a colony for French expatriates in Virginia, with farms, sawmills, stores, schools, and churches. Among the business enterprises envisioned by the elder du Pont were glassware and pottery making, a fast mail and passenger service to Europe (not, presumably, on the *American Eagle),* and a Far East trading company. Headquarters of Du Pont de Nemours Pere, Fils et Cie. were to be nearby in the nation's capital, which was then being constructed to the specifications of Frenchman Pierre l'Enfant.

But those plans, and many other ventures that Pierre had planned, went awry. For one thing, many of the nation's five million inhabitants were clustered in Virginia, and land prices had therefore soared.

It was Irenee rather than his father who eventually stumbled on the business that led to the family's wealth—although the family had to struggle through a century of indebtedness before reaping the real riches. Irenee, on a hunting trip with a French army officer who had served under Lafayette in the American Revolution, wondered why his gun misfired so often. He investigated and found that gunpowder production in America was far behind the techniques he had learned more than a decade earlier in France. He had apprenticed under French chemist Antoine Lavoisier, who supervised the gunpowder plant at Essonne.

After discussing the idea of a gunpowder mill with his father, Irenee went to France to raise some of the $36,000 of capital needed. The rest came from the family company and from two other American investors. Irenee would receive $1,800 a year salary for running the mill, plus one-third of any profits.

Thomas Jefferson, a friend of Pierre du Pont, suggested that the gunpowder mill be set up near Washington, and Irenee explored sites there, as well as near Philadelphia and along the Hudson near New York. But he settled on the Brandywine Creek area, where there was already an established community of French immigrants. The first cotton mill in America had been established there, and although it had burned down, some buildings, roads and a dam remained.

Construction of the gunpowder mill was begun in mid-1802, and not long afterwards Irenee wrote to his father, "We have accomplished an astonishing amount of work since August. In three months we have built a large house and barn of stone and the greater part of the refinery; we have repaired the water-course and the sawmill in which we prepare the wood for our framework. This month we have still to build three mills and one or two other buildings; to dig a new race for one of the mills; to make the drying place, the magazine, the workmen's quarters."

Soon thereafter, the mill was in operation, and the first Du Pont gunpowder was being marketed. But business didn't exactly boom. Irenee found himself a prisoner to his creditors and to the stockholders who insisted on receiving dividends rather than using any profits for capital improvements.

In a letter to a friend, he wrote, "It is cruel to ride 60 miles every five or six days to meet one's notes, and so to waste one's time and one's life. God grant that some day I may get to the end of it." He got to the end of the dividend payments by going further into debt to buy out the investors' shares, but he never got out of debt.

Business picked up nicely with the War of 1812, however, and by 1815 the company had fixed assets of over $106,000. But tragic explosions at the mill wiped out most of the gains. In 1815 nine workers lost their lives in a blast, and in 1818, 40 men died and damage exceeded $120,000. Irenee went further into debt to provide pensions and homes for the workers' widows and orphans.

By the time Irenee died in 1834, the company was about $125,000 in debt, although business was brisk. His eldest son, Alfred Victor du Pont, took over soon after that and ran the company for 16 years. An inventor by nature and training, he was happier designing machinery or experimenting with chemicals than he was running the company. When he retired in 1850, the company's debt had risen to $500,000.

Alfred's brother, Henry, succeeded him as senior partner, and the company's fortunes began to change. Unlike Alfred, Henry relished the day-to-day job of running the company. Boss Henry, as he was called, ran a tight ship, with a weather eye for ways to increase profits. A stern figure, with a bright red beard and a high hat that he wore on most occasions, he nevertheless gained a reputation as a benevolent taskmaster who knew all his employees by name.

Providing no little help for the struggling company about this time were the Mexican War, the westward expansion and, finally, the Civil War. The gold rush of 1849 also led to heavy demand for blasting powder for gold and silver mining. Blasting powder also was needed for building roads and railroads. But the competition became fierce, with more than 200 mills vying for the market.

Since the earliest days of powder making, the system had been basically the one Irenee du Pont had learned in France. Saltpeter, sulphur and charcoal were crushed and then mixed together, employing 75 parts of saltpeter, 15 parts of sulphur, and 10 parts of charcoal. The mixture was sifted, dried, tumbled, and finally sifted again.

The most costly ingredient, of course, was the saltpeter—potassium nitrate. The charcoal was made from willow wood, abundant in the Brandywine Valley. Sulphur, or brimstone, was generally imported, but it was plentiful and cheap. Saltpeter, however, the product of certain organic decay, was found in few parts of the world besides India, so prices were high and supplies undependable.

Thus, it was a considerable breakthrough for the Du Pont mill when Lammot du Pont, Alfred's son and a recent chemistry graduate of the University of Pennsylvania, patented a new formula for making blasting powder. Potassium nitrate would still be needed for gunpowder, but cheaper and more-accessible sodium nitrate (which came largely from Peru and Chile) now could be used for blasting powder, using his formula. The new product, called "soda powder," which was developed in a crude laboratory he had set up, was soon being produced in a new Du Pont mill near Wilkes-Barre, Pa., close to the coal fields that used much of its production for blasting in the mines.

The Civil War wasn't entirely providential for the company, or for the du Ponts, for its strategic position between North and South caused the Brandywine mill to be turned into an armed camp. Moreover, the company had to write off considerable unpaid deliveries made earlier to southern purchasers.

Samuel Francis du Pont, a son of Victor, gained some notoriety during the war as the Navy officer whose charges captured the forts at Port Royal, S.C., but his failure to capture Charleston led to his being relieved of his command. Boss Henry himself was made a general in the state militia, and his son, Henry A., a West Point graduate who later was to be elected a U.S. Senator, became a lieutenant colonel and served in a number of battles in Virginia. Still another du Pont, Victor, a grandson of the original Victor, paid $750 to have a surrogate serve for him in the war.

But it was the chemist, Lammot, whose wartime exploits are best remembered in family history. Large shipments of saltpeter, vital to the Union's war effort, were tied up in Britain, which hadn't committed itself to either side in the Civil War. Lammot, only 30 at the time, was dispatched to London—and ultimately returned with the crucial shipment.

Although Boss Henry ruled Du Pont Co. with an iron hand, holding 20 of the 26 partnership shares, his nephew Lammot continued to make his presence felt after the war as well. In the early 1870s, Du Pont Co. and its chief rival, Laflin & Rand, were heading toward an all-out price war until Lammot helped form the Gunpowder Trade Association, consisting of the two giants plus the Hazard Powder Co. and a number of smaller firms. The association, of which Lammot was the first president, set prices and allocated sales territories.

Not long after the economic downturn of 1873, Du Pont and Laflin & Rand were the only major survivors in the business. Du Pont bought Hazard Powder Co. for $800,000 in cash and notes in 1876.

Around this time, some advances by European chemists were about to shape the future of mankind—and the fate of Lammot du Pont. An Italian named Ascanio Sobrero came upon a liquid explosive of unprecedented power called nitroglycerin—and dynamite came into being.

Far more effective and powerful than blasting powder, dynamite nevertheless was disdained as too dangerous by Boss Henry. It was Lammot who saw the future of dynamite, and he struck a deal with his uncle: Du Pont Co. would provide some of the backing for a new company headed by Lammot to produce the promising new explosive.

Lammot opened the new plant in 1880 on the banks of the Delaware River and named it Repauno Chemical Co., after the Indian name of a creek nearby. The plant, and its dynamite, were instantly successful. But it was here at Repauno, four years later, that Lammot lost his life to the dangerous new product. After being told by a workman about an unusual bubbling in a nitroglycerin vat, Lammot ordered everyone out of the building, and he rushed in to investigate—just before an explosion demolished the plant. It was similar to an incident 23 years earlier, in which Alexis I. du Pont, a son of Irenee, was killed trying to put out a spark in the Brandywine powder mill. Nor would Lammot be the last of the du Ponts to die in the dangerous plants where they typically insisted on working side-by-side with their employees.

A few years after Lammot's tragic death, Boss Henry died, on his 77th birthday—ending a 39-year reign in which the company had risen from heavy indebtedness to a net worth of over $11 million. His son, Henry A., the Civil War colonel, thought he was the heir apparent to run the company, but other du Ponts had other ideas. Henry A.'s brother, William, and their cousins, Eugene and Francis G., sons of Alexis, were the other partners in the firm, and they apparently felt Henry A.'s role in the company had been confined too narrowly to the railroad-shipping business.

Brothers Henry and William didn't get along especially well (Henry once vowed to try to outlive William to prevent his burial in the family cemetery plot), and William ultimately resigned his partnership in Du Pont Co. to devote full time to running Repauno Chemical Co.

It was Cousin Eugene who became the managing partner of Du Pont Co. He was the farthest thing from a Boss Henry, but by now the Gunpowder Trade Association founded by Lammot had evolved into a trust that controlled 90 percent or more of the powder production in America. In the same year, 1890, Eugene invited Lammot's son Pierre, a student at the Massachusetts Institute of Technology, to join the company. It was Pierre more than anyone else of his generation who was to point Du Pont Co. in the direction of the chemical giant that it eventually became.

But this was to be a gradual process, interrupted by antitrust battles and family transition. The colony along the Brandywine remained the homestead for most du Ponts, but some were moving on, including William, whose divorce and remarriage were a scandal among the close-knit du Ponts.

A bigger scandal a year later—perhaps the only large blot on the family's huge and distinguished canvas—made the family forget about William's marital problem. It involved Lammot's brother, Alfred Victor, who had gone to Louisville some years earlier and had become one of its leading and wealthiest citizens. "Uncle Fred's" death in 1893 was at first attributed to a "seizure," but was later said to have been the result of a gunshot wound—administered by the madam of a Louisville brothel, apparently in an argument over child support.

In 1902, when Eugene du Pont died of pneumonia, no one was ready to take over. The senior partners, Francis, Alexis, and Henry A., and the junior partners, Alfred I. and Charles, generally had other things on their minds. At a meeting of the partners, it was first decided to offer the company for sale to its biggest competitor, Laflin & Rand, for $12 million.

But then Alfred, 37 at the time, made the fateful move that was to keep Du Pont Co. in the du Pont family. Although Alfred didn't have the resources to buy out the other partners, he enlisted the help of his cousins, Pierre, 32, and Thomas Coleman du Pont, 37. Largely through Coleman's persuasion, the other partners agreed to accept notes instead of cash—plus 28 percent of the stock in the new company.

Of the new partners, Coleman received the most shares and was named president, Alfred became vice-president, and Pierre treasurer. Coleman's past experience in reorganizing street-railway companies was an asset in his new administrative job, and he was soon putting together a package to buy Laflin & Rand for notes and stock, without paying any cash. The acquisition gave Du Pont Co. majority market shares in powder and dynamite. With that kind of control, the Gunpowder Trade Association was no longer a factor in setting prices, and it was disbanded.

The company's acquisitions and consolidations continued until 1907, when the government sued Du Pont Co. for violating the Sherman Antitrust Act. After a federal court found the company guilty, Du Pont agreed to sell off assets of $20 million, while retaining $60 million. The process involved formation of two new companies to compete with Du Pont—Hercules Powder Co. and Atlas Powder Co. (now a subsidiary of Imperial Chemical Industries). Although Du Pont remained intact, Pierre and Coleman were especially bitter over the matter, with Coleman contending publicly that the company had helped pull the ungrateful government through the Civil War.

The family had other problems about then, when Alfred divorced Bessie Gardner and married his cousin, Alicia Bradford Maddox. Family members took sides in the affair, and some of the rifts never fully healed. Moreover, Coleman and Pierre began to have disagreements about managing the company. Coleman, amid bouts of ill health and heavy involvement in New York real-estate investments, was running short of cash. He offered to sell his stock in the company to the other partners, but Alfred and William rejected the offer.

Pierre made a counter-proposal to Coleman through a syndicate that included his brothers Lammot and Irenee—about $14 million in cash and notes. Coleman accepted, and the deal went through. But the family rift widened as a result.

A number of cousins sued Pierre over the purchase of Coleman's stock, and eventually Alfred I. joined in as a plaintiff. What had always been a shy, almost reclusive, family was about to hang out a lot of dirty linen in court. Family loyalties were being strained not only by the suit but by the lingering effects of Alfred's divorce.

The trial was long and bitter. Among the cousins testifying was Francis I. du Pont, who later founded the large brokerage firm. He said he had decided against joining in Pierre's syndicate purchasing Coleman's stock because Alfred was his friend.

The outcome was an eventual victory for Pierre, for the court ordered that stockholders vote to decide whether the company, rather than Pierre, should buy Coleman's stock—and the stockholders, led by Pierre himself, of course voted against the proposition.

An appeal by Alfred failed, and the public airing of the feud was over. But the two cousins never reconciled, despite some overtures made by Pierre. It had a wrenching effect on the family, but the court case eventually blew over with only a few lasting scars on some du Ponts.

Alfred himself retreated to his estate near Wilmington, which he surrounded with an eight-foot-high stone wall topped with chips of broken glass. The wall, he said, was to keep out intruders— "mainly of the name of du Pont." He later moved to Florida, where he made a fortune in real estate.

With Pierre's branch of the family firmly in control of the company, Du Pont's fortunes began to soar. World War I didn't hurt, either. After the war broke out in Europe, missions from England, France, and Russia descended on Wilmington, seeking to purchase gunpowder and explosives from Du Pont Co. But Pierre, fearing that the necessary plant expansions would be superfluous after the war, drove a stiff bargain. He forced the Allies to cover the cost of the new facilities by paying high initial prices, which would later be lowered.

Huge expansions were undertaken at various plants, and a big plant was built at Hopewell, Va., to increase production of nitrocellulose, a key ingredient in the new technology for making smokeless powder. There was little risk involved for Du Pont, because Pierre's deal with the Allies meant the facilities would be quickly paid off. Indeed, during the war years of 1914-18, the company's revenues exceeded $1 billion, and retained earnings were nearly $90 million.

The money launched Du Pont Co. on the ambitious diversification program that was to transform it from a munitions company into a leading chemical producer. Wartime profits also provided funds for Du Pont's initial $25 million investment in General Motors stock. And when GM's William Durant ran into difficulties in 1919, Pierre du Pont came to the rescue with a complicated transaction calling for Durant to resign and Pierre to take his place as president of GM. Du Pont Co. ended up with 38 percent of GM's stock, and Pierre proceeded to institute the kind of financial controls he had brought to Du Pont.

Pierre, an enigmatic figure, became the family patriarch as well as the company savior. He was affectionately called "Dad" by his nine brothers and sisters, and he was devoted to taking care of them. He didn't marry until he was 45, and then it was to a cousin—in the tradition of many du Ponts before and since. Despite his significant role in shaping two major corporations (Du Pont and General Motors), he never conquered his innate shyness—a trait he said he shared with many of the descendants of his great-grandfather, Irenee.

In their book, *Pierre S. du Pont and the Making of the Modern Corporation,* Alfred D. Chandler and Stephen Salsbury suggest that Pierre's financial ingenuity and Coleman's diplomacy meant that Du Pont Co. didn't have to go to Wall Street or other outsiders in search of capital. Pierre, the authors add, saw the need of bringing in managerial and entrepreneurial talent while keeping the family interested and involved in the company.

With growing wealth, however, came a softening of the old commitments to serving the family enterprise and to the rigors of managing a large corporation. Nevertheless, Pierre almost singlehandedly kept Du Pont and GM humming by bringing together strong outside managers, often of conflicting personalities, and forging them into efficient teams.

There were setbacks, of course. Government antitrust actions in 1907 and 1950 finally forced the sale of Du Pont Co.'s GM stock, although many family members continued as large shareholders in GM. Sen. Gerald Nye of North Dakota held hearings in the 1930s to investigate Du Pont Co.'s wartime profits, calling the du Ponts "merchants of death." The hearings produced evidence, among other things, that the company had nearly agreed to sell munitions to Hitler's Germany.

Even in the Depression, however, the du Pont family's resources —and the company's prosperity and diversification—were such that both were relatively unscathed. Providing Du Pont Co. with the impetus for further growth in this period was the hiring of Harvard chemist Wallace Carothers and pioneering work in basic research.

From the research of Carothers and others at Du Pont came an epochal development. For centuries, scientists had tried to unravel the mystery of natural fibers such as cotton and silk, but not until 1938 were they able to apply the accumulated knowledge to the production of a practical man-made fiber. The new fiber, described at the time as "a new silk, made on a chemical base," was nylon. Highly versatile, it became an overnight success not only for fashionable garments but for many industrial uses as well. It was a "silk" that didn't depend on imports. Supplies of natural silk from Japan were undependable, and fabrics made from it were less durable. In the first year in which they were available, American women bought 64 million pairs of nylon hose.

Commercial development of cellophane, dyes, insecticides, films, and many other products followed. Along with this growth came managerial systems and controls developed by the outside managers first brought in by Pierre. Many of the innovations helped GM as well as Du Pont, as Du Pont supplied GM not only with products but with administrative and financial help. Conversely, GM dividends helped to sustain Du Pont in periods of slow earnings growth.

Du Pont also invested at various times in U.S. Rubber Co., U.S. Steel, and other companies, almost always incurring the wrath of government antitrusters in the process. Like many an industrialist before and since, Pierre du Pont simply couldn't understand the government's opposition to big business. He also couldn't understand why it frowned upon the stock-swap deal he worked out with his long-time associate, John Raskob, after the stock-market crash. The stock sales established tax losses for the year, and the two men then bought back their original holdings from each other. Publicity about that case established that Pierre in 1929 paid $4.5 million in taxes and that his income for the year therefore was over $31 million.

Small wonder that Pierre was a prominent national figure and the du Pont family patriarch. His correspondence with other members of the family dispensed a homey philosophy and often handsome financial help as well.

In one letter, he railed against what he saw as a growing disregard for the law in the U.S. "We are rapidly assuming a position," he wrote, "where we have no laws because what masquerade as such are either so indefinite that no lawyer or court, let alone an ordinary man, can tell what they mean, or are so impossible of enforcement that it is foolish to attempt obeyance."

Despite his vast wealth and national reputation, however, Pierre concentrated his philanthropies in the Brandywine area that was the family's homeland. Considering Delaware's school system to be scandalous, he raised such an outcry that the governor appointed him tax commissioner in 1925, to help raise school funding. As commissioner, he took tax dodgers into court, and within two years the school system had a surplus—and improvements were under way. He also used his own resources, especially for schools for blacks.

A 1927 *Time* magazine cover story about Pierre said he had spent $5 million on Delaware schools, building 86 schools for blacks and 20 for whites, entirely with his own money. He also built the Kennett Pike, a Brandywine-area traffic artery, and opened the Longwood Gardens, at the family estate, to the public. Pierre was also a leading advocate of the repeal of Prohibition.

Illustrating his dislike of the public spotlight, he once said that he had done well in school but was always pleased when a good performance was passed over without undue comment. He also observed in autobiographical notes, "I count that my inheritance of qualities from my ancestors and the teachings by precept and example of my father and mother and grandmother gave to me advantages that were worth more than my school education."

His innate humility and shyness, however, didn't prevent Pierre from earning a reputation for the elegant living that great wealth allowed. The staff of his Longwood estate included three cooks, four other kitchen employees, a headwaiter, a doorman, and four other household employees. Parties for hundreds of guests were

Eleuthere Irenee du Pont (1771 - 1834), founder of the Du Pont Company. *Credit: Du Pont Company*

Du Pont Shield

Workers at the Du Pont mills used wooden tubs and railroad flat cars to move batches of powder from place to place. Despite such precautions as wooden railroad tracks to prevent sparks, accidents were frequent in the mills' early days. *Credit: Du Pont Company*

Du Pont gunpowder mills built on the banks of the Brandywine River near Wilmington, Del., were operated until 1921. These two restored mills were built between 1822 and 1824. *Credit: Du Pont Company*

Immense profits from the sale of gunpowder during World War I triggered a battle for control of the company among cousins (top to bottom) Pierre S., T. Coleman and Alfred I. du Pont. Alfred, who lost the fight, is pictured here in Florida, where he later prospered in the real estate business. *Credit: Wide World Photo (Pierre S.)*

Credit: Du Pont Company (T. Coleman)

Credit: Wide World Photo (Alfred I.)

Pierre du Pont channeled his company's war profits into the development of new products, such as nylon and cellophane. Here, models at an exhibit at the 1939 New York World's Fair display a new product, nylon hosiery. *Credit: Du Pont Company*

Lammont du Pont Copeland, Sr. resigned as chairman in 1971, ending family leadership of the company. *Credit: Wide World Photo*

Irenee du Pont Jr. was the last of the family to hold high office in the company, retiring as senior vice president in 1978. *Credit: Philadelphia Inquirer*

The personal bankruptcy of his son, Lammot du Pont Copeland Jr., in 1970 was the largest on record at that time. *Credit: Wide World Photo*

Pierre S. du Pont IV, Governor of Delaware, at a press conference in 1979. *Credit: Wide World Photo*

regular occurrences at Longwood, and debutante parties for du Pont nieces were legendary. In 1950, he presided over a family-anniversary reunion attended by more than 600 guests—all du Ponts and their in-laws.

Although Pierre was president of Du Pont Co. only from 1915 to 1919, he remained chairman, and then honorary chairman, for the rest of his life, and his influence continued to be pervasive. In the mid-1920s, he set up the Delaware Realty & Investment Co. as a vehicle for transferring his estate. His eight brothers and sisters received the shares of the new company, and in exchange they agreed to pay $900,000 a year to Pierre and his wife, Alice, for the rest of their lives. Besides helping to avoid taxes, the tactic was designed to help keep Du Pont Co. in the family.

Despite this early transfer of much of Pierre's wealth, when he died in 1954 his estate was valued at more than $75 million. Du Pont Co.'s assets in his 40 or so years with the company, moreover, had grown to more than $2.5 billion from less than $12 million.

The professional-management techniques that he instituted at Du Pont "became archetypes for other corporations," says Alfred Chandler, a professor at Harvard University's Graduate School of Business. His bringing in of professional managers, of course, also foreshadowed the decline of the du Pont family in the top echelons of the company's management.

Meantime, his younger brothers, Irenee and Lammot, who in turn succeeded him as president of Du Pont Co., carried on the family tradition of able company leadership. Irenee, known as "Bus," was the most genial and articulate of the brothers, and it was he who is given much of the credit for seeing the company through the period after World War I and through various government investigations. It was also Irenee who was instrumental in the family's purchase of 18 percent of U.S. Rubber, which later became Uniroyal.

At the Nye Committee hearings on alleged war profiteering, the pipesmoking Irenee was the star witness for the defense, arguing that Du Pont Co.'s expertise was sorely needed by the U.S. and the Allies—and that Du Pont Co., among all the government contractors, was probably singled out for censure because of its opposition to Franklin D. Roosevelt.

Despite his great wealth, Irenee's charitable contributions were relatively small. For one thing, he had 10 children to support in the manner to which du Ponts had become accustomed (although two of them died at early ages). He also had expensive amenities like a 60-foot yacht and a Cuban estate with a private landing field and golf course. (The estate, known as Xanadu, eventually was confiscated by the Castro regime and became a tax write-off in Irenee's estate.) Like his brother Pierre and other du Ponts, Irenee married a cousin, Irene Sophie du Pont. With eight debutante daughters, the Irenee du Ponts became notorious for their lavish parties.

When he died in 1963, he left an estate of $200 million, nearly half of which went to taxes. A large part of his assets had already been put in trust for his children, however.

Irenee had been president of Du Pont Co. only until 1926, when he stepped aside for his brother, Lammot, who remained president until 1940. Lammot is credited with pushing basic research at Du Pont—and investing heavily in it, even during the Depression.

A company publication said of Lammot, "Learning to work with his hands gave him a respect and feeling for tools; he likes to chop wood and sharpen the family cutlery on an old treadle stone. Motorists often see him bicycling to work amid heavy traffic. Simple and direct, he has a candor that wins the regard even of those who disagree most with his views."

His "candor" mostly involved speaking out on behalf of the free-enterprise system and against government interference with business. The government's antitrust suit opposing Du Pont Co.'s holding in General Motors was before the public during much of his reign, although the final ruling and divestiture weren't made until some years after his death.

He had eight children by his first wife, none by the next two, and two by his last wife. He had already distributed much of his wealth to his children by the time he died, in 1952, at age 71.

The passing of the three brothers who headed Du Pont also marked the end of an era for the family. They had scaled the heights of corporate achievement, and their descendants could reap the benefits—or the benefits of what was left after taxes and dilution in the successive generations.

Family participation in the company's management did continue for some time, however, and family members didn't give up the leadership until 1971, when Lammot du Pont Copeland Sr. resigned as chairman. The resignation followed his entanglement in the financial affairs of his oldest child, Lammot Jr. Lammot Sr., called "Big Mots" in the family, was the son of Pierre's older sister, Louise. One of the hardest-working of his generation in the family, Copeland concentrated on the financial operations of the company at a time when it was experiencing some setbacks: Corfam, the substitute leather that proved too costly, and a photographic process that didn't quite make it, for example. Copeland sometimes lamented publicly that more young du Ponts didn't take an active interest in the company.

Lammot Jr., called "Little Mots," did sell chemicals for Du Pont for a time in the 1960s. Then he became associated with a man named Thomas Shaheen, and they formed Winthrop Lawrence Corp. In a series of transactions, Shaheen would arrange loans for failing companies, and Little Mots would guarantee the loans. Some of the deals went awry, and creditors began suing Copeland. The result was Copeland's filing a Chapter 11 bankruptcy petition listing assets of $26 million and liabilities of nearly $60 million. Winthrop Lawrence Corp. also filed a bankruptcy proceeding.

The senior Copeland had become involved by lending millions to Winthrop Lawrence and guaranteeing most of his son's loans. As a result, he ultimately resigned as Du Pont Co.'s chairman. Under the bankruptcy settlement, Lammot Copeland Jr. was ordered to repay a portion of his debts. His trust income of over $400,000 a year wasn't legally at stake. Although his personal bankruptcy was one of the biggest ever in the U.S., he didn't end up in the poorhouse, by any means. Today, he is in the joke-writing business.

Although Lammot Copeland Sr. was the last member of the family to lead the company, he wasn't the last to hold high office. That distinction goes to Irenee Jr., who resigned as senior vice-president in May, 1978. Now 66 years old, he still is a Du Pont Co. director, and he also spends time serving on family foundations and puttering around his sprawling hilltop estate outside Wilmington. Passed over for the presidency of Du Pont Co., Irenee Jr. was quoted by the *Wilmington News Journal* in 1973 as saying, "I would have been terribly surprised if anyone had asked me to be president. I know my limitations, Besides, I as a stockholder would have objected to me as president."

But if the du Ponts no longer are active owner-managers, many of them are still owners, and most of them are still rich. The old saw that wealthy American families go "from shirt-sleeves to shirt-sleeves in three generations" doesn't apply to them. If a du Pont is seen wearing shirt-sleeves, it no doubt is purely for reasons of comfort.

The family fortune today is estimated at $5 billion: about $2.3 billion in Du Pont stock, about $1.2 billion in shares of General Motors that remain held by family members after the court-ordered divestiture by Du Pont Co. of most of its GM holdings in 1961, and the rest in private landholdings and businesses.

Some branches of the family are richer than others, and some latterday du Ponts managed their finances and marriages better than others, so the amounts of money that have come down to individual members of the present generation range from many millions of dollars to less than $100,000. But despite their large numbers today, almost all du Ponts begin life with a considerable headstart on the pack.

The diversity of the present-day du Ponts is evident in a look at some of them and their pursuits.

Gov. Pierre S. du Pont IV

"Pete" du Pont, 45, recalls that when his grandfather, Lammot, and Lammot's brothers, Pierre and Irenee, were at the helm of the chemical company, the public perception was that the whole family was involved in Du Pont Co. In fact, he says, the family was no longer especially cohesive then, and certainly isn't now—although the New Year's reunions help to keep the widely scattered family members in touch with one another.

After attending Princeton University, du Pont went to Harvard Law School, which he says was against his father's better judgment. But he did follow his father's advice after that by going to work for the company—from 1963 to 1970. "I worked in marketing and manufacturing positions," he says, "and was quality-control supervisor in a magnetic-tape pilot plant."

But even with a law degree and the name du Pont, advancement was slow. "It's difficult in any organization that big to progress as fast as you'd like, and I thought there were more opportunities elsewhere."

His decision to enter politics wasn't a popular one with his father or with the rest of the family, but he ran anyway, first winning election to the Delaware House of Representatives. There was a little more family criticism later, when he was running for Congress and disclosed his personal finances. There was some public criticism too.

"My name was a tremendous issue in that race," he recalls. "The charge was made that I was going to be terribly conservative, but I've proved that wrong." In his later races, for Congress in 1974, and for governor in 1976, he adds, he stipulated that "all campaign contributions be limited to $100 a person—myself and all my relatives included."

Having won all the elections he has run in so far, Pete du Pont has succeeded in a profession that hasn't been a family forte. "We had two U.S. Senators back in the old days, and Pierre was just about everything for Delaware, but I'm only the second member of the family to be a member of the Delaware bar with the name du Pont," he says.

Gov. du Pont adds, "The values imparted to me and that I try to get across to my children are that whatever you do in the world isn't as important as doing it well. I got the feeling from my parents that there's some obligation to maintain a high performance in whatever you're doing.

"That feeling was certainly there in my father's generation. But if you look at the dollar and time involvement of my generation in civic and community projects, you'll see much less involvement than in past generations. I don't think the younger people are making the commitment. I bet you'll find the boards of charitable organizations have a relatively slim number of younger du Ponts on them. The younger generation's involvement in the Wilmington community is much less, too."

H. Rodney Sharp III

One of the three family members working at Du Pont Co. nowadays, Sharp, 44, is a grandson of Bella du Pont Sharp, a sister of Pierre, Irenee, and Lammot.

"When I started at Du Pont in 1961, there were a fair number of relatives working for the company," he says. "They felt they were being tested for higher things, but competition was very good."

Rodney Sharp heads a team of 35 that maintains computer programs for corporate accounting, and he says he doesn't see much hope of advancing higher in the corporation. For a time, he was transferred to the finance department, but his first love has always been the computer.

"I have vague memories of the 1939 World's Fair—all those little cars going around at the GM exhibit. That world-of-tomorrow business may be why I'm so fascinated with computers and organized gadgets. It's like having a new electric train under the Christmas tree every day you come to work."

Rodney, who describes his life as "very middle-class," received an inheritance from his grandfather, trust income from his grandmother, and gifts of securities from his father. All of which allows him such luxuries as a Porsche auto, a 14-foot sailboat, and private schools for his children. But he considers such things as vacations in Europe too extravagant, so his travel abroad is generally only on business.

He has been president of the family's Longwood Foundation, but shies away from most other civic and charitable positions. When his two daughters entered a private school in Wilmington, the school asked him to go on the board. "If I had just been an ordinary parent, they wouldn't have asked me to do that," he observes.

The two daughters, from his first marriage, will be his primary beneficiaries, he says, but he adds, "It has just become impossible to transmit inherited wealth, so why fight it. The best gift I can give them is to teach them to operate as rather normal people."

When he remarried in 1979, he bought a $110,000 row house in Wilmington rather than moving elsewhere. "I tend to be uncomfortable in new situations, and it would be a transitional shock to go somewhere else," he says. He adds an afterthought: "You tend to get asked to do a lot of things."

Pierre Coleman du Pont

Coley du Pont, as he is called in the family, at age 31 is the only family member with the name du Pont who works for the company —as a supervisor in the photo-products plant at Glasgow, Del. His grandfather, Evan Morgan du Pont, was a younger brother of T. Coleman du Pont, the man who sold out to Pierre.

"My grandfather seemed to make one poor decision after another in trying to make money," Coley notes, "and seemed to be 180 degrees away from T. Coleman."

Which helps to explain why Evan Morgan du Pont's heirs are generally less wealthy than T. Coleman's heirs. Coley's father, James Q., who died in 1973, was a public speaker of some note, talking about family and company history.

James never pushed the company as a career for his son, but Coley, after studying landscape architecture and then business administration, applied for a job at Du Pont Co. in 1971. He became a line-production supervisor at a fibers plant in Richmond, Va.

Now, as an employee-relations supervisor in Glasgow, Del., he is in the field he considers himself best suited for. "I would dearly love to see my family once again have an active role in directing activities of the company," he says. "Our family and ancestors did a lot of things right, and someday I'd like to say I contributed to that. I'd like to be in a position to someday help in running the company."

Meantime, he says, he doesn't enjoy any privileges associated with the name du Pont. "I walk a tight wire," he says. "I'd be the first to go if my performance is bad." And he says he isn't bitter when someone moves ahead faster than he does.

"I look on it as a challenge to convince people that I put my pants on one leg at a time just like everyone else, and I'm not about to waltz through the company on the coattails of my ancestors' ability."

Coley not long ago married Mary Doerr, a research chemist at the Glasgow plant. "As far as I know," Coley says, "we are the first husband-wife team of du Ponts working for the company."

He adds, "I have a little man in me that keeps saying I have to keep the du Pont name important. It would be sort of sad to see Du Pont Co. without any du Ponts in it."

Helen Quinn du Pont

Penney du Pont, as she is known, is the 40-year-old sister of Coley. A graduate of Yale Drama School, she is one of the few family members to go into acting. "It's hard to be an actress in Wilmington," she says, and outside of Wilmington people don't usually make the connection of the name du Pont.

One time in New York, however, when she was trying to line up theatrical work, an agent said to her, "Why don't you just go home and buy a theater?"

She did get work eventually, though, and she has been co-host of a syndicated television talk show. "I think I can truly say that being a du Pont hasn't helped or hurt," she says. "Sports and theater are very democratic. No one cares if you're rich or poor, but just the job you can do."

Alfred du Pont Dent

Alfred du Pont Dent, 46, is too young to remember much about his grandfather, Alfred I. du Pont, but he certainly knows his reputation, including the story about building that wall around his house to keep out du Ponts, among others. He is also aware of how the family was split by the legal fight between his grandfather and Pierre for control of the company.

"My grandfather with William du Pont started their own bank, Delaware Trust, and then built a Delaware Trust building one story higher than the du Pont building just so he could look down on the other du Ponts," Alfred Dent says.

"My father told me that Alfred I. wouldn't ever refer to Pierre without saying to his dog, Yip, 'Yip your cousin Pierre.' "

The president of a small Wilmington investment company, Alfred Dent says he couldn't live without working because he was born too late to be included in his grandfather's will. He did receive an inheritance from his mother, Vicky, however. "I'm not in the category with a great many du Ponts. A lot of people think that if your name is du Pont you're automatically worth $5 million plus. I'm constantly asked to invest in things because of my middle name," he says.

"My grandfather had three yachts and my uncle had six. But there's no way I could afford a yacht. The vestiges of wealth are disappearing very quickly."

Alfred, a trustee of his grandfather's estate, is making some ripples in the family nowadays by joining in a suit against other trustees of the estate, whose income goes to the so-called Nemours Foundation. The estate, valued at $30 million in 1935, now has principal of over $750 million, Alfred Dent says, "and some say $2 billion." It continues to control St. Joe Paper Co., which controls railroad, real-estate and paper-mill properties, mostly in Florida.

The suit seeks to have the foundation sell the St. Joe stock so that more of the foundation's money will become available for the charities it supports. Alfred says his legal fees in the case in 1978 alone were $25,000. "I tell people this is my contribution to charity."

Alfred's investment-company job allows him time for other interests—notably backgammon and golf, and he has gained something of a reputation in backgammon tournaments. "For the last 10 years I've played with good players all around the world," he says. "I get a lot of publicity about that. I'm amazed at the number of people in town who think I do nothing but play backgammon. I probably go to tournaments two or three weeks a year, as a vacation from the brokerage firm."

With typical candor, Alfred tells of hs earlier years. "I went to Tower Hill School, where my seven-year-old daughter goes now, then to St. George's School in Newport, Rhode Island, and then to

Princeton for two years and flunked out. I went into the U.S. Navy, and after I was in boot camp for a week I realized I had made a mistake." But he served in the Navy for two years and then finished up his education at the University of Pennsylvania.

Alexis I. du Pont

Alexis, 51, is the youngest son of E. Paul du Pont Sr., an engineer who quit Du Pont Co. after the Pierre-Alfred feud in 1914. He then founded Du Pont Motors, which eventually went into receivership, and then became president of Indian Motorcycle Co.

Alexis says his father didn't encourage him to work at Du Pont Co., even though the wounds from the family feud had healed. Like some other du Ponts, Alexis has always been interested in aviation, and for a time he also raced cars as a hobby. A number of years ago, he was seriously injured when an antique plane he was flying in with a cousin by marriage crashed as it was landing in a snow-covered field in Iowa.

Nowadays, Alexis and his wife, Anne, own and operate a small airport and museum 11 miles from Wilmington. Among the museum's possessions: A prized Du Pont Motors car and Indian motorcycles.

The airport isn't a big money-maker, and Alexis and Anne say they aren't in a class with the wealth of many du Ponts. "If we had one child," Anne says, "we'd be quite well-off, but with five, they'll manage. They can afford to go to London for school and buy cars and travel a little bit, and they won't starve even if they choose a career not particularly remunerative, but they aren't likely to be in the private-jet class."

Owning the airport causes the du Ponts some worries about potential liability claims. "Our lawyers say it isn't the type of thing someone with the name du Pont should do," Anne says, and Alexis adds, "You have to be careful and sometimes turn away business in the interest of protecting yourself."

"Another problem," Alexis adds, "is people who don't pay their bills because they figure we can afford it. Now we're on a cash-only basis."

Henry E. I. du Pont

A descendant of "Boss Henry," Henry E. I. du Pont, 53, is a son of William Jr. This branch of the family is among the wealthiest, partly because it was less prolific than some other branches.

Henry once worked in the Du Pont Co. mechanical-testing laboratory, but in 1966 he inherited $30 million from his grandfather, William Sr. With his inheritance, he quit Du Pont Co. and started a time-sharing computer company and another company that kept track of stolen and missing securities.

But the business failed. "I hate to think how much I lost on the two companies—about $8 million," Henry says. Two divorces cost him $5 million each, and stock-market losses took another $10 million of his inheritance, Henry says.

So he has had to let go the butler and gardener at his estate near Wilmington and sell his 60-foot ocean cruiser that used too much fuel. Not to worry, however: the du Ponts still have a laundress, a cook, and an "upstairs girl." And Henry is due to receive another $30 million inheritance when an elderly aunt dies.

His wife, Martha Anne Verge, known as Muffin, does worry, though. "We've talked about giving up our citizenship and going to another country with different tax laws," she says, lamenting particularly about how difficult it has become to pass wealth on to children.

Henry adds, "We're currently working with tax experts and looking for a loophole we can jump into."

The du Ponts own 81 acres, on which they breed Morgan horses. Their 16-room home is said to be one of the best examples of Georgian architecture in Delaware. Muffin spends much of her spare time helping to run a shelter for abused children. "We funded it 100 percent at first, probably $1 million in all," she says. "Henry and I feel people like us can help get things like this started, and hopefully we can move on to other things."

In some cases, however, Muffin has learned to shy away from civic involvement. "As soon as you join something, they want to put you on the board," she says. "They aren't looking to honor you, but they're looking at your pocketbook. But when we go on boards, it's often the kiss of death, because the public says du Ponts are on it and let them pay for it."

She adds, "I sometimes feel the disadvantages don't outweigh the advantages of being a du Pont. You could take everything away from me and I'd survive."

Since he let the gardener go, Henry is surviving by doing more of his own outdoor work, and this has led to some interesting encounters.

"When I was putting in a brick walk," Henry says, "a hedge trimmer in the neighborhood came by and asked for a drink. He asked if it was nice working here and if the hours were good and if the owners were nice. I said, 'No problem.'"

On another occasion, a paper deliveryman saw Henry at work and asked how long he had been working there. "I said, '52 years—and I have no complaints.'"

John E. du Pont

Henry's brother John, 41, is seemingly made from an entirely different mold. A bachelor, he lives with his mother and runs the Delaware Museum of Natural History, which he founded and which he calls the second largest natural-history museum to be founded in this century. This avocation began in his youth, when he was an avid collector of seashells and bird specimens.

Recently, he has written several books and articles about birds and seashells, and this, he says, has left less time for his other interests, notably the pentathlon. This sport, which involves swimming, running, pistol shooting, horseback riding and fencing, has engaged his interest for years, and he still competes. He is also an officer of the U.S. Modern Pentathlon Association and was manager of the U.S. team for the 1976 Montreal Olympics.

To further this interest, he had a 50-meter indoor swimming pool built in 1967 at the house he shares with his mother. The pool is often used for training young Olympic hopefuls, just as the barns and property outside are used by natural-history buffs on field trips. Also to further his pentathlon interest, he raises horses. "At one time I had a bunch of racehorses, but no longer," he says. "I just raise a few horses here at my mother's house."

Still another of John's interests is law enforcement. "I'm a county detective in Chester, Pa., and a police officer in Newtown Square. I only get involved in special cases—for no charges. I started out as a firearms instructor for the local departments. I'm interested in intricate burglary rings and homicides. I keep police dogs and use my helicopter for police work like taking aerial photos of the crime scene."

His helicopter, loaded with sophisticated electronic gear, is also used for business trips to New York.

John's outside interests seem to be partly defensive in nature, for if you are a du Pont, people are apt to hound you to contribute to their cause or to invest in their ventures. And if you are a du Pont bachelor, you are in double jeopardy.

"The world is full of people looking for venture capital," he observes with a sigh. But I've finally gotten the reputation of not going along with a lot of wild ideas. It's amazing—they're always trying to introduce me to their daughters. It became a nuisance after a while. But it's not as bad as it used to be. People aren't hounding you to death when you're out there running"—a reference to the fact that he practices about six hours a day to keep in shape for the pentathlon.

S. Hallock du Pont Jr.

Hallock du Pont Jr., 43, whose grandfather, William, was a brother of Pierre, Irenee, and Lammot, lives in Miami in a 12-room house.

An energetic man with many interests, from airplanes to gun collecting and marketing, he calls himself the only du Pont left in the firearms business. He manages his businesses (often wearing Bermuda shorts) from a two-story concrete-and-steel office building across the road from Miami International Airport, where he can watch the planes taking off and landing.

Among other things, Hallock owns part of a bank and a restaurant chain and imports from West Germany trap-shooting and skeet-shooting guns that sell for $3,000 and up. He is also a champion marksman and participates regularly in matches around the country. He also has a sizable collection of antique firearms and du Pont powder cans.

One of his businesses leases aircraft to small airlines, and he still sometimes flies a small jet as a reserve captain for a leasing firm.

He doesn't manage to go north for the du Pont New Year's callings, but he does consider that the du Pont name carries with it certain responsibilities. "People are always watching," he says. "If I don't set the example, they can't expect others to. People look to us to supply a certain amount of leadership."

"It's very nice to start life out with a nest egg," he adds. "But if you don't take what you're born with and pass it on or make more, you aren't fulfilling what you're here for. I feel I will drop dead with a greater amount of money than I was born with."

Francis I. du Pont

A Du Pont Co. dropout, Francis I. du Pont, 53, thinks he has found his life's calling. He lives at Chadds Ford, Pa., on the Delaware border, and has started a land-management business that helps forest owners selectively thin out their trees to promote the growth of the other trees.

His grandfather and namesake was one of those siding with Alfred I. du Pont in the infighting with Pierre, after which the original Francis left the company and set up his own chemical engineering company. Later, he set up the brokerage firm bearing his name, which went bankrupt after his death. His son, Emil F. du Pont, the father of the current Francis, went to work for Du Pont Co. and became manager of the first nylon plant.

"It never occurred to me that I would do anything but go to work for the company," Francis says. "I went to Yale, was in the Navy and then went to work for Du Pont in the Dacron plant in Kingston, N.C. Later, I went into marketing research in Wilmington and into merchandising of Lycra. I had the distinction of calling on the girdle and bra trade for a couple of years."

After a few other jobs, he says, he told management he would like a greater voice in decision making at Du Pont. "I asked what kind of plans they had in mind for me, and the answer came back they didn't have a concrete plan. So I figured I had best spend the rest of my life doing something else."

He is now a consultant to a financial-service organization. "I advise people on capital gains and other financial concerns. I'm not a technical wizard in finance, and what I do best is dealing with people. Everything I've done in life has been in marketing and sales."

Like other du Ponts, Francis is ambivalent about carrying the du Pont name. Most du Ponts, he says, are a little shy and try to avoid the limelight. "But I had this revelation one day," he says, "that the name is either going to work for me or against me. One wonderful advantage of the name is that I can get to see anybody, anywhere, anytime if I want to." This is despite the fact, he says, exaggerating slightly, that "I don't have wealth—zero." The wealth has been dissipated, he explains, by the fact that his father was one of nine children and his grandfather was one of 13.

His interest in land management began in 1977 when he was discussing with management consultants possible jobs in industry. He learned, he says, that companies in agriculture, forestry, and environmental areas all considered "man's intelligent use of land" to be the biggest problem they faced.

He experimented by "custom harvesting" 15 acres of woods on his 100-acre property in Chadds Ford. "Because we let in sunlight by taking out 46 percent of the board feet, we had a better forest left," he says. "You should have seen the forest floor—it was a sea of green. We built a barn from the wood from the property. It cost me less than half of what it would have if we didn't have the raw materials." Now he is offering his expertise to others, and he is also trying to use his own land to better advantage.

"I'd like to get the land I live on to sustain me. I have eight steers, three pigs and 30 chickens," he says, "and I also have a vegetable garden. I like to work outside, and I'm happiest when I'm working the hardest. The first thing I do at 6 a.m. is feed the animals, collect chicken eggs, and sit down to breakfast of my own eggs and bacon."

He is also a trustee of the Brandywine River Museum, director of mutual funds, and treasurer of a cemetery. "You get a certain amount of responsibility dumped on you as you get older," he says. "I call it nonproductive work because you don't get paid for it."

Christopher Treusdale du Pont

A ski buff and former Vietnam war protester, Christopher, 31, lives in Sun Valley, Idaho. His grandfather was A. Felix du Pont, Sr., a brother of the original Francis I. du Pont.

Recently divorced for the second time, Christopher is trying to help start a business that would market shredded newspapers as a straw substitute for bedding for horses. Meantime, he is living primarily off the annual income of $200,000 from his inheritance. "With the inherited money," he says, "I have an obligation to do something responsible, rather than frittering it away."

"I don't have any grand designs to make millions," he adds. "I want to avoid making the mistakes I made in the past. In college I lost $20,000 investing in a motorcycle shop in Putney, Vt. I'm becoming more and more conservative right now, it seems. I want to keep taxes down so the old money lasts."

That's a bit of a change from his college days at the University of Delaware, where he marched off the ROTC field in an anti-Vietnam war protest. "My father has never forgiven me for that," he says. Nowadays he is also realizing the intangible benefits of being a du Pont. "I feel I'm related to something much more cohesive than what many of my friends came from."

As for the tangible benefits, there is the Sun Valley "helicopter skiing." He pays a helicopter pilot to fly him to the top of an otherwise inaccessible mountain so he can ski down.

VII

The Mellons

INVITATIONS TO THE 39th floor of Pittsburgh's Mellon Bank Building aren't easy to come by. There, among quiet offices and plush carpeting, the lawyers and accountants of Richard King Mellon's heirs conduct the family's business. Visitors are discouraged, and the family does not discuss its business affairs with "outsiders."

It is a little different in Washington, D.C., where R. K. Mellon's cousin Paul maintains a suite of offices. Invitations there are not so elusive. As a world-renowned art collector, Paul Mellon is much more accustomed to dealing with inquiring reporters than his Pittsburgh-based relatives are, but information about the way he handles his business is no more available than it is in Pittsburgh. Asked why the family will not discuss its financial affairs, Paul says, "Why should we? After all, we aren't running for office."

That is the way it has been for decades with the Mellons, whose immense fortune long has been one of the largest, and quietest, in the United States. Conservatively estimated at $5 billion, the fortune is linked largely to such "smokestack" industries as oil refining, aluminum refining and fabricating, and the manufacture of industrial equipment. But the Mellons have always stayed in the background, leaving it to professional managers to keep the smokestacks going. And while the family fortune was born and

---

This chapter contains material adapted from a three-part article, "The Mellons of Pittsburgh," originally published in Fortune magazine in 1967.

grew to maturity among the factories of Pittsburgh, the family is so large and dispersed today that many of the Mellons seldom, if ever, even see the smokestacks.

It is difficult to pinpoint the beginning of the Mellon family's fortune, but 1818 is as good a starting point as any. That is when Andrew Mellon arrived in Westmoreland County, Pennsylvania, with his wife, Rebecca, and their five-year-old son, Thomas. They left behind them in County Tyrone, North Ireland, a 23-acre farm that had provided them with little hope for ever improving their station in life. But Pennsylvania promised a much brighter future. On the advice of relatives who had preceded him to the area Andrew purchased a 160-acre tract of farmland. With his farming skills and no small measure of luck Andrew hoped to one day leave his young son Thomas with a prosperous and considerably larger farm.

Andrew had little reason to think that Thomas would not want to take over the farm one day. After all, the boy worked hard splitting rails, plowing, and performing the other endless farm chores. But young Thomas's mind was grasping for new ideas and stimulation as he entered his teens. In his autobiography, entitled *Thomas Mellon and His Times,* Thomas recalls that he frequently carried books or pamphlets with him into the fields to read during lunch breaks or while the plow horses rested. Much of his love for books stemmed from his exposure to them during his infrequent sessions at the local schools, which he attended as the seasonal patterns of farming allowed. He also made occasional trips to nearby Pittsburgh, where he admired the stately mansions and their elegant furnishings while pondering how one achieved such finery. Prodded on by the maxims of Benjamin Franklin's *Poor Richard's Almanac,* Thomas began to think that perhaps he had a choice in the way he would spend his life and that he was not obliged to follow the path his father so clearly intended. Even so, it was difficult to discuss the matter with his father, who viewed anything but farming as slightly disreputable and unfit for an honest man.

The decision finally was forced upon Thomas when he was 17

years old. For some time Andrew had been discussing the purchase of a nearby farm, but neither Andrew nor the farm owner had pursued the sale seriously. That is, until Andrew hit upon the idea of purchasing the farm as a grubstake for Thomas. As Thomas wrote in his autobiography, "this he supposed would extinguish my foolish hankerings, as he regarded them, after merchandising or a learned profession." At length, Thomas reluctantly agreed and a price was set. Andrew and Peter Hill, the seller, set off for the county seat of Greensburg to complete the transaction, leaving Thomas to his farm chores on a hill overlooking the property that soon would be his. The deal that was to be sealed, Thomas knew, would tie him irrevocably to the soil, "making an honest, frugal living by hard labor, but little more." The thought was too much. "I suddenly realized the tremendous importance of the moment. The utter collapse of all my fond young hopes thus suddenly precipitated nearly crazed me. I could stand it no longer. I put on my coat, ran down past the house, flung the axe over the fence into the yard, and without stopping made the best possible time on foot for the town. . . ." Catching his father barely moments before the deal was closed, an exhausted Thomas could only blurt out that "I had come to stop it and it must be stopped so far as I was concerned."

With farming eliminated once and for all as a career, Thomas was still faced with the question of what to do with his life. An education, he decided, might help him set some goals, and he began classes at Western University, the forerunner of what is today the University of Pittsburgh. Although he was an ambitious student, Thomas's financial circumstances required that he continue to work on the farm, and the constant interruptions made his college studies doubly difficult. When he finally was graduated, Thomas concluded that his college education was valuable only in that he was certain at last that a college education was not very valuable. "Had I not gotten such an education," he wrote later, "I have no doubt that I would have always have greatly overrated my loss." As for the diploma he had worked so hard to acquire? "After obtaining the bauble which I had so eagerly sought for it was laid away as any other child's plaything . . . in my forty years of subsequent experience in the legal profession it never occurred to any one among my numerous clients to inquire whether I had a diploma, or as to the kind of preliminary education I had received."

Despite his best efforts at college, however, Thomas was no closer than before to knowing what he wanted to do. He briefly considered the ministry. While far from being a fanatic church-goer, Thomas enjoyed pondering the great questions of theology and morality, as is reflected in the substantial portion of his autobiography devoted to religion. But the drawbacks of the ministry were serious. For one thing, ministers did not get rich. For another, they were constantly at the beck and call of their sometimes fickle congregations. The law seemed to be Thomas's other option. But there, too, he had his qualms. The eloquence of the lawyers impressed Thomas, but he was concerned that "success in that line by one so nervous and diffident as I was seemed too uncertain." Only later did Thomas find that "the money-making part of the business lay in the background, and not in the line of speech making to any great extent. . . ." In any event, the law eventually prevailed and Thomas became a law student in his early 20s, supporting himself by serving as clerk of the court. A year and half later, he passed his bar examinations, and in 1839 he set up his law office.

By his own reckoning, Thomas was a good lawyer. Indeed, he boldly notes that his own ability surprised him. He had entered into his law practice intent upon accumulating some $1,500 or so within five years. But as he checked his books at the end of his first year in practice, he happily noted he had already surpassed his goal. He reached the conclusion that in forecasting his future he had not taken into account such factors as his "mature judgment" and his "earnest, cautious, and painstaking disposition."

But probably more important was Thomas's deep concern for his clients. Either he believed totally in his client or he refused to take a case. And once committed to a case, he regarded the loss of that case as something of a tragedy. "Indeed," he writes, "I have often found that the loss of a case annoyed me more than it did the client."

Two other character traits developed during Thomas's days as a lawyer that were to stand him in good stead in his subsequent business career. One was his decisiveness, best illustrated in his unusual desire to take on a case and get it resolved. Unlike other lawyers of his day (and of modern times) who sought constantly to delay or frustrate justice, Thomas Mellon pushed his cases resolutely toward a conclusion. When he abandoned the law for the world of business, this decisiveness gave him the upper hand in many transactions in which opponents hesitated. The other trait was his reluctance to exploit his clients. While Thomas recognized that he frequently undercharged his clients, he noted that the goodwill generated by such a gesture brought him a great deal of repeat business that some of his greedier associates lost. What's more, he discovered that a client, asked to pay whatever amount he thought Thomas's services were worth, almost invariably paid more than Thomas would have charged.

B Y   T H E   T I M E he was 30 years old Thomas's law practice was thriving, his other investments were swelling his bank account, and he had every right to be content and somewhat proud of himself. But a vague sense of unease and loneliness kept nagging at him. At first he tried living in different quarters—a boarding house, then a hotel, and eventually with a family in a private home. Then he purchased his own house and persuaded his parents to move in with him. But his father was uncomfortable in the big city and soon returned to the country. Thomas, faced with the choice of living alone in a house too large for him, or finding someone with whom to share it, decided the time had come for him to be married.

As with almost everything else he did, Thomas turned his quest for a bride into something akin to a major business decision. "It was an enterprise new to me," he noted, "but as I had succeeded in others more difficult I undertook it without any apprehensions of failure." But he quickly found that his earlier dedication to books and the law had left him woefully lacking in the social graces that women of the day sought. Also, the introductions he obtained early in his search were discouraging at best. "Some were too gay and frivolous or self conceited; others too slovenly and ungainly, and others again too coarse or stupid," he decided.

Thomas had begun to give up hope until a friend, Dr. R.C. Beatty, complained to him about a young Pittsburgh woman whom Dr. Beatty had tried to court. The problem, Dr. Beatty explained, was that she was too independent, "had no elasticity in her composition, and did not seem to appreciate gentlemen's attentions." Those particular qualities piqued Thomas's curiosity and eventually he managed to secure a formal introduction to Miss Sarah Negley, the rather homely daughter of a deceased member of Pittsburgh's gentry.

The courtship of Miss Negley was a vexing time for Thomas. Unsure of himself, his task in wooing her was not eased by any cooperation from Miss Negley. Each time Thomas attempted to bring the conversation around to the discussion of their personal relationship, Sarah invariably introduced a new subject. After three months of such coyness, Thomas was rapidly losing patience with the whole procedure. "I no longer possessed the amiable mood of a wooer," he recalls. "Impatience and baffled expectation annoyed me, and at each successive visit I usually left in a temper entirely unbecoming a lover and unsuited for expression in her presence."

Finally Thomas decided to force the issue. During one of the brief periods in which he and Sarah were left alone in the parlor of her home, he pulled a chair up close to her, explained that he was fully satisfied that she would make a good wife, and asked her intentions. There was no answer. Thomas leaned slowly forward, kissed her, told her that her lack of resistance to the kiss indicated to him a willingness to have him as a husband, and then fled, too unnerved to continue the conversation.

Within a week they were negotiating a wedding date. Thomas wanted the wedding within a week or ten days. Sarah insisted on six weeks. A compromise was reached on a month and the wedding— described by Thomas in his autobiography as the consummation of the "transaction"—was held August 22, 1843. Though love clearly bound the pair together over the many years that followed,

Thomas nevertheless points out in his memoirs that had his proposal been rejected, "I would have felt neither sad nor depressed, nor greatly disappointed, only annoyed at loss of time."

D URING THE NEXT 16 years, Thomas Mellon consolidated his position as both businessman and family man. He and Sarah had eight children, but three died in childhood and one at age 27. The four survivors—Thomas Alexander, James Ross, Andrew William, and Richard Beatty—were raised in a household that stressed honesty, integrity, and the value of a dollar. In business matters they had no better teacher than their father, who continually taught them that they would receive only that for which they worked. He set the perfect example during their youth, pursuing with increasing vigor the various business ventures in which he was engaged. And as Thomas's interest in business grew, his interest in his law practice waned. In 1859, as an escape from the time-consuming chores of running a law office, he sought and won election as a judge of the Court of Common Pleas of Allegheny County.

For 10 years Judge Mellon meted out justice—somewhat harshly, by his own account—and conducted his own business affairs. During those years he also set his two eldest sons on the paths that would eventually lead to their own fortunes, mostly through wise investments in coal, lumber, real estate, and their own little bank. Only after the economic boom that followed the Civil War was well under way did Judge Mellon leave the bench to pursue business with single-minded devotion through his own bank, T. Mellon & Sons, which opened its doors in 1870.

At first Thomas operated the bank mostly with his second son, James Ross Mellon. But as J.R.'s own business interests exerted an increasing pull on the young man, the judge gradually brought his third son, Andrew William Mellon, into the bank. A.W. was a frail youth with a slight stammer, and he made little impression on his friends and classmates at Western University. But he was alert and bright, and during vacations from school he worked in his father's bank, where he was given increasing responsibility. Finally, with

J.R. anxious to devote himself to his own affairs, A.W. quit school at the age of 17, only a few months shy of graduation, and went to work full time in the bank, serving as his father's agent in various transactions in distant cities. He did so well in those tasks that the judge decided to test him further with a business of his own. In 1872 he lent A.W. $40,000 to build a lumber yard and suggested that A.W. take as his partner his younger brother, Richard Beatty Mellon, then only 14 years old. The two built the lumber yard into a thriving business over the next 18 months and then, sensing trouble in the nation's economy, sold out just before the Depression of 1873 hit Pittsburgh.

If Judge Mellon had been impressed by his son's ability to manage and build the lumber yard, he was doubly taken by A.W.'s shrewd sense of timing in selling the business. In 1874 the judge offered A.W. a one-fifth interest in the bank and a monthly salary of $75. Over the next several years father and son invested substantially in Pittsburgh real estate, coal lands, and various small businesses. The bank began to take a more prominent role, too, in financing the industrial boom that was sweeping the nation and settling in such prime manufacturing areas as Pittsburgh. Indeed, T. Mellon & Sons was instrumental in providing the money that established and built the fortunes of two other great industrialists, Andrew Carnegie and Henry Clay Frick, who together turned Pittsburgh into the steel capital of the world.

Finally, in 1882, Judge Mellon left the bank entirely, turning over its reins to 27-year-old A.W., with the tacit understanding that at some point he would bring his younger brother, R.B., into the bank as a partner, too. If any single decision should be deemed the turning point in the Mellon family's history, it is the judge's decision to give A.W. free rein at the bank.

Under Judge Mellon the bank had fulfilled the classic role of banks everywhere—lending money and collecting interest on it. To be sure, there had been ventures in which the bank took an equity position, but they were relatively small, and the judge had preferred to risk his money mostly in ventures where he maintained virtually complete control. A.W. and R.B., though, were not content to run the bank along traditional lines. Rather, they were interested in the more aggressive approach that called for the bank to provide money to worthy men in exchange for a piece of the action. It was a considerably riskier policy than lending money against collateral, but it could be far more lucrative if one backed the right sort of enterprises.

The two younger Mellon brothers formed one of the most remarkable business partnerships ever. Superficially, they could not have been more different. A.W. was shy, frail, deadly serious, and formal in even his most intimate friendships. R.B., on the other hand, was a hearty man with a booming laugh, always ready to have a good time, and always looking to meet someone new and interesting. But in their business dealings the two brothers operated as one. Decisions were almost always made jointly, and even if one of the brothers had not been consulted, Pittsburghers knew that the other nevertheless could commit his brother to a venture. They even shared a checking account and bank books. Yet, despite the many critical decisions they were called upon to make over the years and the vast amounts of money they handled, the Mellon brothers were never heard to argue or dispute one another, and the partnership functioned perfectly, R.B. serving as liaison with the business community, encouraging local men to place their accounts at T. Mellon & Sons, and A.W. astutely judging the worth of a man's character before committing the bank's money to any ventures.

The first of the major moves that the Mellon brothers made on their way to elevating the family from the ranks of the merely wealthy to the rarefied atmosphere of the superrich came in 1889. A.W., as usual, was at his desk in the bank when three men approached him seeking a $4,000 loan. The loan, they explained, would pay off another bank's note, part of a debt they had run up developing an electrical reduction process to smelt aluminum out of bauxite ore.

A.W. was intrigued by the unique properties of the hunk of aluminum the men showed him. It was surprisingly light in weight, easy to work, and did not rust like steel. He paid a visit later in the week to their little smelting plant to see for himself how the process worked and to get an idea of the economics of the business. Satisfied that there were commercial possibilities in the production of aluminum, A.W. called the three men back to the bank. A mere $4,000 would not do it, he told them. They needed considerably more capital than that to build the process to a sufficient size to be self-sustaining, and he was prepared to advance them $25,000 in exchange for stock in the Pittsburgh Reduction Co., the predecessor of Aluminum Co. of America. The three men accepted the offer, and today Alcoa is the largest producer of the metal in North America. Its aluminum-skin headquarters building stands only a block from the Mellon Bank Building, symbolic of the role the Mellons played in the development of the modern aluminum industry.

The Mellon brothers' second big opportunity came in 1895. T. Mellon & Sons had begun to acquire a reputation as a bank willing to hear out a man with an idea, and one day an inventor named Edward Acheson turned up at the bank to show A.W. a man-made "diamond." It was not a true diamond, of course, but it possessed some characteristics similar to a diamond, particularly its hardness. It was the result, Mr. Acheson explained, of the fusion of sand, coke, and limestone under high temperatures in an electric furnace. If this silicon carbide could be produced in sufficient quantities at a reasonable price, its peculiar properties would make it an ideal abrasive for shaping all that steel Pittsburgh was producing.

Convinced that Acheson was onto something, and knowledgeable about the economics of electrical power through his role in Pittsburgh Reduction Co., A.W. bought into the company that became Carborundum Co. Although Carborundum never reached the financial pinnacles that the other main Mellon businesses reached, over the years it served the family well as an economic indicator. When sales of its abrasives began to drop, trouble surely was brewing in the industrial sector of the nation's economy. (The Mellons finally relinquished their sizable position in Carborundum in 1976, when Kennecott Corp. offered to pay more than a half-billion dollars for the company.)

At the turn of the century, the Mellons' businesses were booming. They included streetcars, shipbuilding, steel construction, and railroad-car manufacturing. The brothers even broke their father's tacit taboo on getting into the steel business, first by trying to buy the Carnegie Steel Co. and later by making a large investment, along with steel magnate Henry Clay Frick, in Union Steel Co. But so wary had businessmen become of the Mellons' competitive instinct that rather than run an unacceptable risk, the other owners of the budding industrial empire known as U.S. Steel bought them out of the steel business for $75 million.

Meanwhile, the banking scene in Pittsburgh had been changing. In the 1880s, A.W. had joined Frick and some other Pittsburgh businessmen in setting up Union Trust Co., originally intended to handle the transfer of corporate securities. But the company eventually entered the general banking business, and by the turn of the century it had eclipsed T. Mellon & Sons in volume of business. Even so, Union Trust was not large enough to handle the biggest and most-demanding corporate appetites for capital, and the Pittsburgh bank was losing business to the bigger banks in New York and Philadelphia.

In one of his shrewdest moves as a banker, A.W. proposed a solution to everyone's problem—consolidate T. Mellon & Sons with Union Trust. True, it would mean making the family's bank subordinate to a larger institution. But given the interest A.W. already had in Union Trust, coupled with both his and R.B.'s interest in T. Mellon & Sons, the Mellon brothers would emerge as the largest shareholders in the new and more powerful institution. Today, the Mellons still hold their commanding position in what is now called Mellon National Corp., the holding company for one of the nation's largest banks.

The Mellons had been into and out of the oil business in the late 1800s, but by 1900 it had not amounted to much in the way of return on their investments. But that year they were persuaded to lend an oil-speculating concern, J.M. Guffey Co., $300,000 to finance a drilling venture in an unproved area near Beaumont, Texas. On Jan. 10, 1901, the speculators hit oil, one of the biggest strikes in

U.S. history. The Mellons advanced more capital for the development of the field in exchange for a one-third interest in the newly organized J.M. Guffey Petroleum Co. The Beaumont strike was the beginning of the great Texas oil boom, and the Guffey Petroleum Co. was the beginning of Gulf Oil Corp.

The last of the Mellon brothers' seminal deals did not occur until World War I was underway. Years earlier, U.S. Steel Corp. had brought Dr. Heinrich Koppers to the United States from his native Germany to build batteries of his coking ovens for U.S. Steel's mills. Coke ovens are giant ovens in which coal is baked to remove many of its volatile elements and to make it useful in the steelmaking process. Dr. Koppers's ovens were far superior to the type that the steel industry in the United States had been using, but the inventor lacked both the marketing talent and the capitalization to strike out on his own until the Mellons took a hand. In 1915, in exchange for more than a one-third interest in Koppers Co., the Mellons set Dr. Koppers up in business, and the company today is still a major supplier of coke ovens, as well as hundreds of other industrial products and chemicals.

Thus it was that over a period of three decades, working from the base their father had provided them in T. Mellon & Sons, A.W. and R.B. built the foundation for the Mellons' fabulous fortune. No other family in American history has had such a forceful impact on so many basic industries, and it is hardly conceivable that any future family will ever be in a position to lay so much of the groundwork of a nation's economy as did the Mellon brothers.

D ESPITE A.W.'s immense success in the world of business, in 1920 he was not very well known outside Pittsburgh. It was during that year that President-elect Warren G. Harding was casting about for a Secretary of the Treasury. Someone, perhaps Senator Philander C. Knox of Pennsylvania, suggested as a likely candidate Andrew Mellon.

"Who?" asked Harding.

It did not take Harding long, though, to find out just who Andrew Mellon was. What he discovered was that A.W. represented many of the values that the new President would need as he assumed office in the wake of Woodrow Wilson's liberalism, among them a firm view of how the world should work and a reputation as a man who could make it work that way. Basically, A.W. was an advocate of the "trickle down" theory of economic growth. That particular school held that to the extent that the wealthiest of the citizenry prospered, the middle classes and eventually the lower classes would also prosper. Heavy taxes on the wealthy, A.W. believed, merely discouraged them from the kinds of risky ventures that led ultimately to the creation of more jobs and better incomes for the masses. By reducing taxes on the wealthy, he figured, the government would recoup the lost revenue through the prosperity of the working people. Thus it was that in 1921, at age 65, A.W. resigned from the boards of directors of some 60 corporations and set out for Washington to take up the position that would eventually cover his carefully cultivated reputation for financial acumen with a deep layer of tarnish.

The first eight or so years of A.W.'s tenure as Secretary of the Treasury firmly placed the old man's star on the ascendency. It was the era of Big Business and A.W. was given much of the credit for the prosperity of the 1920s, whether he deserved it or not. Among his most notable accomplishments during that period was a sharp reduction in the nation's war debt and an even sharper reduction in the government's expenditures. A.W. managed to crown that with a personal victory on the tax front—the maximum income tax was reduced from 73% to 25%. Those victories didn't come easily, however, and A.W. was the frequent target of criticism from liberal populists, many of whom charged that his advocacy of lower taxes on great wealth was not aimed so much at the benefit of the nation as the benefit of Andrew Mellon.

Perhaps the high point of A.W.'s stewardship in Washington came in 1928. With the economy perking along strongly, A.W. was one of the most respected public figures in the nation. He was widely heralded as "the greatest Secretary of the Treasury since Alexander Hamilton." His fame and policies persuaded Republican party leaders to give considerable thought to A.W.'s chances of obtaining the Presidency that year, and for some time A.W. did nothing to indicate he would not accept the nomination if it were offered, despite his advancing years. Finally, though, he acknowledged the inevitable and bowed out of the race in deference to Herbert Hoover, secure in the thought that he would be kindly treated in the history books.

But times changed. The wealth that A.W.'s tax policies had fostered sought more wealth, and the result in the late 1920s was increasing speculation in the stock market. Everyone wanted to be rich, and for a while it appeared that such a goal was possible. Stock prices rose to phenomenal levels, and real-estate values shot up, too. Credit rapidly became the foundation for speculation by anyone who could convince a banker to lend him money or a broker to sell him stock on margin. The speculation began to foreshadow a gigantic bust, and anyone intimately familiar with business might have seen it coming, especially such an astute businessman as Andrew Mellon. Yet, even as the signs became increasingly evident that something had to give in the stock market, A.W. suggested only that perhaps bonds might be a better investment for those of lesser means. As the Great Depression developed, A.W. with few exceptions merely urged restraint by the government in order to let the economy purge itself in a "natural" cycle. To a nation panicked by the extent of the collapse and the suffering it caused, such a view was nothing short of brutal. No longer did anyone refer to Andrew Mellon as second only to Alexander Hamilton for his role in the nation's economy. Deeply troubled despite his conviction that his was the correct course, A.W. quietly accepted an appointment as ambassador to Great Britain in 1932.

No one can be sure just how much Andrew Mellon should be blamed for the Great Depression. But whatever his liability, it was sufficient to make him the Roosevelt Administration's primary target for revenge. The trouble began in 1933 with charges that A.W. had cheated the government in his 1931 income-tax return. The Justice Department began an immediate investigation. The newspapers carried frequent stories concerning the investigation and an audit was conducted. Apparently nothing was amiss. A.W.

was relieved that the obvious political vendetta against him had borne no fruit. But then another rash of newspaper stories discussing the continuing investigation of the tax return appeared and finally, in March, 1934, Attorney General Homer Cummings announced that he was submitting the results of his department's investigation of Andrew Mellon's 1931 tax return to a grand jury to obtain an indictment against the former Treasury Secretary for tax fraud.

A grand jury convened that year in Pittsburgh to study the government's case against A.W. and came back from its deliberations with a solid victory for the 79-year-old A.W.—a refusal to indict. Once again A.W. relaxed, confident that his retirement would be peaceful.

But the Roosevelt Administration was not easily dissuaded from pursuing the man it held largely responsible for the Great Depression. If Roosevelt could not nail A.W. on a criminal charge, he would try to destroy the man through civil proceedings. The Treasury Department lodged a notice of tax deficiency against A.W.'s 1931 return. No matter the outcome, A.W. would not go to jail. That much was certain. But a decision against him would go a long way toward ruining his already tattered reputation, and the implication would surely be that the Pittsburgh grand jury, far from being persuaded of A.W.'s innocence, had failed to indict him out of either fright or loyalty to a native son.

The government's move put A.W. in a vexing position. Either he could accept the government's claim, pay up the $3.1 million it claimed he owed (it was not as if he could not afford it), and be done with the matter, or he could fight the notice in an appeal to the board of tax appeals, in which case he knew he would be forced to bare his financial soul. Despite a lifelong desire for privacy, A.W. chose to defend his reputation.

The issues before the board of tax appeals involved financial transactions of mind-boggling complexity. There was, for instance, the question of whether the sale in 1931 of McClintic-Marshall Construction Co., a venture in which the Mellon brothers had invested heavily in their early years in the bank, constituted a reorganization and thus was liable for heavier taxes than A.W. had paid. Associated with that issue was the matter of valuation of the stock in McClintic-Marshall so that A.W.'s profits on the sale could be calculated. Other questions involved the sale and subsequent repurchase of interests in a number of companies—transactions that benefited A.W. because he claimed the sales resulted in losses that ultimately reduced his tax bill.

While the trial disclosed some of the complex workings of a personal financial empire, it also pointed up the curiously simplistic approach that A.W. took toward his tax planning and his proper place in society. According to David Koskoff's biography *The Mellons,* A.W. argued that in 1931 he easily could have taken sufficient deductions to wipe out entirely any tax bill. But, he insisted, his circumstances enabled him to pay a substantial tax and he wanted to do his fair share. Thus, he said, he had decided upon what would be a "fair" amount to pay the government and had simply stopped taking deductions when his tax bill had been whittled down to that amount.

Although aspects of some transactions discussed during the four months of A.W.'s trial were questionable, the final decision by the board was that he owed the government about $400,000, primarily because of the unintentional overvaluation of the McClintic-Marshall stock, which had resulted in a lower recorded profit on the sale than the tax board thought was proper. No attempted fraud was implied. In essence, the decision was a total vindication of the former Treasury Secretary, and he left it to his estate to pay the bill.

If Andrew Mellon's public life ended for him in sorrow, his personal life was an even deeper tragedy. In Thomas Mellon's autobiography, published in 1885 when A.W. was 30 years old, the old man takes note of the status of each family member. Andrew, he writes, lives at home with his parents and "manages my banking business with eminent ability and success. Although of a proper age for marriage he shows no desire to change his condition." That, Thomas concludes, is the result of the lingering sickness and subsequent death in 1883 of a young woman to whom A.W. had become engaged. "Since then," Thomas writes, "he has gone but little into ladies' society, and become more and more absorbed in business pursuits."

Andrew remained single until he was 45 years old. It was then, in 1889, that A.W. joined his friend Henry Clay Frick for a cruise to Europe. While aboard the ship Frick introduced A.W. to Alexander McMullen, the owner of the English brewery that made Guinness Stout, and to his daughter, 19-year-old Nora. A.W. was smitten by the young lady. She, in turn, fell in love with the more mature and clearly very wealthy man. In September 1900 the couple was married at the McMullen's ancestral castle in England.

In her innocence Nora had no real grasp of what she was embarking upon when she married A.W. On her wedding day she knew nothing of the grit, grime and smoke of Pittsburgh and she apparently gave little thought to the vast age difference between herself and her husband, or to his obsession with business affairs and what that might hold for her over the years. But she was not long in learning her mistake. The birth of their two children—Ailsa in 1901 and Paul in 1907—doubtless relieved the tedium of life with A.W. and the dreariness of Pittsburgh. But children alone were not enough. Nora began clandestinely seeing a young Englishman, Alfred Curphey, and as the affair became increasingly public, relations between A.W. and Nora deteriorated.

In August 1909 the couple agreed to separate quietly. But in a dispute over custody of the children, the agreement broke down and for nearly a year A.W. and Nora lived together in thinly-disguised hostility. It finally became too much for A.W. His deep desire for privacy notwithstanding, A.W. filed suit in 1910 for divorce on the grounds that his wife had committed adultery with Curphey.

The divorce trial was a battle of wills. In an effort to protect his privacy A.W. used his vast wealth and influence to ram through the Pennsylvania legislature a bill granting strict privacy to divorce proceedings. Nora countered by having the judge declare that because A.W. had filed his divorce suit prior to the privacy bill's passage, it would remain public. Fights also occurred over custody

Judge Thomas Mellon and Sarah Jane Negley Mellon, his wife, in 1908. Their sons Andrew W. Mellon and Richard B. Mellon built the family fortune.

Richard B. Mellon a hearty man with a booming laugh. In partnership with his brother Andrew he encouraged local men to place their accounts at T. Mellon & Sons, and Andrew astutely judged each one's character before committing the bank's money to any ventures.

When his father, Richard B. Mellon, died in 1933, Richard King Mellon shouldered the family's financial empire alone. Like his father and uncle, he left the day to day management of the Mellon companies with hand-picked professional managers.

Andrew W. Mellon, a frail youth with a slight stammer who made little impression on his friends in college. But he may have been the best businessman the United States has ever produced.

Founder of "In-'N' Out" hamburger restaurant and Rubatub, a maker of rubber bathtubs, Paul Mellon established his entrepreneurial weakness early in life. He became a world renowned art collector.

Ailsa Mellon, daughter of Andrew W. Mellon.

of the children, Nora claiming that A.W.'s business pursuits precluded him from serving as their guardian, and A.W. charging that Nora was poisoning the children against him. Nora broke first. Apparently realizing that her position was weak and that her best chance would be to appeal to A.W.'s desire for privacy, she opened negotiations for an out-of-court settlement. A.W. agreed to change the basis of his suit to desertion instead of adultery, to divide custody of the children equally between the parents for six months each, and to provide Nora with a trust fund. The amount of the trust fund remains secret to this day. The divorce was granted in 1912.

D ESPITE BOTH THE praise and opprobrium heaped upon Andrew Mellon for his performance as Secretary of the Treasury, relatively few Americans today are even certain what office the man held, much less how he handled it. Fewer still know A.W. as an enthusiastic art collector. But art collecting was one of the man's few perennial pleasures and he is among the most important figures in American art, not so much for his taste and knowledge of art as for his fantastic spending on it. He assembled at great expense to himself, then donated to the American public, one of the finest art collections ever amassed and built the monumental structure to house it in the nation's capital.

A.W.'s interest in art was kindled by his close friend Henry Clay Frick, himself a skilled and enthusiastic collector who left an important collection in his New York City mansion, now a museum. At first A.W.'s frugal nature did not permit him to pay the vast sums for art that Frick paid. And because A.W.'s first forays into the art market were aimed at acquiring art he liked rather than art that was important or rare, dealers tended to dismiss him as something of a lightweight.

Over time, however, A.W. became a more sophisticated collector, realizing the investment potential of fine art and seeking advice from experts. As his willingness increased to pay the immense sums necessary to acquire really fine art, his status among the dealers rose, too, until he became the most desired customer—

target, some said—for dealers skilled in putting together transactions of awesome value. Thus, in the late 1920s, when the Soviet Union let it be known that it wished to bolster its sagging economy through the sale of some of the Old Masters in its Hermitage collection, A.W. was notified. There were political obstacles to the deal. For one thing, it was not politic to be dealing with the Soviet Union and A.W.'s post as Treasury Secretary made such transactions doubly sensitive. Moreover, with the U.S economy in shambles, the expense of purchasing the Hermitage collection seemed unusually self-indulgent. Nevertheless, it was A.W.'s greatest collectin coup. For $6.7 million he acquired 21 paintings that formed the nucleus of the collection he planned to give the nation.

It is not exactly clear when A.W. began planning for the National Gallery of Art. It is clear, however, that as an up-and-coming collector, he was embarrassed by the nation's lack of a prestigious gallery. He was mentioning the possibility of donating his growing collection to the public in his correspondence in 1926, and by 1928 he was known to be considering various sites for the gallery. While he was negotiating the purchase of the Hermitage paintings, A.W. privately asked President Hoover to reserve a site for the gallery in Washington, and shortly thereafter, he made a gift of the Hermitage art to his A.W. Mellon Educational and Charitable Trust.

As plans moved forward for the gallery, A.W. began to spend more and more money on art. Dealers, naturally, were delighted, and none more so than Joseph Duveen, one of the world's foremost art dealers. It had taken years for A.W. to shed his distrust of dealers, but over the years his relationship with Duveen had solidified. Aware of A.W.'s intentions to build the gallery, Duveen took full advantage of his client's trust. He leased an apartment in Washington and filled it with paintings and statuary, and then turned the key over to A.W. The strategy worked perfectly. Rather than reject any of the treasures, A.W. decided to purchase the entire roomful for $21 million.

In 1936, in a letter to President Roosevelt, A.W. formally offered to donate his collection to the American people and build a gallery to house it. He also offered to provide sufficient funds to operate the gallery and to make future acquisitions. While A.W. wanted to retain some control over who would direct the gallery's activities, he insisted only that the new gallery be called something that implied public ownership. A.W., his businessman's mind clearly at work, reasoned that other art collectors would be much more inclined to contribute their collections to a national gallery rather than to a Mellon gallery.

The National Gallery of Art building alone cost $16 million, and the collection he gave the gallery was valued at $50 million. But A.W. did not live to see it completed. He died at the age of 82 in 1937, four years before the gallery opened its doors to the public. His donation is commemorated today on the gallery grounds at a small fountain with a plaque that bears his name and the dates 1855 and 1937.

The stormy divorce that ended A.W.'s marriage and the terrible suspense of the later tax trial left a lasting impression on A.W.'s only son, Paul Mellon. From his mother he developed a love of things English and a distaste for his native Pittsburgh, with all its grime and greed. The tax trial convinced him that he wanted nothing to do with the world of business that so fascinated his father and uncles. The result was that he set out on a path quite different from that of his forebears. He became the first Mellon to concentrate not so much on making money as on spending it. That is not to say, however, that he took the role of playboy. Rather, he preferred to concentrate on his studies, specializing in literature. At Yale he directed his studies toward English literature specifically, and he later persuaded his father to let him spend two years at Cambridge before returning to Pittsburgh in 1932 to assume his place in the bank. During the summer vacation between the years at Cambridge, Paul worked in the bank to get his first taste of business life. He was not impressed and candidly passed on his observations to journalists who questioned him about his future plans. Banking and industry did not appeal to him, he said, and he doubted he would be much of a success at either.

Judging by two of his early ventures as an entrepreneur, related in Burton Hersh's biography, *The Mellon Family,* he was absolutely right. The first was a restaurant. A former Yale classmate convinced Paul that Pittsburgh needed a good hamburger stand that could offer a filling lunch at a low price. The result was called the "In-'N'-Out," and as a business venture it was exactly that. The youths were in for six months, then out. Nobody, it was reported, could eat the hamburgers.

The other go at business resulted from Paul's conclusion that bathtubs were a primary cause of household injuries. A bathtub made of rubber, he figured, would be infinitely safer than the porcelain and steel affairs that proved so slippery and unyielding. The Rubatub Corp. was no more successful than the In-'N'-Out.

Paul did work in the bank after he returned from Cambridge, but a great deal of his time was taken up assisting his father in planning the National Gallery. He married a divorcee named Mary Brown in 1935, and the couple spent increasing amounts of time at A.W.'s farm in Upperville, Va. When A.W. died in 1937 Paul moved to the farm permanently to raise horses and otherwise spend his fortune.

Paul spent World War II first as a cavalry officer, then as an intelligence officer. He returned to the farm soon after the war ended, only a few months before a fatal asthma attack claimed his wife. Left with two small children, it was not long before Paul married Rachel Lambert, a divorced heiress, and the two of them continued to enjoy their wealth. Over the years they acquired a number of homes, including one on Cape Cod, one on the Caribbean island of Antigua, one in New York City, and another in Paris. He had early disavowed any interest in business affairs and chose instead to hire a professional staff to keep an eye on things for him. The inheritance that Paul and his sister, Ailsa, received from their father easily established them as the most wealthy of the Mellons and assured that they would never need to husband their resources.

Like his father, Paul has an abiding interest in art. His ties to England led him, while a young man, to begin collecting English art, at the time apparently an unappreciated genre. To grasp the extent of his enthusiasm one only has to note that when he gave much of his collection of English art to Yale University in 1977, the collection was valued at some $200 million. What's more, Paul built the museum to house the array of paintings.

His abiding interest in British art notwithstanding, Paul's importance as an art collector stems mainly from his careful assembling of a large number of French Impressionist paintings, works he began to collect only after Rachel encouraged him in the late 1950s. His French Impressionist collection, valued at well over $100 million today, is by far the most important in private hands.

Paul also chose to follow his father's example in donating art to the public. Consequently, while his sister, Ailsa, was still alive, the two of them made arrangements to finance the construction of an East Wing for the National Gallery of Art. The wing, completed in 1978 at an estimated cost of nearly $100 million, is a vast, modernistic structure housing a collection of art much more recent than the Old Masters that dominate A.W.'s gallery. Characteristically, there is little to remind an observer of the donors. Indeed, the name most often associated with the East Wing in news accounts is that of I.M. Pei, the architect, and probably few outside the art world realize the Mellons' role in creating the East Wing.

W HEN ANDREW MELLON went to Washington to take up his duties as Secretary of the Treasury, he left the Mellon businesses in the hands of his younger brother, R.B. Although R.B. had never shown the kind of financial genius that A.W. had so often demonstrated, he was a competent overseer, and the companies prospered during the 1920s. More important to the future of the Mellon family, however, was the education that R.B. was giving his son, Richard King Mellon.

Born into vast wealth, R.K. grew up in Pittsburgh in a huge mansion that was unmatched in its extravagance, yet reflected his father's sometimes-plebian tastes. In the foyer, there was a gigantic hatrack constructed entirely of buffalo horns that R.B. had collected during some early business ventures in Montana. And staring down on social gatherings from a wall in the drawing room was half of a huge buffalo head that R.B. had mounted.

R.K.'s formal education consisted of the standard training provided a monied Pittsburgher's children at Shady Side Academy and a stint at Culver Military Academy in Indiana, which R.K. attended in hope of pursuing a military career. He entered Princeton in 1918 after the Navy rejected him as underage and after a brief stint in the Army before the war ended. But he remained at Princeton for only a little over a year. The practical education he got listening to his father and uncle discuss business made an impression on R.K. Shortly after R.K. entered the bank, A.W. set off for Washington to take up his government work, and R.B. and R.K. were running the businesses. R.K. served as his father's assistant and, in due course, took his place on the Mellon company boards and those of other Pittsburgh businesses.

When the Depression struck, the Mellons were ready. A few years earlier, R.B., in anticipation of government authorization to open branch banks, had shored up the positions of the many small country banks in which the Mellons had minority interests and in 1929 assembled them all in a holding company called Mellbank, which R.K. was given the task of managing. Of the many hundreds of banks around the country that closed their doors forever during the Depression, none was owned by the Mellons. The story goes that one of the Mellon bank managers halted a run on his bank merely by putting a sign in the window that read, "This bank is owned by the Mellons of Pittsburgh."

Not only did the father-and-son team keep the scourge of the depression from the doors of the Mellon businesses, they also created a little-known, but very prestigious, social institution, the Rolling Rock Club. The club had its genesis in R.B.'s passion for the outdoors. To escape the press of business in Pittsburgh, R.B. and his son frequently traveled the 50 or so miles east of the city to the Laurel Highlands, where R.B. owned vast tracts of farm land and pastures. It was there that R.B. decided to build a lodge to house his family and the dozens of business cronies who joined him for weekends of hunting and riding. The result was the Rolling Rock Club, a sprawling, rustic-looking clubhouse with elegant appointments. Not only did R.B. pay for the club's construction with his own money, he also established a fund to pay for its operation. Until his death in 1933, members were assessed no dues, and even today the membership fee, for those few invited to join, is reportedly low by any standard.

R.B. laid the groundwork for the club, but it was R.K. who turned it into a social institution. R.K., running a pack of imported English foxhounds, got the Rolling Rock Hunt officially recognized by the Masters of Foxhounds Association of America, and R.K. himself was named a master of foxhounds. Steeplechase became one of the favorite pastimes at the club, too, and today the Rolling Rock Races are a major event on Pittsburgh's social calendar.

When his father died in 1933, R.K., then 34, was left to run the family's financial empire alone. His cousin, Paul, wanted as little as possible to do with business, and A.W. was preoccupied with his tax troubles and the National Gallery. The 1930s moved along peaceably enough for R.K., although he was surely disturbed by the tax liability that his father's estate carried. R.B. had not taken the broad hint that Congress had given in the 1920s when it first adopted a gift tax and then repealed it. Instead of using the repeal as a chance to pass along virtually all of his wealth to R.K. and R.K.'s sister, Sarah, R.B. had retained a sizable portion of it, and the death tax claimed much of that. By the time World War II erupted, however, R.K. was married to Constance Prosser McCauley and the Mellon affairs were in good order.

During the war it became clear to R.K. that if the family was going to have a strong leader, it would have to be he. Binding together a widely dispersed family, however, was a problem. Only after the war did he arrive at a strategy. T. Mellon & Sons, named after the bank that had launched the Mellon fortune, would be used to help bring the family together. The organization served largely as an umbrella for discussion, although some observers believed it may have functioned more as a holding company for their immense investments, exercising some power beyond individual members' votes. In any event, T. Mellon & Sons did bring Paul and his sister, Ailsa, to Pittsburgh for meetings, and it gave family members a chance to observe the way the companies were being managed.

As R.K. demonstrated his ability to oversee the giant corporations that formed the foundation of the Mellon wealth, he was invited to take other roles as well, and he supplemented his position as leader of the Mellons with posts on the boards of the Pennsylvania Railroad, Pan American World Airways, and General Motors. Like his father and uncle, R.K. left the day-to-day management of the Mellon companies to hand-picked professional managers. His response to the question of what he did for a living reflects the Mellon management philosophy—"I hire company presidents."

After World War II it became evident that Gulf Oil Co. was in a bind. It was not making the best of its opportunities for distribution or exploration and was threatening to wither away in the face of competition from other oil companies. R.K. hired Sidney Swensrud in 1945 to correct things, but in his six years at Gulf, Swensrud failed to remedy the problems. Then, in 1951, R.K. brought in William K. Whiteford, an American oilman who had been working for British-American Oil Co., which was controlled by Gulf. Whiteford moved dramatically to reverse Gulf's course, and by the time he retired in 1965 the giant company was once again more profitable and on a steady course. But it was also involved in a heavy program of secret contributions to political campaigns through a slush fund that Whiteford had established in 1959, apparently without R.K.'s knowledge, much less his approval.

The existence of the slush fund first surfaced in 1973, three years after R.K.'s death, when Gulf admitted that it had given $100,000 to Richard Nixon's 1972 presidential campaign. Then, in 1975, Gulf Chairman B.R. Dorsey advised the board that the illegal contribution was only the tip of an iceberg, and that the total contributions channeled through the fund over the years were more like $10 million. Frightened by the Securities and Exchange Commisson's interest in the slush fund, Gulf directors named a special committee headed by John J. McCloy, a New York lawyer, to investigate. McCloy's report, delivered in January, 1976, prompted a two-day board meeting that led to the ouster of Dorsey and three other high executives. News reports generally credited the Mellon-affiliated directors with leading the efforts to dismiss the executives.

Even so, the disclosures that the fund was set up virtually under R.K.'s nose and that it paid out such large sums of money without the directors knowing it suggest that the family had little control over the daily affairs of the company and over the management it had picked. One Gulf insider gave R.K. his due, however. Had R.K. still been alive in 1973, there would have been no special committee to investigate slush funds—"There would have been new management in 1973 or 1974."

I F T H E M E L L O N companies prospered in the postwar years, so did Pittsburgh. R.K. had been taught by his father to love Pittsburgh, and once during a visit to New York the youngster was given a tour of the city with special emphasis on the homes of former Pittsburgh industrialists like Frick who had made their money in that city and then left for New York to enjoy their wealth. It wasn't proper, R.B. had told his son, to take the honey and leave the hive.

When World War II ended, Pittsburgh was in trouble. The city was so befouled with its own grime and smoke that the big corporations that had been created there were considering moving to other cities where it would be easier to attract the young executives who would one day run the companies. After all, what bright young man would want to work in a city where he had to carry a clean shirt to the office so that he could change at noon because of the layer of soot that would gather during the morning?

Concerned over Pittsburgh's economic health and thus, by extension, his own wealth, R.K. joined forces with one of Pittsburgh's most dynamic political leaders, Mayor David Lawrence. With pressure being applied by both Lawrence and R.K., the area industries began cleaning up their smokestacks and waste-water outflows. Funds were raised to build new office buildings and to replace with an attractive park the slums and warehouses that lined the waterfront at the juncture of Pittsburgh's three rivers.

The process took some 20 years. But the result is that although Pittsburgh still has occasional days when temperature inversions shade the hills with a smelly haze, the city once again is an attractive place for young executives to seek their fortunes.

R.K. died in 1970, at the age of 71, the last of the leaders that the family is likely to have. Judging by his will, signed barely a month before his death, he learned his lesson about death and taxes much better than his father had. The will, a deceptively simple document of less than 30 pages, left half his estate to his widow, Constance, and the other half to the Richard King Mellon Foundation. But that brief document doubtless was only the capstone of a series of complex legal and financial maneuvers that R.K. must have engaged in for years before his death, all with the aim of passing along as much wealth as possible to his heirs and as little as possible to the Internal Revenue Service. He obviously accomplished his goal: neither bequest was subject to federal taxes, and estate planners generally agree that most of his millions had been passed on quietly to his four adopted children and his grandchildren long before his death, with little, if any, tax consequences.

P AUL MELLON, NOW in his 70s, is the last of the "main Mellons," the ones whose enormous wealth bestows upon them the certainty of fame and influence. Paul is the titular leader of the family, but any powers that might have accrued to the title over the years have long since withered from lack of use. And while he may be the last of the "main Mellons," plenty of other members of the family are spread far from the Pittsburgh-Washington axis that he and R.K. inhabited.

One of the most intriguing of the far-flung kinsmen is Dr. William Larimer Mellon Jr., the grandson of Judge Thomas Mellon's second son, James Ross Mellon. Now also in his 70s, Larry, as he is known, was a rambunctious youth who rebelled at the patterns his forefathers had set. He dropped out of Princeton, married secretly at the age of 19, and went to work first in the bank, then at Gulf Oil. He liked none of it, and in 1935 abandoned Pittsburgh for a huge ranch he had purchased in Arizona, leaving his wife behind.

Ranching suited Larry's tastes for something other than the financial worlds of Pittsburgh and New York. He took an active hand in running his sprawling ranch and eventually met Gwendolyn Grant Rawson, a divorcee living at a nearby dude ranch. They were married and Larry began to take less and less of an interest in the ranch. By the time he was in his mid-30s he was once again casting about for something different. Inspired by the example of Albert Schweitzer, who had become a medical missionary in middle age, Larry and Gwendolyn sold the ranch and moved to New Orleans, where they entered Tulane University in 1948, Larry to study medicine and his wife to study nursing.

As David Koskoff relates it in his biography of the family, while Larry and Gwen were getting their degrees, they were also studying the globe with an eye toward finding a place in dire need of medical help. Haiti offered itself as a logical possibility, and Larry, still a student, proposed to Haitian President Paul Magloire that he be allowed to open a small hospital in the Artibonite Valley, one of the most desolate places on earth. The request was granted, Larry was given a piece of property that was being abandoned by United Fruit Co., and in 1956 he and Gwen opened the doors of L'Hopital Albert Schweitzer.

It cost him some $2 million to set up the hospital, and most of the rest of his funds were set aside to satisfy operating expenses at the hospital. Now, nearly a quarter of a century later, the hospital operates almost independently of Larry, who is devoting his energies to aiding the development of the Haitian economy under "Baby Doc" Duvalier. Gwen, however, remains on duty at the hospital, and it appears that the two of them will live out the rest of their lives helping Haiti in one way or another. Koskoff says that, at least among the younger Mellons, Larry is the most admired of the "older" generation.

Another Mellon who strayed far from the paths cleared by his ancestors is William Mellon Hitchcock, another of James Ross Mellon's many descendants. Hints of what was to come surfaced in 1957 when, at the age of 18, Billy told police that someone had tried to kidnap him and was demanding the payment of $100,000 to be delivered at a certain place on a certain date. Undercover agents surrounded the "drop site" at the appointed hour, but no one showed up. Only later did they learn that it was all an elaborate hoax that Billy had concocted.

Much more serious, however, was his later association with illegal drug manufacturers. Billy had become a broker with the securities firm of Lehman Brothers in the early 1960s, and in 1963 he became friends with Dr. Timothy Leary, the LSD guru. Billy allowed Dr. Leary to rent his sprawling mansion in Millbrook, N.Y., and eventually Billy helped put together a manufacturing operation that began turning out LSD in sizable quantities.

The scheme began unraveling in 1969 when one of Billy's associates told customs agents on returning from overseas that the large sum of cash he was carrying belonged to Billy. While the Internal Revenue Service was investigating the source of those funds, Billy's wife filed for divorce, alleging in a deposition that her husband had maintained a large Swiss bank account in which he deposited the profits from his drug operation. Only by turning state's evidence in exchange for immunity did Billy avoid an almost certain prison term. He did receive a five-year suspended sentence and a $20,000 fine for income-tax and securities violations. Robert Scully, one of Billy's friends, was implicated in Billy's testimony and received a 20-year prison term.

T HE CONTROL ONCE exercised by the Mellon family over the great corporations that formed the basis of their fortune is symbolized today in the physical proximity of the four corporate headquarters buildings. Kopper Co.'s art-deco headquarters stands directly across Seventh Avenue from the Gulf Oil headquarters. A block away, Alcoa's building rises on one side of a block-square park donated by the Mellons during Pittsburgh's Renaissance. The Mellon Bank Building occupies a site on the opposite side of the park.

The family's interest in those companies, considerably diluted nowadays, remains impressive. It is impossible to come up with an exact figure on how much stock the family owns or controls in the

"Big Four," but a conservative estimate based on proxy statements issued by the companies would be that the Mellons own stock worth more than $1 billion and receive annual dividends totaling about $70 million. The Pittsburgh side of the family—R.K.'s heirs—have been periodically reducing their holdings in the main companies over the past few years with an eye toward diversification of their investments. Paul, on the other hand, continues to follow his father's advice—"put all your eggs in one basket and then watch the basket."

Although the family fortune is still substantial, time has diluted the power the Mellons once wielded. Proxy statements indicate that the family owns or controls about 15 percent of the stock of Mellon National Corp. and slightly more than 16 percent of Gulf Oil. The family's holdings amount to about 6 percent of Koppers and about 2½ percent of Alcoa. Such influence in four immense corporations by one family is impressive, indeed, but one has only to recall the extent of the Mellons' interest in those companies when they were founded to realize how the family's power has waned over the years.

Also, the figures in the proxy statements can be misleading because the family is such in name only. It began to unravel in the 1930s with the deaths of Judge Mellon's sons, especially A. W. Richard King Mellon managed to keep up at least the semblance of cohesion through the creation of T. Mellon & Sons, but his death in 1970 marked the end of that organization. After Paul left T. Mellon, it was renamed Richard K. Mellon & Sons, and today it acts as a meeting ground and financial instrument of R.K.'s widow and their four adopted children.

The family's breakup has even been noted legally. The Gulf Oil proxy statement warns that the stock held by various family members, their trusts, and foundations, is sufficient that "if they were to act together" the Mellons "might be in a position to exercise a controlling influence in the management of the company." But, of course, the family does not act together. As one Gulf employe explains it, "you have to remember that you are talking about third, fourth, and fifth generation Mellons and a bunch of trusts and foundations. They do not take any day-to-day interest, or even a very general interest, in how the company is run."

Paul acknowledges it, too. "We see the other side socially," he says of his Pittsburgh kin, "and they are fine folks. But we do not act together."

It is difficult to say, then, where the Mellons are headed. The fortune, while still substantial, is split among various factions of the family and taxes are drawing an ever-tighter noose around it. More than half of the Mellons who ever lived in the United States are alive today—some 80 in all—and that insures that whatever wealth remains after the IRS gets its cut will be widely dispersed over the next few generations.

Yet there remain among some of the family members remnants of the entrepreneurial spirit that launched the fortune years ago. One of the most aggressive of the "younger" generation is Richard Mellon Scaife, R.K.'s nephew. In 1969 he bought the *Greensburg Tribune-Review* in Pennsylvania for $5 million and has since started a city magazine called *Pittsburgher*. He also bought a chain of small California newspapers. So far, though, he has been frustrated in efforts to take over larger, more prestigious publications.

Paul Mellon's son, Timothy, also is an entrepreneur. According to his father, he set up his own computer consulting company several years ago and more recently formed a concern that specializes in a new method of preserving wood for railroad ties. While Paul agrees that the fortune his father and grandfather built is probably doomed to extinction because of taxes, he takes wry pleasure in his son's endeavors.

"Who knows," he says, "someday the railroads may make a great comeback, and Timmy's business will take off."

VIII

The Fords

FROM ITS BEGINNINGS, Ford Motor Co. was the private domain of the Ford family.

Auto pioneer Henry Ford dominated its founding years with his ingenious mechanical and engineering ideas and his ceaseless efforts to recruit financial backing to supplement his own small savings. When the company finally got off the ground, he quickly and cleverly pushed out the "outsiders" who differed with him, consolidated the family's burgeoning wealth, and personally seized complete control of the company and its fortunes. For generations, the leadership of Ford Motor Co. remained a family affair.

Management succession in the company seemed natural and preordained. Henry's only child, Edsel, labored in his father's shadow and assumed the presidency of the company at 25, shortly after Henry left the company in a rage following a bitter fight with minority stockholders. Edsel's own three sons considered little else but someday going to work for the company and perhaps eventually running it. And after Edsel died suddenly in 1943, his wife and mother soon maneuvered his eldest son, Henry Ford II, into the driver's seat.

The world's second-largest automobile company "has been my life," Mr. Ford said as his 35-year tenure as its chief executive and chairman came to a close. As the family's patriarch, he says running Ford Motor Co. has been "a personal and family responsibility—a private and public trust."

The Ford family's dominance of one of the world's best-known enterprises is one of the most celebrated corporate dramas in modern times. It has been grist for novelists, journalists, historians, and even Hollywood screenwriters. It has also been embellished from time to time with occasional glimpses of the family's colorful private life and public interests. Henry Ford II was dubbed America's "Last Tycoon," as he reigned over its largest corporate dynasty.

From the start, the family has always fiercely protected its holdings in Ford Motor Co. As Henry I ruthlessly squeezed out his early associates, he also quickly moved to put himself squarely in the seat of power. Later, when the federal government's tax laws threatened to take a hefty chunk of the family's wealth in the 1930s, Henry Ford immediately moved to establish the Ford Foundation to shelter his tremendous stockholdings in the company for future generations of his family.

What's more, as the founder's life drew to a close, he and his son had their wills carefully drawn so as to pass Ford stock to their descendants in a way to incur the least tax. Then, when the Ford Foundation first moved to sell off some of its huge Ford Motor Co. stockholdings to the public in 1956, the family worked out a plan giving it a special class of Ford Motor Co. stock that in effect ensured that it would retain 40 percent of the voting power for many years.

The family's dominance, nevertheless, has eroded in recent years —and the erosion is likely to continue. Indeed, there isn't any certainty that a Ford will ever again reign over the vast corporate empire that has been closely identified with the family for more than three-quarters of a century. Even if a Ford eventually does reach the top of the corporate ladder again, he unquestionably will never attain the sovereignty of the last two Henrys.

The Ford family perforce is in the midst of conflicting currents of family tradition and a dramatically changed corporate world. Similar forces have altered the succession of other clans that founded and led major U.S. corporations. But while the changing of the guard at Ford may signal the end of an era in American business, it isn't a complete break of the family's long-standing presence in the company.

For one thing, Henry II plans to remain on the board until he reaches 70 in 1987. Moreover, as the fourth generation of Fords matures and looks to its own aspirations, it continues to have a large ownership stake, and it may find another niche for the family in the company's top executive ranks.

The gradual change that the family faces was reflected in Henry II's thoughts as he ruminated about the future upon his retirement as chief executive in 1979. On the one hand, he said he was fully aware of the strains of running a publicly-held company that operates in 200 countries and U.S. territories, employs 500,000 people, and has 350,000 stockholders. No longer, he said, can the company be run on the basis of family domination. He said future leaders of the company will be promoted for merit, and contrary to the strong opinion of his grandfather, he professed not to have any "goddamned hang-ups" about outsiders at the top of Ford Motor Co.

But on the other hand, Henry Ford II is conscious of the legacy he himself guarded during his own tenure in the company and his role as the head of the family. "It's meaningful to have some Ford at the top of the company, somewhere," he said, but he is not sure who that should be after he and his brother, William Clay Ford, are gone, or precisely where they should be. Lest there be any doubt, though, he said he would "like to see" his own son, Edsel B. Ford II, up there someplace, someday.

The conflicts in Henry Ford's own thinking reflect the fact that the succession situation today is far more complex than when his grandfather moved to consolidate family control. Although the Fords control 40 percent of the voting power (their stock is worth between $500 million and $600 million), the family isn't the small, tightly-knit group it once was. It now includes 13 fourth-generation heirs and a number of husbands and wives. Many live far from the family seat in Detroit's elegant Grosse Pointe enclave. They see each other rarely and have widely different degrees of interest in the business started by their great-grandfather.

Although at least two of the heirs freely admit they would like to run the company someday, and observers say that a third family member is a likely aspirant as well, none of them will rise to power quickly. Over the next few years they are welcome to come to work in the company, Henry II says, but, like everybody else, their promotions will be based on performance, not on their name.

As this process evolves, Henry Ford remains a director, and his brother, William, a longtime Ford vice-president and director, remains a top executive. William Ford says that though he may retire from active management when he reaches 65 in 1990, he will stay on as a director until he turns 70.

Beyond that, however, the picture is unclear, because none of the younger Fords appears in line to assume a position of leadership in the company. Many company observers blame Henry for this. They say he was so completely in charge of Ford Motor Co. affairs that he cast even his brothers aside when they showed any interest in the business, encouraging them to do whatever else they wanted to do.

In fact, until 1977, William Ford spent more than half his time running both the pro-football Detroit Lions, which he owns, and a Florida land development near Palm Beach. Although he was then a vice-president of Ford Motor Co., he went to the company offices so rarely that Ford managers routinely parked in his designated parking place at the Ford Design Center. Another brother, Benson, who died in 1978 at age 59, was also a vice-president and a director, but he had an even lower profile in the company.

A sister, Josephine Ford (she married Walter Buhl Ford II, who isn't a relative), never worked for the company. She and her children have accumulated more Ford stock than Henry and his family —but not as much as William Ford, the family's largest Ford Motor Co. stockholder.

Ford Motor Co. has been a big part of all of their lives. Company affairs and family affairs often have been intertwined. "Going back to day one, all I can remember around our family is Ford Motor Co.," says William Ford. "You couldn't escape it." Different kinds of cars were always around the grounds of the huge lake-shore mansion that was his parents' home. He recalls that even when the family traveled for pleasure, the trip often included a visit to a nearby Ford plant.

Henry Ford and his brother Benson used to play on weekends in Ford Motor Co.'s giant Rouge plant and engineering laboratories in Dearborn as young boys—running railroad engines, upsetting the payroll department, and, says Henry, "generally screwing everything up as much as we possibly could." He adds, "It was a private domain. There were no public stockholders. So grandfather always wanted us to stick our noses in and sort of gave us free rein to play around and do anything we wanted to. And he didn't care. He sort of encouraged us."

The older members of the family say they never seriously considered anything else but working for the company. "Having a name like that, it's pretty hard to duck," says William Ford. "Your subconscious directs you that way from the time you're able to comprehend what it means." After Henry Ford left Yale University (he says he flunked out), "it was just a matter of coming back and going to work somewhere (in the company), wherever that might be."

But going to work in the family business isn't considered appropriate for eight of the 13 offspring of Henry, Benson, Josephine, and William, in the family's eyes. The eight are women, and to date none of them has shown an interest in climbing the executive ladder.

"I think you have to discount the girls (as future Ford managers), because I don't think any of them wants to work at Ford Motor Co.," Henry says. The idea has been discussed informally, he adds, but never seriously. "What I call real interest is going to work, and I haven't seen any evidence that they want to turn to and go to work (at the company)."

Henry's daughter, Charlotte, the oldest of the 13 great-grandchildren, agrees. "The auto business is really a man's business in this country," she says. She quickly adds that her father's "head isn't in the direction of women" taking a major role in the company.

Nevertheless, the women in the Ford family have played key

roles in times of crisis. Henry II's mother, Eleanor, and his grandmother, Clara Ford, engineered the family decision that put him
in power, and prior to that, Clara reportedly convinced her cantan-
kerous husband, Henry I, to recognize the United Auto Workers
union in 1941, and put an end to bloody labor battles at Ford plants
and elsewhere.

What's more, until her death in 1976 at age 80, Eleanor Ford was
the true family matriarch. She would frequently summon the
family to special meetings at her home or in the boardroom atop
the company's headquarters on Saturdays to discuss family matters. For important executive appointments, Henry II sought her
counsel.

Eleanor Clay Ford was also one of the Motor City's best-known
matrons. Her father was related through marriage to the family
that founded the city's leading department store, J. L. Hudson Co.
(the Fords get a standard 20 percent employe discount), and she
grew up in the city's prominent social circles. She played hostess
to some of Detroit's most elaborate parties. "You would never drop
in" on her, recalls her eldest granddaughter, Charlotte. "You were
received."

Mrs. Ford was frequently seen around Grosse Pointe in white
gloves and a tasteful hat. She lunched occasionally at the area's
exclusive clubs, and she seemed to relish being bold and forthright.
She dealt with the social press personally. Reporters recall, however, that at social events at her home, members of the press were
limited to the grounds and not allowed to enter the home itself.

Of the family's current generation, Charlotte Ford is a likely
leader despite her father's and her own disclaimers. She is as firm
and as plain-spoken as Henry II, and though he says she is ignorant
of the ways of the auto industry, she is a shrewd and forceful
woman who could take it upon herself to close the family's ranks to
press for something she felt strongly about. She admits to a growing interest in the company. Her brother Edsel once said that
Charlotte "had the macho" that characterized young Henry II's
tenure. At the 1979 Ford Motor Co. annual meeting, Charlotte

spoke for her generation in publicly thanking her father for his service to the company.

Of the five male Fords, Henry's son, Edsel, seems the most likely candidate for leadership in the company, mainly because he has worked at the company longer than anyone else in his generation, and his father mentions him frequently as the Ford in the company's future.

In his early years, Edsel hardly demonstrated much aptitude for big business. Though he was always interested in cars, and is a racing fan, he did poorly in school. He had a lackluster academic record through prep school and was admitted to Babson College, near Wellesley, Mass., a small, private school with a business and finance emphasis in its curriculum.

At Babson, Edsel stumbled through his first year and contemplated quitting altogether to go to work for the company. He decided against that, friends say, because he knew that lacking a college degree would hurt his chances later for responsibility in the company. Instead, he took a year off after his freshman year and went to work in the product-planning area at Ford. His ideas "were not monumental contributions," recalls Harold K. Sperlich, then a Ford vice-president who oversaw Edsel's work. "But he was trying to learn."

Edsel eventually finished school at Babson and did so with an apparently well-earned reputation for throwing lavish parties. While he was at Babson, one professor who knew Edsel, Larry Godtfredsen, encouraged him to do some serious thinking about his future. "I told Edsel he should make a contribution for himself (outside the company) because he'd always be overshadowed and he'd always be the old man's son."

In fact, Godtfredsen says he gave the same advice to Henry Ford during a visit to the campus. "I essentially told him that you're a tough act to follow, Mr. Ford, and Edsel ought to do something altogether different." He says Henry Ford thought that was a good idea and encouraged his son to make his own decision.

Henry Ford also encouraged Edsel to seek some early experience in the European banking community, or perhaps later on to enter politics. "He's very good on his feet, without notes and without any preparation," his father says. And he adds, "I encouraged him to look as far afield as he wanted, to look without feeling inwardly that he had any obligation in any way just because his name was Ford."

But Edsel didn't take his father's advice, and at an elaborate party aboard a yacht cruising Boston Harbor in 1973, Edsel proudly announced to the guests, including his father and his father's second wife, Cristina, that he intended to come back to Dearborn to succeed his father someday. (Dress for the party was black tie and sneakers, and Henry Ford showed up wearing just that.)

Edsel joined the company as a product analyst in 1974 at age 25, worked on a special marketing project in Los Angeles, at another sales job in Boston, and in 1978 was transferred to Australia, where he was named assistant managing director of a company subsidiary. From that job, he said he would possibly like to be moved to Ford's European operations, or perhaps to a nonautomotive area, such as the glass division in Dearborn.

All of this, Edsel hopes, will win for him his ultimate goal. "My aspiration is to run the company," he says flatly. "I want to be a vice-president by 40 and chairman by 50."

If he succeeds, friends say, Edsel will do so with a sharply different style than his father. "He isn't as tough as his father," says William Chapin, a long-time school chum of Edsel and himself a grandson of auto pioneer Roy Chapin. Edsel "is a lot more soft-spoken, and he believes that wielding the hard stick is not the way to get things done." Adds Prof. Godtfredsen, "Edsel is a gentle gentleman."

Recently, family and friends say, Edsel has matured considerably, shucked his playboy image, and is dedicated in his drive to take over the company someday. His sister Charlotte says she used to have to plead with him to stay for a long weekend at her home in Southampton, but he would usually insist that he had work to do and would head back to his job in Boston. William Chapin says that many times he calls Edsel at home in Australia to chat late in the evening, and Edsel's wife, Cynthia, says that Edsel is still at work.

The only other young Ford now working in the company is

Walter Buhl Ford III, Josephine's oldest child. He joined the company in 1978 after tries at moviemaking and other jobs, and after a divorce. He also had trouble in college. He took the job at the company after asking his Uncle William for it. Buhl, as he is called, worked for a while in Ford's parts and service division, often handling phone complaints from frustrated Ford owners. (He didn't give his last name to the callers.) His uncle, William Ford, says Buhl doesn't have any expectations of getting a top-management job at the company.

Shortly after he graduated from Princeton University in 1979, William Clay Ford Jr. joined the company. He had a summer job in Ford's marketing research area and at the design center, in which his father has a keen interest and some responsibility. Though he is one of the youngest heirs, he is considered one of the brightest. "Keep your eye on young William," says Pierre V. Heftler, a Detroit attorney who for years handled the family's private affairs. "He's a very smart kid."

Alfred B. Ford, Josephine's youngest child, isn't pursuing any job with the company. He devotes much of his time to the Hare Krishna religion in Detroit, where he has taken the Hindu name "Ambarish Das" after a famous, saintly king in Hindu scriptures, who was known for his administrative qualities and religious advancements. In 1975, he donated about half the money needed to buy a $300,000 mansion (originally built for Lawrence P. Fisher, an early General Motors Corp. executive) to serve as a temple and local headquarters for the religion. In 1979, Alfie, as he is called, opened a store in Detroit's Renaissance Center that sells Far Eastern arts and crafts.

Friends say Alfie isn't interested in working at the company, preferring instead to develop his own interests and hobbies, which include collecting antiques, many of which he has used to furnish his large Grosse Pointe home. "Alfie isn't interested in working for the company, but he is interested in making sure that whoever does work for the company does a good job," says William Chapin, who lives down the street from him.

Benson Ford Jr. isn't in the company either, but he'd like to be.

In fact, he too would like to be considered for chairman someday. He believes his chances for that kind of leadership will be enhanced if he can vote a large share of Ford Motor Co. stock his father owned.

His father, Benson Sr., was a company vice-president and a director when he died in 1978. He was also the third-largest individual stockholder in the company, behind William and Josephine, with shares valued at about $85 million. In 1978, less than four months after his father suffered a fatal heart attack aboard his yacht, Benson launched a much-publicized campaign to win a voice in the company. He petitioned a Detroit probate court for permission to contest his father's will, which gave his mother voting control directly over Ford stock and named her trustee for Benson Jr.'s and his sister's holdings. He also wrote to his Uncle Henry asking to be named to succeed his father on the company's board.

Both Henry and William Ford attempted to meet privately with Benson about his future in the company, but as the hostile opinions of the senior members of the family toward his legal action and request became known, Benson called off the meeting. Then, less than a week before the annual meeting in 1979, Henry Ford sent a letter to Benson telling him that a committee of outside Ford directors (but chaired by Henry Ford) unanimously rejected his request to join the board.

Over the years, Benson had drawn farther and farther away from his family, and his move to rejoin their inner circle jarred many of the senior members. After stints at various prep schools, where he was a poor student, Benson entered Whittier College near Los Angeles, mainly because it was the first place that accepted him. There he was instantly taken by the warm climate and the informality of California life. He says Michigan winters depress him, and his cloistered environment in Dearborn, Detroit, and Grosse Pointe didn't allow him the kind of life he enjoys.

He did poorly in college, too, and dropped out for a year to work in a machine shop. He graduated from Whittier nine years after entering. But during the course of his stay he became closely associated with two men, Louis Fuentes and Elliott Kaplan, to whom his parents took strong exception. Elliott Kaplan dated Benson's sister, Lynn, who was, for a short time, also a student at Whittier. But Elliott says Ford family pressure finally ended the courtship. Louis Fuentes, a wealthy Mexican-American who owned a psychiatric clinic next to the Whittier campus, befriended Benson and counseled him. Benson also moved in with Fuentes's family for a time while he went to Whittier, and they became close friends and, later, business partners.

Benson's father worried that this close relationship between his son and Fuentes was potentially harmful to Benson, as he sensed that Fuentes and Kaplan were only interested in using the young heir's money. Gradually, Benson Sr. and his son drifted apart, and the father frequently insisted that Ben return to Michigan. Lawyers for the Ford family in California secretly observed young Benson's activities and reported them to Pierre Heftler, the family attorney in Detroit. After Benson Ford had seen enough, he quietly rewrote his will to pass his fortune to the offspring of his son and daughter, rather than give his own children full control of their share of his estate. (Family lawyers defend this, contending that such a step was merely "generation skipping," a commonly-used technique for lessening estate taxes. After all, they argued, Benson Jr. and his sister, Lynn, had already inherited millions from the estates of their grandparents and their great-grandparents—not to mention large cash gifts given to them by their parents.)

Benson Jr. failed to object formally to his father's will within the legal period of time required by Michigan law. He apparently tried to work out an agreement with his mother, but he says she didn't want to deal with the matter shortly after his father's death. So he ultimately filed for permission to contest the will belatedly, and after three days of court argument, publicized in the national press, Benson lost the case.

The whole effort, however, further chilled his relationship with the family. Especially irritating to the family was Benson's choice of Roy M. Cohn as his lawyer in another, separate legal action against the Fords. Cohn, the controversial New Yorker who had gained national prominence in the early 1950s as chief counsel to Sen. Joseph McCarthy in his anti-Communist investigations, was an arch-critic of Henry Ford II.

Cohn sued Ford shortly before he stepped down as chief executive of Ford Motor Co., in a dissident-shareholder complaint that accused Ford of misuse of company assets, paying bribes, and accepting kickbacks from suppliers. The suit was later thrown out by a New York court, and the case was settled with a payment of $200,000 by Ford Motor to Cohn and another lawyer.

Family members met with Benson at William Ford's Grosse Pointe home to get his explanation of his actions, but one of those present says that trying to get answers from Benson was exasperating. The family member adds, "He has cut himself off from the rest of the family—and he's the only great-grandchild who has."

Benson's ambition to be chairman of the company someday puts him squarely in competition with Edsel, his cousin. The two know each other fairly well, they lunched a few times when Edsel was working for the company in Los Angeles, and both are car buffs, though Benson prefers off-road racing. "Time will tell if they'll be partners or rivals," says someone who knows them both. This source believes that if one of them can achieve a family consensus —long the family hallmark—he will run the company. "If not," he says, "it'll be a zoo."

Despite their ambitions, the heirs aren't assured of anything, and they claim to be aware of that. The company has changed so much that merely being a Ford doesn't guarantee a role in the stewardship of the company. In a pointed farewell address to shareholders at the 1979 annual meeting, Henry Ford warned that "there are no crowned princes in Ford Motor Company." To the cheering crowd meeting in Detroit's Henry and Edsel Ford Auditorium, he declared: "Ownership of Class B (family-held) stock is no passport to a top position in Ford."

That isn't the way things used to work. Henry Ford says that when it came time for his grandfather, the founder, to relinquish some of his duties, "Father (Edsel I) was naturally going to suc-

ceed" as president, and Henry II's own appointment after his
father's death was, he says, "just a family decision."

In some ways, the younger generation seems to recognize that
the family and the company are shaping a new relationship that is
changing the kind of management succession their parents accepted. "I ought not to get anything unless I earn it," says Edsel Ford,
adding that he wouldn't want to be "plopped down" in some key
job if he weren't ready for it. His sister, Charlotte, has a similar
belief: "I don't think there is anybody qualified to appoint to the
board now," she says of the younger generation. "God knows my
brother won't get on the board for years."

At the same time, the family, including the younger generation,
is affected by a sense of history and pride in the company that has
been instilled in the Fords. "My great-grandfather founded the
company, and my name is on all the cars we build," says Edsel
Ford. "I just feel that if it is Ford Motor Co., then one or two Fords
ought to be participating."

Charlotte Ford adds: "We've come this far. It's very rare to have
a public company with a family behind it," after so many years.
And her father echoes that: when it comes to dealing with customers, dealers, government officials, and labor unions, "It's better to
have someone there," he says, "than not to have anybody there."

That kind of thinking would have brought a twinkle to great-
grandfather Ford's eyes. For if there was an important concern to
Henry Ford it was that the Ford Motor Co. should remain the
business of the Fords. Indeed, that notion is reflected in his thinking and his actions from the earliest days of the business.

H ENRY FORD'S INTEREST in automobiles came rela-
tively late in his life. He was a 30-year-old night engineer at the
Edison Illuminating Co. power station, a job that helped to satisfy
his curiosity about machines. At night, he crawled through the
powerhouse, repairing steam boilers and tinkering with the machinery, all for $45 a month, a third of which paid the rent on a small
flat in Detroit.

In his spare time, both at work and during the day at home, he constantly repaired things or took them apart and put them together. At the Edison plant he made himself a small hideout in the storage room, where he spent hours trying to make a one-cylinder gasoline engine out of scrap. His work on the engine usually took place on Saturday nights, and his friends would go to the power-house in the evenings just to chat with him and see his progress.

During the winter of 1893, Henry was promoted and transferred to the company's main power facility in downtown Detroit. With his salary almost doubled and with a son only a few months old, he set off to look for a new home.

Shortly before Christmas, the Fords moved into the now-famous home, then located on Detroit's Bagley Avenue. Behind the house, Henry converted an old shed into a workshop and resumed work on his engine. One Christmas Eve, with his wife Clara's kitchen cluttered with fixings for the next day's meal, Henry came clamoring in from the shed wanting to start the little engine using an electrical outlet in the kitchen because the shed lacked electricity. He also wanted Clara to drip gasoline into a tiny metal cup he had fashioned on the engine which served as a carburetor.

Henry put the engine, which was mounted on a wooden board, next to the kitchen sink and spun the flywheel. It sputtered to life, coughing exhaust and giving off fumes of gasoline.

He kept the car for two years before he sold it to his first customer, Charles Aynsley of Detroit, for $200. Ford later said that he had built the car strictly to experiment with, and that he hadn't intended to sell it. But with the offer of $200, he decided that he might as well continue his experiment by building another car.

Even then, Ford realized there was a far wider market for automobiles than could be filled just by building cars by hand for the wealthy. He looked for ways to build his "car for the multitudes."

Building a second car was an expensive undertaking for a utility-company engineer with a family. So Henry needed to find someone willing to help him. William C. Maybury, who was a friend of the Ford family, had recently been elected mayor of Detroit and was impressed with Henry Ford's sense of purpose. During the winter of 1896-97 he obtained for him a lathe that Henry used in shaping several pieces of his new car.

And the Mayor did more than that. He also helped recruit three men who each advanced the auto pioneer $500 for his work on a so-called motorwagon.

The second car was completed by the middle of 1899, and it attracted some modest attention in the Detroit press, which gave it high marks for being light (875 pounds) compared with many European models of the day. The attention also attracted more investor interest: William H. Murphy, a wealthy Detroit lumber merchant, offered to put up some money to manufacture Henry Ford's car. Murphy then joined Mayor Maybury and the other small band of investors and, on Aug. 5, 1899, formed the Detroit Automobile Co., the first auto maker in Detroit. All told, the firm was capitalized at $150,000. It included the four backers of Ford's second car and at least seven other Detroit businessmen. Henry Ford was a stockholder in the company, but he didn't put up any money.

Along the way, Henry was forced to choose between his experiment with the gasoline-powered car and his job—now as chief engineer at the power plant. He chose the car, of course, for he was determined to see his dream of a car for the common man realized.

That dream turned quickly into a nightmare, and about a year into business, the Detroit Automobile Co. came to an abrupt halt. Though the car the company made was competitive and incorporated most of the primitive technology of its rivals, much of the assembly was done by hand, components were complicated, and the car was generally unreliable. Mr. Ford later explained that the company folded because the cars wouldn't sell. He wanted to develop a better car, but the stockholders who controlled the company refused to finance any such attempts. In 1900, the company went out of business.

Shortly after the closing of the Detroit Automobile Co., Henry Ford turned his energies to building a racer. That was a task he could finance almost by himself and, in the early days, auto pioneers were spotlighting their work and their products by racing cars and setting speed records. The publicity from the races brought financial backing and notoriety to the car builders, and Ford saw this as the only way to make a name for himself. "I never thought anything of racing," he later said, "but the public refused to consider the automobile in any other light but a fast toy."

Ford's racing days are legendary chapters in automotive history books. In 1901, at the Grosse Pointe Race Track east of Detroit, he won a 10-mile race by beating the popular, and heavily favored, Alexander Winton, who also drove cars he built. The nationwide publicity for Ford's surprise victory catapulted him into national prominence for a short spell. Later he vowed to build a car that was capable of moving at a mile a minute. He fell short of the goal in 1902, when the celebrated Barney Oldfield, who first raced bicycles, guided the "999" built by Ford and named for a fast New York Central train, to victory in Grosse Pointe, covering five miles in five minutes and 28 seconds, just short of the mile-a-minute goal. (In 1904, a car driven by Henry Ford set a world's speed record of 92 miles an hour.)

Ford's racing activities made him an important figure among automotive pioneers and, as he hoped, attracted new car-making interest. In 1902, Alexander T. Malcomson, a member of the Episcopal church that Clara attended and a prosperous coal merchant, signed an agreement with Henry Ford to develop a car. Less than a year later, ten other investors, including Malcomson's cousin, Vernon Fry, joined the effort and, on June 16, 1903, the Ford Motor Co. was incorporated in Michigan.

Henry Ford, Malcomson, and his clerk, James Couzens, set about lining up financing for the company and getting production in place. At that time, with the automobile industry in its infancy, no self-respecting Wall Street banker or speculator would even consider putting up money for an auto-making venture. Con artists gave the business a bad name by seizing any opportunity to profit from the speculative nature of the business. On a number of occasions, shares of stock in an auto-making company were sold by alleged representatives of some firm or another, but the stock would later prove worthless.

For that reason, the first president of Ford Motor Co., ironically, wasn't a Ford. It was John S. Gray, Malcomson's uncle and a Detroit banker who knew Malcomson's sometimes precarious financing arrangements. Mr. Gray could also lend a sense of financial stability and stature as head of the auto maker. Henry Ford was given the title of "engineer."

From the very beginning, there were suspicions in the Ford family that later proved to be the motivating factor for wresting control from the outsiders. About the time Ford Motor Co. was being organized, Clara Ford, in a letter to a relative, worried that the rich outsiders were going to profiteer from Henry's long, hard work—and it might take all that he had someday to stop it.

Ford Motor Co. set up its first assembly line on Detroit's Mack Avenue in an old wagon-making shop near one of Malcomson's coal properties. Included in the company were two stockholders who later became celebrated auto pioneers themselves: John F. Dodge and his brother, Horace E. Dodge. The Dodge brothers operated a machine shop that was well-known in the Detroit area. They built engines and chassis for Ford Motor Co.—to Henry's specifications—and later became important minority shareholders in the company.

Orders came in first in a trickle, then in a steady stream, and the business rapidly expanded. Henry Ford was named a vice-president, as Gray's connection with the company at this point was in name only. Henry Ford handled the production and manufacture of the car, while James Couzens handled the accounting and business chores of the auto maker.

Henry Ford and Alexander Malcomson together held more than 50 percent of the stock in the company. But not surprisingly, despite some product successes, dissension between the two major shareholders started to grow. Henry Ford, demonstrating his own self-interest and a drive to realize his dreams of building the kind of products he wanted, moved swiftly to increase his holdings in the company. He also moved to squeeze out Malcomson, the only other large shareholder, who was becoming more and more of a roadblock in Ford's path.

Malcomson, whimsical by nature, became convinced in 1905 that the potential for market growth lay in making a big, expensive car. But Henry Ford held fast to a principle that would become the centerpiece of the empire he later built: Make just one type of car, make it simple and reliable, and, most important, make it easy for the typical American to buy and use. Thus, the stage was set for a confrontation in the fledgling auto company.

At this point, Ford was having trouble building a cheap car to compete with such cars as the Oldsmobile, with a list price of $650. Part of the problem was that as an assembler of cars, Ford had to rely on firms like that of the Dodge brothers for many parts. Henry Ford believed that he could reduce his production costs by doing many of those jobs himself.

That notion, coupled with the confrontation that was coming to a head between Ford and Malcomson, prompted the formation in November, 1905, of the Ford Manufacturing Co., which was mostly a cleverly disguised ploy to get rid of Malcomson. Officially, Ford Manufacturing Co. made engines, gears, and other auto parts that Ford Motor Co. had formerly bought from outside suppliers. A second purpose of the manufacturing company was to make those parts solely for the less-expensive car that Henry Ford insisted on —not for the big, expensive car that Malcomson wanted. Ford made himself president of the manufacturing company.

Allan Nevins and Frank Ernest Hill, who produced a three-volume work on Ford Motor Co., speculate that the point of Henry Ford's scheme was to drive up the cost of producing Malcomson's pet project by forcing him to buy expensive parts from outside sources rather than from the manufacturing company. As the price of the car, which was originally $2,000, would creep up over time, sales would falter. And as the sales of the car ran into trouble, so would the earnings—and dividends—of Ford Motor Co., which represented Malcomson's only return on his investment.

Henry Ford apparently never intended to continue to operate two different companies. All he wanted was to rid himself of Malcomson and his idea for an expensive, large car. In fact, John Gray, who was still president of Ford Motor at the time, assured observers, "I have Mr. Ford's promise that when they get things straightened out with Mr. Malcomson, the Ford Manufacturing Co. is to be taken into the Ford Motor Co., just as if it never existed."

That was exactly what happened. In about a year, the two companies merged and Alexander Malcomson was bought out by Henry Ford. (Malcomson, to the amazement of his Ford Motor Co. associates, had quietly become a major investor in another auto maker. Because of his conflict of interest, he was forced to sell his interest in Ford Motor Co.) But, surprisingly, Henry Ford tolerated Malcomson's beloved Model K in the Ford Motor Co. lineup for a while after its promoter was gone. It was never much of a seller, though, as the company tended to promote its less-expensive and more-versatile Model N, a forerunner of the famous Model T.

A BOUT THIS TIME, the Ford family was beginning to enjoy some of the prosperity of the company. In 1907, Henry Ford built a large home on Detroit's fashionable Edison Avenue. The red brick house, with a wide porch and stone columns, had three upstairs bedrooms and extensive servants' quarters, including a special dining room. The location of the house reflected the new-found status of the Fords. Indeed, the great homes of the so-called Boston Boulevard-Edison Avenue district (which now is in the shadow of the General Motors building) were built by the city's aristocrats. The house, including Clara's extensive landscaping, cost nearly $285,000.

Clearly, the simple life of the tinkerer in the storage room at the power plant had passed. Now the Fords had some of the luxuries of their new class. Mrs. Ford had a spiffy electric car that was used for shopping trips and runs around the neighborhood. Young Edsel, now 15 years old, was enrolled in one of the city's most prestigious secondary schools, Detroit University School, and he too had a car (a Model N) and a keen interest in the family business. He often came by the company's plant and helped process the mail or headed for his father's private laboratory, where Henry Ford was usually engaged in some type of work with an experimental car.

The family prospered with the company. When John Gray, the

Detroit banker and Ford Motor Co. president, died, Henry Ford succeeded him in the presidency and gradually bought up his shares with the dividends he and Clara had saved. With that, the Fords became majority shareholders, holding more than 50 percent of the stock. The rest of the shares were spread among several other employes and investors, and a large portion belonged to the Dodge brothers, who still supplied Ford with engines, chassis, and other automotive parts.

In 1907 Henry Ford renewed his drive for a simple, reliable, utilitarian car that might catch the fancy of the public. He and his engineers retired to the back room at the company's Detroit plant and began the lengthy task of designing a totally new kind of car. During most of the year, they labored into the night, first designing the car, then building an experimental model. The inspiration was largely Henry Ford's. He drew the first sketches of the car on a blackboard and guided its development for many months, sitting in his mother's old rocking chair as he gave orders to his workers. (Henry Ford, who was very fond of his mother, believed the old rocker would bring him good luck.)

What finally evolved, of course, was the venerable Model T, a funny-looking car (even for its day), powered by a four-cylinder engine. It eventually fulfilled Mr. Ford's fondest dreams of a car for the masses. The car embodied several innovative concepts that startled the automotive world. Both the transmission and the engine were enclosed; it was a spartan 1,200 pounds; and, most attractive of all, its list price was a highly competitive $825 for the least-expensive version. (As Model T demand grew in later years, that price was more than halved.)

Almost immediately, public reaction to the car was enthusiastic. The first printed notices on the Model T were circulated in 1908, and the incoming orders outstripped the company's ability to meet demand. Shifts were added on the production line, plants were enlarged, and, later, huge new production facilities were built.

As Ford Motor Co.'s Model T production grew, the family took on even greater wealth. In 1909 the company's sales totaled more than $9 million, and it earned slightly more than $3 million. More significantly, it paid out eight separate cash dividends that year, totaling $1.3 million. Ford Motor Co., catapulted into prosperity and fame by the "Tin Lizzie," had become one of the foremost auto makers in the land.

The Ford family's wealth, produced by the success of the company, gave Henry Ford new stature as a national and international figure. His opinions on the political, financial, and industrial issues of the day became front-page news. Henry Ford became a folk hero, though many newspapers editorialized against his controversial views and his unusual, strongly individualistic ideas.

Nonetheless, Henry Ford was being touted as the world's "first billionaire," a distinction he openly scoffed at. Still, Ford Motor Co. rolled up huge profits through the years during World War I and on into the 1920s. It had paid its first million-dollar dividend in 1910, made a $10 million payout in 1913 and again in 1915. In between these years, the company continued to pay dividends amounting to about $300,000 four or five times each year, and almost 60 percent of all that went to the Ford family. Small wonder then that one day, while going through Henry's pockets, Clara discovered a check written to her husband for $75,000 that he had forgotten about.

Coupled with the company's emerging prosperity were the broadening powers of the man whose name was on the building. Ford Motor Co. was run like an autocracy. Henry Ford cared little for the opinions of his coworkers and fellow stockholders. He gradually tired of consulting them and frequently made major decisions involving huge sums of money without asking permission of the directors.

Ford's personality also took on the full-blown individualism and arrogance that made him a legend in his day. A complex genius who had little time or patience for the administrative chores of running the business, he left much of that to others and chose to contemplate problems and ways to solve them. His instinct for machines and ways to harness them to do manual work astounded his rivals and overjoyed the public who came to buy his products. David L. Lewis, a well-known Ford historian and University of Michigan

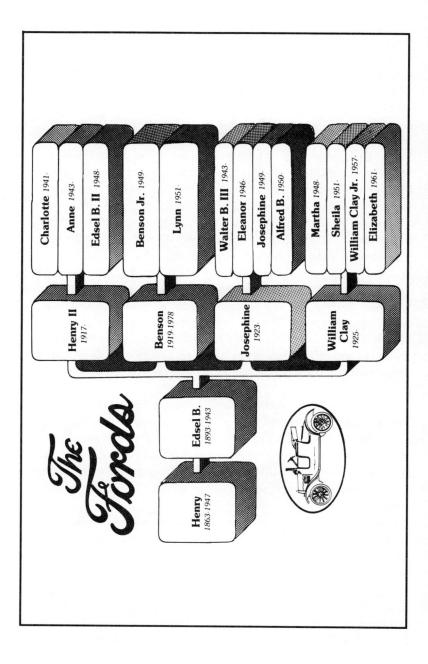

The Fords

Henry 1863-1947

Edsel B. 1893-1943

Henry II 1917-
Charlotte 1941-
Anne 1943-
Edsel B. II 1948-

Benson 1919-1978
Benson Jr. 1949-
Lynn 1951-

Josephine 1923-
Walter B. III 1943-
Eleanor 1946-
Josephine 1949-
Alfred B. 1950-

William Clay 1925-
Martha 1948-
Sheila 1951-
William Clay Jr. 1957-
Elizabeth 1961-

Three Ford Generations: From left, Henry II, the founder, and Edsel B. Ford, the founder's son. The photo was taken at the World's Fair in New York in 1939. The previous year, young Henry was named a director of the company. *Credit: Ford Motor Company*

A 1920 Ford Model T. Roadster. *Credit: Ford Motor Company*

1928 Model A Roadster. *Credit: Ford Motor Company*

Camping in the Maryland countryside (1921): From left, Henry Ford, Thomas Edison, President Warren Harding and Harvey Firestone. *Credit: Ford Archives/Henry Ford Museum, Dearborn, Michigan*

Henry II poses with his grandparents only 34 days before the death of his father. Henry Ford, then 79 years old, is at left, next to his wife, Clara, and Henry II. Young Henry, then a navy lieutenant, was awaiting orders when his father died. *Credit: Ford Motor Company*

The Edsel Fords on the steps of their Grosse Pointe mansion in 1937. From left are Edsel, then president of the company, his wife, Eleanor Clay, Henry II, Benson, Josephine and William Clay. *Credit: Ford Motor Company*

The family matriarch celebrates her 75th birthday, and her children gather for a rare picture. From left, the late Benson Ford, Josephine Ford, William Clay Ford, Mrs. Edsel Ford, and Henry II.
Note: Josephine Ford is correct. She married a Ford who wasn't related.

Two adversaries in a rare, cordial pose. At left is Henry II, then a vice president of the auto maker. On the right, Harry Bennett who claimed he had a document that would give him control of the company. *Credit: Ford Motor Company.*

The young prince chatting with assembly workers in 1945. In that year, young Henry was maneuvered into the presidency of the company by his mother and grandmother. *Credit: Ford Motor Company*

Henry Ford II, 61 years old, chairman and chief executive officer, acknowledges a standing ovation at the company's 1979 annual meeting in Detroit, the last meeting at which he said he would preside. *Credit: Ford Motor Company*

Edsel B. Ford II, the only son of Henry Ford II. *Credit: Ford Motor Company*

professor, tells a story about Henry Ford inspecting six seemingly identical carburetors laid on a table, five good and one defective. Ford, the story goes, spotted the faulty one by doing little more than looking at it.

It was his mechanical intuition that led to development of what is hailed as his most sophisticated and important contribution— mass production. To Ford's mind, mass production meant more than a moving assembly line that enabled a plant to turn out completed cars by the hour. Rather, mass production was an exacting combination of accuracy, continuity, speed and repetition, producing an efficient and reliable product. In the case of a car, it could be started for the first time at the end of the line and driven away.

Ford's first use of mass production techniques came in 1912 at the Highland Park, Mich., plant, where Henry installed a moving assembly line with overhead conveyors on which auto parts, including heavy engines, were hung. Although today's plants have greatly refined that method, the basic idea is intact not only in Detroit but in a variety of other kinds of manufacturing operations in different industries around the world.

Ford Motor Co. and Henry Ford also advanced certain ideas that broke new ground in the work place. In 1914, Ford Motor Co. stunned the world by announcing it would pay a minimum wage of $5 a day and reduce the working day to eight hours from nine. Instead of paying out a year-end bonus to production workers and managers, as had been its practice, Ford adopted a policy of dividing up a share of the auto maker's expected profits at year-end and sharing it with the workers. The pay boost, spread over the whole year, was included in the company's semi-monthly payroll.

Forty years after the announcement, the *London Economist* called the idea the most dramatic event in the history of wages. Tens of thousands of workers, many of whom were besieged by a national economic depression, left their homes in the East, South and Midwest and headed for Detroit. When Ford decided it could hire only a fraction of the applicants, workers who were camping near the company's main plant took to the streets of Detroit in riots. But the $5 day became a milestone in America's economic history. In its first year, the program distributed more than $10 million over what would have been distributed in straight wages.

 H ENRY FORD'S IDEAS soon crossed the boundaries of the industry he had helped foster. As World War I broke out in Europe and threatened to involve the U.S., Ford adopted a pacifistic stance for which he was roundly criticized by some who believed the multimillionaire was a fuzzy-thinking idealist. Others believed the hard-driving Henry Ford didn't want a political dispute to disrupt the automotive business he cared so much about.

One of Henry Ford's most-publicized nonautomotive projects arose in late 1915, when he pushed an idea for the "Peace Ship" that would sail to Europe with a cadre of notable American dignitaries, including Ford; they were to set up a peace council in Europe to negotiate a settlement of the differences.

The idea was bitterly attacked by many in the U.S. as nothing more than a publicity ploy to sell Model Ts. Ford went to Washington to sell the idea to President Woodrow Wilson, who refused to endorse the project. Undaunted, Ford left the White House, chartered the Oscar II, a large, ocean-going Danish liner, and scouted up a roster of peace-seeking celebrities, including his good friend Thomas Edison, John Wanamaker, and several other luminaries. (Most of the 115 distinguished Americans invited to make the journey declined.)

Though the American public generally considered Ford's bizarre venture well-meaning, press reports implied that he was, if anything, a well-meaning buffoon. The ship set sail less than a month after Ford began promoting the idea. It docked in Oslo 13 days later. When it arrived, after a trip that included some dissension among the peacemakers, Ford disappeared for five days.

Later, when he called his first press conference, he stayed true to his unpredictable nature. Instead of talking about peace and the need to bring an end to the fighting in Europe, Ford talked about his new Fordson tractor that hadn't yet been introduced in the U.S. Soon afterwards, he boarded another ship bound for America and abandoned the peace crusade. The rest of his delegates stayed on without him and formed a commission that met at The Hague until February, 1917. At that point, they gave up and came home. Ford paid the bill: $500,000.

Later in his career, Henry Ford took on another international crusade for which he was roundly criticized and bitterly resented. From 1919 to 1927, he published a weekly magazine, the *Dearborn Independent,* which seemed to be his own weapon to fight back against the sector of the press that he believed misinterpreted his controversial opinions. A regular weekly feature in the magazine was a section entitled "Mr. Ford's Own Page," an opinion section that he collaborated in writing.

In May, 1920, the magazine launched a searing, emotional anti-Semitic campaign for 91 weeks. Ford charged that an "international Jewish banking power" had started World War I and kept it going, that Jews were conspiring "to destroy Christian civilization," and that most Jews were "mere hucksters, traders who don't want to produce, but to make something out of what somebody else produces."

In this campaign of defamation, the nation's Jewish communities fought back as best they could. Boycotts of Ford cars were organized in some areas, and businessmen filed libel suits. Henry Ford never retracted any of the accusations; he contended that the articles had forced Americans to consider possible evils. In 1922, the campaign was dropped. The magazine, sold mainly by Ford dealers, reached a circulation of nearly a million at its height.

As HENRY FORD emerged as a world-famous industrialist, he was, of course, becoming Detroit's favorite citizen. His home on Edison Avenue was a well-known landmark and was constantly invaded by passers-by who wanted to see him, asking for everything from money to advice on their inventions. He grew tired and impatient with most of the attention, and his sharp temper often flared.

Much of that was ignored by the Detroiters who revered him. He had built an industry that had given many of them work, prosperity, and a mode of transportation they could afford. His Highland Park plant employed nearly 19,000 workers in 1915, and the rapid expansion there brought endless news stories and increased interest in his activities. Thus, when Henry Ford began buying up a huge piece of land in Grosse Pointe, along Lake St. Clair, and another large tract of land southwest of Detroit, the local press speculated wildly as to his possible use for the lands.

Was it another factory? A new home for Detroit's most famous industrialist?

Ford had indeed outgrown the home on Edison Avenue, and he quietly began looking for land and an architect who would build him a home with all the privacy and comfort a man of his position required. But when he openly dismissed public chatter about a palatial mansion with baronial trappings, it only fueled speculation.

At first, Ford set out to build a home for himself in Grosse Pointe, but he never got much past the stage of looking over the 300 acres he had purchased. When he discovered that his neighbors expected him to take part in the property-owners association and mingle with them at social functions—many of which were the area's societal events of the year—Ford promptly refused. With that, he discarded any thoughts of living in Grosse Pointe and set out to build his 15th and final home west of Detroit in Dearborn's woods. (Ironically, Henry's son, Edsel, settled in Grosse Pointe, had architect Albert Kahn design a huge home nestled on a point jutting out into the lake, and brought up his family there. In fact, no Ford makes a permanent residence in Dearborn today. If they live in Michigan, they live in Grosse Pointe.)

Henry Ford's Fair Lane mansion in Dearborn cost about $2 million to build. And while it is certainly expansive, and well-appointed with rich, dark wood panelling, hard-carved handrails, and parquet floors, it lacks the splendor that characterizes homes of great industrialists like Morgan, Vanderbilt, or Carnegie. With its gardens and wooded hills, it comprises 1,250 acres, most of which Henry Ford used as a natural bird and game sanctuary. (He had a telescope perched on the sun porch to view deer he let loose on the land.)

His yearning for privacy is reflected in the fact that he had a great stone gatehouse erected more than a mile from the front door of his home. No longer would he be pestered by a beggar or backroom inventor (which he used to be), as he was at his Edison Avenue home. At Fair Lane, he and "Calley," as he called Clara, could relax in solitude and socialize as they saw fit.

Ford's notoriety in Dearborn at first was not great. After all, the town was almost entirely dirt paths lined with hitching posts through its main section. The Ford home was far from the center of town, nestled in the woods. Eventually, he became Dearborn's favorite son, as he was, after all, born there on the family farm in 1863. Many of the Dearborn townspeople personally witnessed the coming of the automotive age, and he quickly became their hero. They celebrated his birthday with him in huge public pageants in open fields that he owned, including a several-day affair with a play called "The Man From Dearborn," which marked his 75th birthday.

In return, Ford invited many of the townspeople to his dances on Friday nights, held on the sharply polished dance floor in his main engineering laboratory.

Through the 1920s and 1930s, Ford held two dancing parties each month, usually on Fridays. He had taken to early-American dances and believed they were a fine way to teach young children and adults the social graces. He had the huge Ford Orchestra play the music at the parties. A group of dance masters that he hired went around to the Dearborn public schools to teach youngsters how to dance. For many of them, that was their first contact with the wealthy man who lived in town and built cars in the big factory buildings.

Ford danced at many of his parties, and one of his dance masters recalls that he danced "vigorously, but not particularly smoothly." Ford loved his dancing parties, attended nearly all of them with his wife, and prided himself on knowing nearly all of the 200 guests at each party by name. But in keeping with his taste for privacy—and his moody shyness—he didn't like people to approach him at the parties. "If he wanted to see you, somebody would let you know," says Richard Moore, a dance master who worked for Ford. "He was there, but you weren't to fall all over him when you met him."

Ford's independence and power brought on inevitable conflicts with the people he employed to manage his company. James Couzens, who had started with Ford Motor Co. when his boss, Alexander Malcomson, sent him over to keep Henry's books, became increasingly entangled with Henry Ford's stubborn ways. In 1915, during the height of the public controversy over the Peace Ship venture, the equally strong-willed Couzens began to part company with Ford over the matter.

Although the personalities of Ford and Couzens were strikingly similar, the eventual conflict wasn't surprising. Ford's increasing control of the company and his autocratic ways frustrated an equally demanding Couzens who, much to his chagrin, didn't own the business. Ford naturally exerted a heavy influence on those matters in the business he cared about. However, he left many of the executive and administrative chores to competent talent he trusted.

By 1915 he grew slightly more willing to take on increasing administrative responsibility for the company, and he became suspicious of Couzens. (He later even had Couzens tailed.) Couzens, who no doubt longed for independence from the industrial tyrant he labored under, eventually quit active management but remained on the board for a time. He later ran successfully for the U.S. Senate from Michigan.

Conflict also arose between Ford and the Dodge brothers who, after witnessing Henry Ford's remarkable success at building cars, wanted to give it a try themselves. By an agreement, in 1915, the Dodges kept their stock in Ford Motor Co. and still sold the company some of its parts, but they went off to make cars to compete with Ford.

That arrangement didn't last long, however. In fact, the day after Edsel Ford was married, in 1916, the Dodge brothers, who had attended the wedding, filed suit in a Michigan court to enjoin

Henry Ford from investing the profits of the company in a variety of expansion projects instead of paying larger dividends. In the suit, they claimed Henry Ford had plans to buy a fleet of lake ships and had acquired iron mines in northern Michigan to mine ore for his new steel mill.

They had also learned of Ford's plans to erect another manufacturing plant in Dearborn that would dwarf the sprawling Highland Park plant, and the suit charged that such construction would waste company funds.

The Dodge brothers' suit, which brought on a lengthy and much publicized trial, aimed to compel the distribution of about 75 percent of Ford Motor Co.'s cash surplus, or nearly $40 million, as dividends. The Dodges wanted their share of the money to further their own car-making operations.

The trial was a sensational event in Detroit, and when Henry Ford took the witness stand to defend his actions, Detroiters followed the case with much the same fascination as is aroused by a celebrity's trial for murder or divorce. Ford coyly defended his policies and confounded high-priced lawyers with his sly wit and frequent sarcasm.

On the stand, Ford laid out much of the industrial and economic philosophy that became the legacy he later left the world. He explained how certain economies could be achieved by making more and more of the parts for a car within the auto-making company. He stoutly defended his decision to make steel and glass alongside his assembly plant in Dearborn, and he denied the idea represented a waste of company profits.

He also defended his idea eventually to phase out production at the Highland Park plant in favor of a giant, more efficient complex on the banks of Dearborn's River Rouge and within sight of the sun porch at Fair Lane.

Though all of his arguments were played out in the press around the world, the judge ultimately embraced many of the arguments advanced by the Dodge brothers' attorneys. It seemed clear that Ford Motor Co. was the private domain of Henry Ford, and no other shareholder held any sway with him.

The judge ruled that Ford Motor Co. dividends, despite Henry Ford's good investment intentions, had been unreasonably withheld from other stockholders. He ordered that Ford Motor Co. distribute to the Dodge brothers more than $20 million in dividends, and interest. The amount was about half of what the Dodges had originally sought, but the ruling was a clear victory for them and their business.

The decision in the case, handed down in late 1917, made Henry Ford fume, and he contemplated what he could do about it. Though he owned more than half of the company's stock, he was frustrated by not having complete control. Never mind that the company was under his rule or that the projects the Dodge brothers had objected to were eventually carried out anyway. A judge had made very clear that Henry Ford didn't have total domination.

Ford pondered plans that might give him complete control. In 1918, he resigned as president of Ford Motor Co., and his resignation was accepted by the board. On Jan. 1, 1919, Edsel Ford, then only 25 years old, succeeded his father. Henry said he intended to start a new auto company, in which his independence wouldn't be threatened by outsiders who seemingly insisted on having a part in everything.

But Henry Ford soon proceeded quietly, with help from his son, to work on a plan to buy out the minority shareholders in Ford Motor Co. and take complete, unchallenged control of the company's operations. The prospect of Henry Ford competing with Ford Motor Co. was too much for Ford's extensive dealer group and other Ford supporters to take, in any case. Edsel, as president, worked to calm dealers through personal letters. Historians such as Nevins and Hill credit Edsel with devising the plan to buy out the minority stockholders in an effort to get his father back into the company.

Stuart W. Webb, a vice-president of Old Colony Trust of Boston, secretly completed arrangements under which Henry Ford would obtain options to 41 percent of the Ford stock he didn't already own. Unless all of the shares could be obtained, he wouldn't purchase any, under the terms of the secret agreement with the bank.

The secrecy surrounding the plan was so effective that in Detroit there were rumors that Webb was really seeking to buy shares for the reorganizing General Motors, which Detroiters thought might want an ownership stake in Ford.

Webb agreed to offer $12,500 a share for all holdings except those of Couzens, who was to receive $13,000 a share. All told, for 8,300 shares Henry Ford paid an astounding $105.8 million. Couzens received more than $29 million, and the Dodge brothers, who had been trying to end their ties to Henry Ford for years, got $25 million. In July, 1919, some seven months after Henry Ford had resigned the Ford presidency, he owned the company totally. Though he didn't reassume the presidency until after his son died, he finally had the company and its operations in the palm of his hand. Investment bankers estimated the total value of Ford's holdings, conservatively, at $225 million.

All at once Henry Ford, as a result of the clever buy-out, was in a class that might have been envied by other great industrialists of the era. John D. Rockefeller, for instance, never held as much as 30 percent of Standard Oil Co. stock, and J.P. Morgan, who helped found U.S. Steel Corp., owned only a small percentage of its shares, according to Nevins, the historian. Henry Ford's complete ownership of an enterprise the size of Ford Motor Co. was an accomplishment unmatched by anybody then or now.

Ford Motor Co. continued its prosperity. In 1915 it had built its one-millionth car, after 12 years in the business. Only seven years later, it built its 10-millionth car. Along the way, the genius of Henry's invention, the Model T, was changing the face of the American landscape. Folk songs were sung about the car, and tales of travels in the old Tin Lizzie were spun from coast to coast. Rapidly increasing production slashed prices to as low as $345, and Henry Ford's dream of a car for the multitudes was finally being realized.

But in the early 1920s other competitors started gaining shares in the part of the auto market dominated by Ford—the low-price segment. By 1925 Ford Motor Co. sales were in trouble, largely because it had clung to one product, the Model T, far too long. Back in 1912, while Henry Ford was on his first trip to Europe, his head engineer had quietly devised a number of improvements for the Model T. When Henry returned, the engineer showed him the special car he had fashioned with a few new components, which would have been the first major change in the Model T in at least four years. Henry at first circled the car and then began ripping and kicking every new part. He requested a sledgehammer and personally smashed the vehicle to pieces in front of his head engineer and several members of his staff. There would be no changes made to the Model T unless, of course, Henry made them himself.

But after customers started to notice that the Model T had passed its prime, they turned to Chevrolet and Dodge, among others. Ford dealer morale, once very high, sank.

By 1927 the last Model T rolled off the assembly line. Fittingly, Henry and Edsel Ford jumped in it and drove it off the line. The production run, spanning nearly 20 years, totaled 15 million cars. Within months, Ford tooled up to build a new car to respond to the competition.

The 1920s, auto historians note, proved to be the auto industry's decade for the survival of the fittest. Ford Motor Co.'s Model A, which succeeded the Model T, came a bit late, and its entry was poorly executed. It managed to succeed, nonetheless, and the company began to rebuild, while many of its smaller rivals dropped out of sight. The Big Three auto makers were already taking their place. General Motors, having acquired Olds, Chevrolet, Oakland (later named Pontiac), Buick and Cadillac, was the largest in the industry. Right behind were Chrysler (which was formed in 1925, when Walter P. Chrysler split from GM) and Ford.

Through those years, the Ford family's role in the company was never seriously threatened. Henry was the stubborn autocrat. His gentle, articulate son, Edsel, as company president, lived in the constant shadow and under the tyranny of his strong-minded father.

The company continued to have its successes—and failures. It introduced the first mass-produced V-8 engine in the industry in 1932, the same year the Model A production came to a halt. (From then on, Ford had an ever-increasing array of coupes and sedans. It added the Mercury to its line in 1938.)

THE FIRST THREAT to the Ford family's tremendous wealth and its long-term ownership of the company had come in 1916, but the family never really took any action on it until 1936. The federal government's inheritance tax instituted in 1916, setting high rates on bequests, was a clear sign that great wealth concentrated in any individual family was in jeopardy. No longer, it seemed, could a large fortune be passed from one generation to another without incurring a stiff tax that gradually would diminish the fortune itself.

The Fords had only one child, and thus the fortune would be passed simply to Edsel and his four children.

Other families, like the Rockefellers and the Carnegies, took action to protect their fortunes from taxes. They established foundations to shelter their stock so that their heirs wouldn't so often be forced into selling off large blocks to pay federal inheritance taxes.

Henry and Edsel Ford similarly established the Ford Foundation in New York in 1936. The final motivation apparently came with the so-called Wealth Tax in 1935, which set high rates for income and estate taxes. The latter rose to 50 percent for amounts over $4 million, and 70 percent for all income over $50 million.

The intention of the Fords in setting up the foundation, and in drafting their wills at the same time, was primarily to maintain control of the company in the family. To ensure that the family holdings didn't erode when they died, the foundation would hold the bulk of the stock and use the dividends for philanthropic work.

The Fords took their entire block of stock and classified the first 95 percent of it as "Class A" nonvoting shares. The wills of Henry and Edsel at the time took the remaining 5 percent of the stock and classified it as family-held "Class B" shares, with voting rights. In Henry's will, he gave all his Class A stock to the Ford Foundation and all his Class B shares to his son and four grandchildren: Henry II, Benson, Josephine, and William. Edsel signed a similar will: he left his Class A stock to the foundation and his Class B shares to his wife, Eleanor, and their children.

The result: The Ford Foundation ultimately held 95 percent of the stock in Ford Motor Co. For all intents and purposes, the foundation was a Ford family enterprise, as its board included Henry and Edsel, family lawyers, and other close associates.

The wills, however, had a key provision that underlined the family's purpose for the foundation all along. Both Henry's and Edsel's wills provided that inheritance taxes on the shares of voting stock, as they were passed along, were to be paid by selling the nonvoting stock to the foundation. Thus, family control of the company was to be preserved. In fact, in 1948, the year after Henry died, 90 percent of the company's stock went to the foundation and the rest went to Edsel's family and Clara. Had it not been for the foundation, inheritance taxes would have swallowed up nearly 80 percent of the auto magnate's estate. As it was, the taxes amounted to $42 million, all of which the foundation paid.

Another challenge to the Ford family's preserve had come in the aftermath of the sudden death of Edsel at age 49 in 1943. Henry Ford immediately resumed the presidency of the company at age 80. But the firm was in disarray, crippled by in-fighting as key executives jockeyed for power, mindful of the fact that the founder's anointed successor was dead and the aging founder couldn't hold on much longer. To make matters worse, the company was poorly organized, as it was immersed in production of B-4 bombers needed for World War II, and its administrative controls were so lax that in one department invoices were weighed by the pound. The company had been in the ultimate charge of one man for so long that its enormous size had overcome his direct, personal style of management. He had also driven out able associates throughout his career, and now there was nobody to succeed him.

One of the power centers in Ford Motor Co. was kept by Harry Bennett, the company's security chief. He had managed to gain favor with Henry Ford and disfavor with Mrs. Ford by lining up a band of burly security men to combat the United Auto Workers' organizing attempts in Ford plants. Bennett, a gun-toting associate of Detroit underworld characters, had also hinted openly that Henry Ford had drafted a codicil to his will that would, over a period of time, turn over control of the company to Harry Bennett and his men.

The managerial chaos at Ford was grave. Some observers estimate the company was losing as much as $10 million a week. The situation worried the federal government because Ford Motor Co. was a prime defense contractor. Shortly after Edsel Ford's death in 1943, the Secretary of the Navy had Henry II discharged and sent to Dearborn to try to put the Ford ship back on course. But things were so bad when he arrived that Henry II carried a pistol to and from his office. His mother, Eleanor, wanted her oldest son to succeed her dead husband, and grandmother Clara supported that move. However, Henry Ford would not near of it. "I won't hear a word against Harry Bennett," he was quoted as saying, which infuriated Clara.

A nucleus of a team began to rally round Henry Ford II, whose easy good nature and eagerness quickly won him support among the hourly workers as well as the managers who opposed Harry Bennett. He was a quiet, blue-eyed, chubby-cheeked six footer who was made a Ford director shortly after his 21st birthday in 1938. Though he was looked upon as the hope of the company, he had little in his background to recommend him. He says he flunked out of engineering at Yale, and afterward flunked sociology. ("The fellows said that was a snap," he says ruefully.) He was finally tossed out of the university when he submitted a paper he didn't write. During his brief service in the Navy, he wrote Ford managers constantly in an effort to keep up with production schedules and chart the activities of the company.

Though he joined the company at age 26 in 1943, his presence there wasn't noteworthy. His grandfather, now in his dotage, tried to run the company, but his failing health prevented him from spending more than a few hours at the office each day.

But slowly, over the next year, Henry II's effectiveness, particularly in marketing and sales, began to show. He was promoted to executive vice-president, and he began to be seen as the successor to his grandfather.

A confrontation between Harry Bennett and Henry II was inevitable, however. As Henry began to hold more sway in company matters, he brushed up against Bennett and his followers, and the atmosphere grew tense. They hinted at knowledge of a secret codicil that Henry I was said to have drawn up after Edsel's death giving Bennett the title of secretary of a board that would control the company for 10 years after old Henry's death. None of the Ford grandchildren would serve on this board.

David Lewis, the Ford historian at the University of Michigan and author of *The Public Image of Henry Ford,* says "Harry Bennett held a strong poker hand, but Henry II had all the aces, if he had the insight and the nerve to play them." For one thing, Henry II was widely considered the heir apparent because of who he was. He also had the unwavering support of two family members who were taking a greater role in the company's affairs, Clara and her daughter-in-law Eleanor, Edsel's widow.

Actually, the first moves to begin Harry Bennett's ouster had begun earlier. After Henry II returned home in 1943 and went to work for the company, he learned of the document related to his grandfather's will that would give control of Ford Motor Co. to Harry Bennett and his lieutenants. The discovery dumbfounded and infuriated young Henry. In mid-1944, he turned to John Bugas, a trusted confidant, for help.

Bugas had been gaining young Henry's respect and trust over the months following the heir's return to Dearborn. The two men, and sometimes others, huddled in private dining rooms at the posh Detroit Club downtown to plot young Henry's moves.

Bugas eventually went to see Harry Bennett about the purported codicil to the senior Ford's will. Bennett took out the original and a copy from his desk. He threw the original on the floor and burned it. He put the ashes in an envelope and gave them to Bugas, saying, "It wasn't any good anyway." Henry Ford I had scribbled notes on it, including passages from the Bible. Later, it was learned that the document had never been signed.

It soon became clear that young Henry's rapidly developing sense of purpose and responsibility was winning support within the family and from other power blocs at the company. Lower-level managers believed he was the inevitable heir to the executive suite. His own mother, who attributed her husband's untimely death to the rigors of his job, fought hard for the promotion of her eldest child. But Henry I often seemed to have other ideas.

The movement to get Henry II into the driver's seat began making progress at the Fair Lane mansion in Dearborn, where, time and again, Clara would discreetly try to reason with her stubborn husband to transfer the presidency to her grandson. But the maneuvering reached a peak when Eleanor threatened to sell her Ford Motor Co. stock unless Old Henry gave her son the nod. Mrs. Edsel Ford held nearly 42 percent of the company's stock, and because of Henry I's fierce desire to keep the stock from falling into outsiders' hands, that ultimatum worked.

On Sept. 20, 1945, young Henry was called to Fair Lane by his grandfather, who offered him the presidency. Henry II, who was 28 years old, was fully aware of the lion's den in the company offices, so he insisted that he be given a free hand in running the company. "We argued about that, but he didn't withdraw his offer," Henry II later said. The next day, a meeting of the Ford board was called.

Of the seven members present at the meeting, three were Fords: Henry, Eleanor, and Henry II. (Benson Ford, also a director, wasn't present.) Henry Ford I's letter of resignation (his second in his career at Ford) was quietly read, but before they could get past the first sentence, Harry Bennett ran for the door. The directors prevailed on him to stay to make the vote unanimous. After that, he angrily congratulated Henry and stormed out of the room.

After the meeting, the new president told Bennett that he would be kept on the payroll until he qualified for retirement benefits in about a year and a half. But within minutes after the board meeting, Henry II moved to purge the auto maker of Bennett's men.

Later on, John Bugas and Harry Bennett had a confrontation. Bugas, carrying a .38 caliber automatic inside his coat, just in case, went to Bennett's office apparently to say good-by. As Bugas, a tall, athletic-looking man, approached Bennett's desk, Bennett jumped up screaming, "You're to blame for all this!" and pulled a gun from his desk drawer. Bennett slammed the weapon on his desk and continued his tirade. After it began to wind down, Bugas told him to clean out his desk and leave, then turned and headed for the door. "I guess my shoulders were braced a bit, waiting to take a shot, but nothing happened," Bugas later said.

Bennett soon left Detroit and returned only in 1951, when he was a reluctant witness at a U.S. Senate hearing concerning Detroit's underworld. He died in 1979 in Las Vegas.

The reconstruction of Ford Motor Co. has become one of the most colorful success stories in American business. Henry II, eager to learn and anxious for results, put in long hours himself and set out to hire good, college-educated talent and knowledgeable auto-industry veterans. Among them was Ernest Breech, a respected industry executive who, before World War II, had been a General Motors vice-president. Breech, who eventually rose to become chairman of Ford, helped guide Henry II in his early years as president.

With the older talent also came the young. The famed "Whiz Kids" were hired after the war ended when Henry II set out to find aggressive, well-schooled talent to analyze the company's problems and recommend changes that would bring it up to date. Included in the group (sometimes referred to as the "Quiz Kids" because of their probing questions to Ford staffers) were several men who later became top Ford Motor Co. vice-presidents, and at least two of them, Robert S. McNamara and Arjay Miller, became presidents of Ford.

Within four years the company had shown clear signs that it had righted itself. Manufacturing had vastly improved, and the finance department had, as one observer noted, "passed from chaos to efficiency." Furthermore, the long-sought plan of administrative organization seemed to be taking hold, and Ford was once again becoming a stronger rival to General Motors.

M ANY YEARS BEFORE, when the suggestion was made to old Henry that the Ford Motor Co. sell stock to the public, he refused even to consider the idea. But in the mid 1950s, the Ford Foundation, the very organization established to preserve family control of the company, began pressuring the family to permit selling off a mountain of stock it had accumulated. Having received more shares after Clara died in 1950, the foundation sought to diversify its holdings. As it was, the foundation relied on Ford Motor Co. dividends for 80 percent of its income, although it had no say in company matters.

It came as no great surprise when the foundation directors began seeking a public offering of some Ford Motor Co. stock. For its part, the Ford family now believed that such a sale was prudent. After all, times had changed and a company the size of Ford couldn't forever continue to be closely held by a single family.

In 1955 the foundation announced it would soon sell some seven million common shares of Ford Motor Co. stock to the public. These new shares would have voting rights of one vote per share. The public's first opportunity to own a share of Ford Motor Co. drew great attention among stock buyers.

But the Ford family wasn't prepared to give up control of the company altogether. In arranging the stock offering, lawyers devised a method whereby the family would continue to hold 40 percent of the voting stock in the company because family-held Class B shares would carry more votes than the common shares sold on the market. The family's holdings and its votes would be adjusted as the number of publicly-held shares increased, so the family, at least for a while, would continue to hold the largest block of voting stock.

The first block of stock went on sale in January, 1956, for $54.50 a share, and was believed to be the largest one-shot corporate offering up to that time. Brokerage houses from New York to Los Angeles were flooded with orders. The New York Stock Exchange began trading in the shares at $68.50 a share, and they closed that day at $70.50. Within days, the Ford Motor Co., which the founder had fought to keep private and independent for so long, was owned by 350,000 people—each with a vote on certain company matters.

Through the years since that public offering, the company has sold some stock on the open market. After Eleanor's death in 1976, for instance, and after other Ford deaths, more family stock was converted to public shares that were sold in the company's employe stock program.

The public offerings did a lot more than just spread the ownership of the company among thousands of investors. "The whole relationship of the family to the company changed dramatically," says Henry II. The Ford Motor Co. board meetings no longer look like a family reunion. Only two of the 19 directors are Fords; the rest are non-family, professional managers in the company and outside directors.

What's more, Henry Ford now discounts the notion that the 40 percent of the voting stock still held by the family actually holds much sway in company matters. "I don't know what the family vote amounts to. It has never been tested," he says. "I have always looked on the vote as something that is nice to talk about, but it really isn't a control mechanism." He claims that over the years a "mythology has been built up about all this, that goes far beyond what the practical situation is."

That may be so, but the fact is that Henry Ford will remain an influence at the company for as long as he is alive. "I don't think he'll be able to cut it off completely, and I don't think he'd want to," says Charlotte Ford, his daughter. Adds John Bugas, now retired: "If he's in good health, I see him staying in close touch with the important policy issues of the company."

But Henry Ford says he will henceforth be in the audience at the company's annual meetings, not at the podium. If he has to decide to do anything, "I'll do what I damn well want to do, not what somebody else wants me to do or something that I think I should do because of my position." He rules out any possibility that he would again take over the chief executive powers for any reason. "I'm too old" for that, he says. "I wouldn't be prepared for it mentally or physically." Besides, he adds, "If it's being run well, you don't want to stick your nose in it and screw it up."

Because Henry Ford has run Ford Motor like a czar, most observers believe that as long as he attends the board meetings, he will have a large voice in company affairs.

Throughout his 35-year reign at Ford, after all, he had always had the final say. "My name is on the building," he once said, and that was all that needed to be said. Over the years, when he had conflicts with top company managers, he never hesitated to fire them. Ernest Breech, the former GM executive brought in after World War II to teach Henry how to run the business, was discarded in 1960. As the story goes, Ford walked into Breech's office and bluntly declared: "Ernie, I've graduated." Henry Ford soon named himself chairman, and Breech later left the company.

In 1968, Arjay Miller, then president of Ford, was moved aside when Henry, striving to attain the stature of a GM, secretly hired Semon E. (Bunkie) Knudsen, a top GM officer, as Ford president, in a move that shook the industry. But only 19 months later, Henry Ford apparently changed his mind and canned Knudsen in favor of Lee A. Iacocca, a super-salesman who had spearheaded marketing efforts for the Ford Falcon and later the Mustang.

Not surprisingly, Iacocca was unceremoniously yanked from the presidency in 1978, apparently after a long-simmering feud, and resurfaced at Chrysler Corp. Henry Ford had decided that he wanted a new man in the job, who would also be his successor after he retired as chairman and chief executive. That was Philip Caldwell, the first non-family member to head Ford Motor Co. since John Gray in 1903.

Henry Ford's managerial style has often been blunt and flamboyant. In none of the firings has he ever fully explained his reasons. "I don't want to talk about that," he said several times when questioned about the Iacocca firing. But firings and management changes are so much a part of Ford Motor Co.'s executive suites that there is a Ford "Alumni Club" of former executives that meets twice a year in New York for luncheons. For like his grandfather, Henry II quickly disposed of managers he didn't need or didn't trust.

Nevertheless, the family leaves a colorful and memorable legacy. The personal lives of both the founder and his grandson have been chronicled by several biographers. Henry II's stocky, barrel-chested form, outfitted with trim monogrammed shirts bearing "HFII," all have been distinctions of his class and his own legacy. His power at the company was so extensive that even his tastes influenced those around him. When Henry Ford took to wearing silk pocket squares, Ford executives rushed out to get a supply of their own. When he wore aviator glasses, they suddenly became a common sight around Ford's so-called "glass house" world headquarters in Dearborn.

In Detroit, the Fords have a zealous following. Ford buffs packed a courtroom in 1978 to see Henry testify in a bizarre court hearing involving his divorce from Cristina, his second wife, which was made final in 1980 with a multimillion-dollar settlement. Other Fordophiles flock to family weddings and funerals to snap pictures of Fords as they come and go from the church. And many of the buffs gather every year on the founder's birthday on July 30 at his Fair Lane home, now the property of the University of Michigan, to pay tribute to him, sing a round of "Happy birthday, dear Henry," and swap old tales about Henry Ford and the family.

To many of them, the Fords at close range in Detroit have been bigger than life. Henry Ford II frequently rides his bicycle unguarded through the neighborhood streets in Grosse Pointe. His coming-out party for Charlotte in 1959 was so huge (it cost an estimated $250,000) that it was front-page news in Detroit and was billed around the country as "The Party of the Century." For the occasion, a Grosse Pointe country club was redecorated with an 18th-century Versailles palace motif by an interior decorator on retainer for a full year prior to the party. Flowers alone cost $60,000, and scores of cases of Dom Perignon champagne were emptied before the long night was over. (When Charlotte eloped a few years later to marry Stavros Niarchos, the Greek shipping magnate who was older than her father, that too was front-page news in Detroit.)

Henry Ford seemed to relish having a good time and to shrug off the embarrassing publicity some of his pranks gained in the press. Once in a neighborhood restaurant in Grosse Pointe, Ford blew a shrill toot on a whistle to tease the diners and interrupt a pianist. On the Riviera, he chased a nobleman up a tree with a soda water siphon while the seemingly defenseless victim resorted to lobbing scoops of ice cream back at Henry Ford. And once, to bring a fitting end to a backyard party, he instructed the dance band to follow him around the grounds of the estate playing "When the Saints Go Marching In," as he led the musicians right into the swimming pool.

With the retirement of Henry II as chairman and chief executive, the mantle of leadership may be gone forever from the Ford family. Unless a younger Ford is able to climb the corporate ladder at Ford Motor Co., the family's role at the company founded by Henry Ford may slowly diminish. If so, the Ford family will only be following the course of most other leading industrial families in U.S. history. Members of the families typically find other pursuits more to their liking and drift away from the companies that brought them their fortunes.

No matter what happens to the Fords as administrators at Ford Motor Co., their ownership and voting role is likely to be diluted as time goes by. When Benson Ford died in 1978, the first of his generation to pass away, the family had no choice but to sell off a huge block of his Ford Motor Co. shares to the public to pay a hefty $35 million estate tax. Gone was the mechanism of selling the stock to the foundation, which would in turn pay the estate taxes. The foundation has only a limited amount of Ford Motor Co. stock and wants to keep it that way.

So more and more Ford stock is likely to be sold to pay estate taxes, leaving less and less for future generations of the family. One family lawyer now speculates that within a few more generations the family's holdings will have dwindled to an inconsequential amount. And the Fords' dominance of the company will be history.